# modern american poetry:

## ESSAYS IN CRITICISM

*Edited by* Guy Owen

# EVERETT / EDWARDS, inc.

133 SOUTH PECAN AVENUE
DELAND, FLORIDA 32720

Library of Congress Catalog Card Number 69-18875
Everett/Edwards, inc., DeLand, Florida 32720

© 1972 by Guy Owen
All Rights Reserved
Published 1972

First edition limited to 500 copies
Printed in the United States of America

*For Sam Ragan and Richard Walser,*
*friends of American literature*

# About the Author

Guy Owen was born and educated in North Carolina, earning his Ph.D., at the University of North Carolina at Chapel Hill. He has taught at Davidson College, Elon College and Stetson University and served as writer-in-residence at Appalachian State University and the University of North Carolina at Greensboro. He is currently Professor of English at North Carolina State University, where he edits Southern Poetry Review and teaches courses in creative writing and modern literature, specializing in contemporary American and British poetry. He has published articles on such poets as T. S. Eliot, John Crowe Ransom and Vassar Miller, as well as the Beats. A collection of his poems, The White Stallion, was published in 1969, and he edited A Decade of Poems and co-edited with William E. Taylor Southern Poetry Today. In addition, he has written four novels, including The Ballad of the Flim-Flam Man (made into an award-winning movie) and the recent The Flim-Flam Man and the Apprentice Grifter. In 1971 his Journey for Joedel was nominated for the Pulitzer Prize. Mr. Owen's poems, stories, reviews and critical articles have appeared in dozens of magazines, including Poetry, The American Scholar, Saturday Review, The Kenyon Review, and The Southern Literary Journal. Winner of a Breaf Loaf Scholarship and a Yaddo Fellowship, he has also received the Henry Bellamann Foundation Literary Award, the Sir Walter Raleigh Award, and the North Carolina Award for his fiction. Guy Owen and his wife Dorothy and their two sons live in Raleigh, North Carolina.

# Contents

# *Preface*

In a time when too many books and non-books are being published, perhaps a few words of explanation, even justification, are due on issuing a new collection of essays on American poetry. First, when this project was begun, there was no work such as this covering the exciting years from E. A. Robinson and Robert Frost to the Beats, unquestionably the most exciting period in American poetry. There have been unavoidable delays, and other books with similar aims have been published — but fortunately there has been less overlapping than one might expect.

In any case, it is highly unlikely that any two editors would choose to emphasize the same poets or approach them in the same way. Moreover, my collection is, frankly, a highly personal one, with prejudices close to the surface. You will find here no treatment of the so-called Chicago Renaissance, because I feel that Carl Sandburg and his fellows are of minor importance. There is only a short essay, but I think a helpful one, on E. E. Cummings, because I think his reputation is overly inflated; the essay on Robert Frost stresses his limitations. On the other hand, I have included Karl Shapiro's long study of William Carlos Williams because he has been the most important seminal influence on poetry in the 1960's and 1970's.

No doubt, too, there is a Southern bias in the collection — though I have let John Crowe Ransom stand for the whole Fugitive movement. Perhaps this is inevitable. I teach, write and edit *Southern Poetry Review* in the South, and on occasion I have simply turned to my friends, like James Dickey and Richard Calhoun, for help.

For obvious reasons, I make no claims for including the "best" essay on a given poet — nor have I always gone to the recognized experts. I have chosen essays that are clear, readable (with enough quotations to suggest the voice of the poets), and above all, helpful in understanding the total career of the subject, rather than a narrow facet of it. I have tried to avoid the usual pedantic work filled with the almost inevitable critical jargon that turns most readers away from both criticism and poetry. All of the essays have been tested on undergraduates in my classes in modern poetry. My search for enjoyable, authoritative essays has led me away from native writers on two occasions. I am grateful to be able to include the English critic A. Alvarez on Hart Crane, and the Irish Denis Donoghue on Randall Jarrell. (Is it an accident that so many of the essays included here — such as those by Radclire Squires, James Dickey and Karl Shapiro — are written by critics who are also practicing poets?) I have kept one other thought in mind: the essays should add up, so far as possible, to a complete history of what is significant in American poetry since World War I.

To conclude, this book is not intended for the specialist, but rather the undergraduate or lay reader interested in poetry. If these essays stimulate the reader, sending him back to the poetry, my purpose will be accomplished.

# *Acknowledgements*

Acknowledgements are gratefully extended to the following poets, agents and publishers for their kind permission to quote from copyrighted poetry:

Edwin Arlington Robinson: The Macmillan Company for permission to quote from Edwin Arlington Robinson's *Selected Poems*, copyright 1965.

Robert Frost: Henry Holt and Co., Inc. for permission to quote from *Complete Poems of Robert Frost*, copyright 1930, 1949.

Wallace Stevens: Alfred A. Knopf, Inc. for permission to quote from Wallace Stevens' *The Collected Poems, Opus Posthumous* and *The Necessary Angel*, copyright 1954, 1957 and 1951 respectively.

William Carlos Williams: Beacon Press, Inc. for permission to quote from William Carlos Williams' *I Wanted to Write a Poem*, reported and edited by Edith Heal, copyright 1958.

New Directions for permission to quote from William Carlos Williams' *The Collected Earlier Poems*, copyright 1938, 1951.

Ezra Pound: New Directions, Publishers for permission to quote from *The Cantos of Ezra Pound*, copyright 1948; *Thrones: 96-109 de los Cantares*, copyright 1959; *Personae*, copyright 1954.

Marianne Moore: The Macmillan Company for permission to quote from Marianne Moore's *Collected Poems*, copyright 1951.

Robinson Jeffers: Random House, Inc. for permission to quote from Robinson Jeffers' *Roan Stallion, Tamar and Other Poems*, copyright renewed 1953 by Robinson Jeffers.

T. S. Eliot: Harcourt, Brace and World, Inc. for permission to quote from T. S. Eliot's *The Complete Poems and Plays 1909-1950*, copyright 1952.

John Crowe Ransom: Alfred A. Knopf, Inc. for permission to quote from John Crowe Ransom's *Selected Poems*, copyright 1963.

E. E. Cummings: Harcourt, Brace and Co. for permission to quote from E. E. Cummings' *Poems, 1923-1954*, copyrighted 1954.

Theodore Roethke: Doubleday and Co., Inc. and to Beatrice Roethke for permission to quote from Theodore Roethke's *Words for the Wind*, copyright 1958, and *The Far Field*, copyright 1962 by Beatrice Roethke as Administratrix of the Estate of Theodore Roethke.

Randall Jarrell: The Macmillan Company for permission to quote from Randall Jarrell's *The Lost World*, copyright 1964.

Robert Lowell: Harcourt, Brace and Co. for permission to quote from Robert Lowell's *Lord Weary's Castle*, copyright 1946; and *The Mills of the Kavanaughs*, copyright 1951.

Farrar, Straus and Cudahy for permission to quote from Robert Lowell's *Life Studies*, copyright 1959.

Cummington Press for permission to quote from Robert Lowell's *Land of Unlikeness*, copyright 1944.

Richard Wilbur: Harcourt, Brace and World, Inc. for permission to quote from *The Poems of Richard Wilbur*, copyright 1963.

James Dickey: Wesleyan University Press for permission to quote from James Dickey's *Poems 1957-1967*, copyright 1967.

# Edwin Arlington Robinson:
# The Many Truths

*by* JAMES DICKEY

A reevaluation of the work of a poet as established as Edwin Arlington Robinson should involve us in some of the fundamentals we tend to forget when we read any poetry that happens to come to hand — the poetry that is thrust upon us by critics and in courses in literature, as well as the poetry that we seek out or return to. As should be true of our encounter with any poetry, reevaluation requires that we rid ourselves of preconceptions and achieve, if we can, a way of reading an established poet as though we had never heard of him and were opening his book for the first time. It requires that we approach him with all our senses open, our intelligence in acute readiness, our critical sense in check but alert for the slightest nuance of falsity, our truth-sensitive needle — the device that measures what the poet says against what we know from having lived it — at its most delicate, and our sense of the poet's "place," as determined by commentary, textbook, and literary fashion, drugged, asleep, or temporarily dead.

Like most ideal conditions, this one cannot be fully attained. But it is certainly true that an approximation of such a state is both an advantage and a condition productive of unsuspected discoveries in reading poets we thought we knew, particularly poets whom we thought we knew as well as Robinson. In Robinson's special case it is even more difficult than usual, for the course of poetry has to a certain extent turned away from him, making his greatest virtues appear mediocre ones and directing public scrutiny from his introspective, intellectual, and ironic verse toward poetry in which more things seem to be taking place in a smaller area — poetry in which the poetic line is compressed and packed to the point of explosion and the bedazzlement of the reader is considered synonymous with his reward.

Robinson achieved unusual popularity in his lifetime. When he died in 1935, at the age of sixty-five, he had won the Pulitzer Prize three times and had gained a distinction rare for a poet — his book-length poem *Tristram* had become a best seller. But in the public mind, Robinson has during recent years been regarded as only his vices of prolixity, irresolution, and occasional dullness would have him. Yet if we could manage to read Robinson as if we did not know him — or at least as if we did not know him quite so well as we had believed — or if we could come to him as if he were worth rereading, not out of duty and obedience to literary history but as a possible experience, we would certainly gain a good deal more than we would lose.

Suppose, eager only for the experience of poems, we were to look through this book before reading it, noting only the shapes of the poems on the page. We would see a good many short, tight-looking poems in different structural forms, all of them severely symmetrical, and page after page containing long vertical rectangles of blank verse. Though this selection leaves out the Arthurian poems on which Robinson's popular reputation was made, as well as the other later narratives of his declining years, there are still a number of middling-long poems that no editor interested in Robinson's best work could possibly eliminate. The chances are that we would be inclined to skip these and first read one of the shorter ones. What would we find if it were this one?

We go no more to Calverly's,
For there the lights are few and low;
And who are there to see by them,
Or what they see, we do not know.
Poor strangers of another tongue
May now creep in from anywhere,
And we, forgotten, be no more
Than twilight on a ruin there.

We two, the remnant. All the rest
Are cold and quiet. You nor I,
Nor fiddle now, nor flagon-lid,
May ring them back from where they lie.
No fame delays oblivion
For them, but something yet survives:
A record written fair, could we
But read the book of scattered lives.

There'll be a page for Leffingwell,
And one for Lingard, the Moon-calf;
And who knows what for Clavering,
Who died because he couldn't laugh?
Who knows or cares? No sign is here,
No face, no voice, no memory;
No Lingard with his eerie joy,
No Clavering, no Calverly.

We cannot have them here with us
To say where their light lives are gone,
Or if they be of other stuff
Than are the moons of Ilion.
So, be their place of one estate
With ashes, echoes, and old wars —
Or ever we be of the night,
Or we be lost among the stars.

It is a poem that opens, conventionally enough, with a reference to a place — one suspects from the beginning that it is one of those drinking places where men gather against the dark and call it fellowship — where there were once parties or at least conviviality of some sort; of that company, only two are left, and one of these is speaking. We feel the conventionality of the theme because we are aware that the contrast between places formerly full of animation and merriment with the same places *now* is one of the most haggard of romantic clichés and the subject of innumerable mediocre verses (though infrequently, as in some of Hardy, it can be memorable and can serve to remind us that such contrasts, such places, do in fact exist and *are* melancholy and cautionary). Yet there is a difference, a departure, slight but definite, from the conventional. This difference begins to become apparent as we read the last two stanzas, which are mainly a roll call of the missing. The Robinsonian departure is in the way in which these dead are characterized. What, for example, are we to make of the reference to "Clavering/Who died because he couldn't laugh?" Or of "Lingard with his eerie joy"? What of these people, here barely mentioned, but mentioned in connection with tantalizing qualities that are hard to forget, that have in them some of the inexplicably sad individuality that might be — that might as well be — fate? I suspect that one who began as even the most casual reader might wish to know more of these people, and he might then realize that in Robinson's other poems, and only there, he would have a chance of doing so.

A first perusal of "Calverly's" might also lead the perceptive reader to suspect that the poet is more interested in the human personality than he is in, say, nature; that he is interested in people not only for their enigmatic and haunting qualities but also for their mysterious exemplification of some larger entity, some agency that, though it determines both their lives and their deaths, may or may not have any concern for them or knowledge of them. Of these men, the poet cannot say "where their light live's are gone," and because he cannot say — and because there is nothing or no way to tell him — he cannot know, either, what his own fate is, or its meaning; he can know only that he himself was once at Calverly's, that the others who were there are gone, and that he shall follow them in due time. He cannot say what this means or whether, in fact, it means anything. Though he can guess as to what it might mean, all he finally *knows* is what has happened.

This condition of mind is a constant throughout all but a very few of Robinson's poems. It links him in certain curious ways with the existentialists, but we are aware of such affinities only tangentially, for Robinson's writings, whatever else they may be, are dramas that make use of conjecture rather than overt statements of ideas held and defended. It is the fact that truth is "so strange in its nakedness" that appalled and intrigued him — the fact that it takes different forms for different people and different situations. Robinson believed in the unknowable constants that govern the human being from within; in addition, he had the sort of mind that sees history as a unity in which these human constants appear in dramatic form. This explains why he had no difficulty at all in projecting Welsh kingdoms and biblical encounters out of houses and situations he had known in New England, much as his own Shakespeare was able to fill "Ilion, Rome, or any town you like/Of olden time with timeless Englishmen."

The unity of the poet's mind is a quality that is certain to make its presence felt very early in the reader's acquaintance with Robinson. One can tell a great deal about him from the reading of a single poem. All the poems partake of a single view and a single personality, and one has no trouble in associating the poems in strict forms with the more irregular ones as the products of the same vision of existence. The sensibility, evidenced by the poems is both devious and tenacious, and it lives most intensely when unresolved about questions dealing with the human personality. Robinson is perhaps the greatest master of the speculative or conjectural approach to the writing of poetry. Uncertainty was the air he breathed, and speculation was not as much a device with him — though at its best it is a surpassingly effective technique — as it was a habit of mind, an integral part of the self. As with most powerful poets, the writing proceeded from the way in which Robinson naturally thought, the way he naturally *was,* and so was inextricably rooted in his reticent, slightly morbid, profoundly contemplative, solitary, compassionate, and stoical personality and was not the product of a conscious search for a literary "way," an unusual manner of speaking which was invented or discovered and in which the will had a major part.

Robinson's tentative point of view was solidly wedded to a style that has exactly the same characteristics as his mind. It makes an artistic virtue, and often a very great one, of arriving at only provisional answers and solutions, of leaving it up to the reader's personality — also fated — to choose from among them the most likely. Thus a salient quality of Robinson's work is the extraordinary roundness and fullness he obtains from such circumlocutions of his subjects, as though he were indeed turning (in William James's phrase) "the cube of reality." One is left with the belief that in any given situation there are many truths — as many, so to speak, as there are persons involved, as there are witnesses, as there are ways of thinking about it. And encompassing all these is the shadowy probability that none of them is or can be final. What we see in Robinson's work is the unending and obsessional effort to make sense of experience when perhaps there is none to be made. The poet, the reader, all of us are members of humanity in the sense Robinson intended when he characterized the earth as "a kind of vast spiritual kindergarten where millions of people are trying to spell God with the wrong blocks."

It is through people that Robinson found the hints and gleams of the universal condition that he could not help trying to solve. Like other human beings, he was cursed with intelligence and sensibility in a universe made for material objects. "The world is a hell of a place," he once said, "but the universe is a fine thing," and again, "We die of what we eat and drink,/But more we die of what we think." Robinson has been perhaps the only American poet — certainly the only one of major status — interested *exclusively* in human beings as subject matter for poetry — in the psychological, motivational aspects of living, in the inner life as it is projected upon the outer. His work is one vast attempt to tell the stories that no man can really tell, for no man can know their real meaning, their real intention, or even whether such exists, though it persistently appears to do so. In all Robinson's people the Cosmos seems to be brooding in one way or another, so that a man and woman sitting in a garden, as in "Mortmain," are, in *what* they are, exemplars of eternal laws that we may guess at but not know. The laws are present in psychological constitutions as surely as they are in physical materials, in the orbital patterns of stars and planets and atoms, only deeper hid, more tragic and mysterious, "as there might somewhere be veiled/Eternal reasons why the tricks of time/Were played like this."

Robinson wrote an enormous amount of poetry (how one's mind quails at the sheer *weight,* the physical bulk, of his fifteen-hundred-page *Collected Poems!*), but at the center of it and all through it is the Personality, the Mind, conditioned by its accidental placement in time and space — these give the individuations that make drama possible — but also partaking of the hidden universals, the not-to-be-knowns that torment all men. In these poems "The strange and unremembered light/ That is in dreams" plays over "The nameless and eternal tragedies/That render hope and hopelessness akin." Like a man speaking under torture — or self-torture — Robinson tells of these things, circling them, painfully shifting from one possible interpretation to another, and the reader circles with him, making, for want of any received, definitive opinion, hesitant, troubling, tentative judgments. The result is an unresolved view, but a view of remarkable richness and suggestibility, opening out in many directions and unsealing many avenues of possibility: a multidimensional view that the reader is left pondering as the poem has pondered, newly aware of his own enigmas, of what he and his own life — its incidents and fatalities — may mean, could mean, and thus he is likely to feel himself linked into the insoluble universal equation, in which nature itself is only a frame of mind, a projection of inwardness, tormenting irresolution, and occasional inexplicable calms.

. . . she could look

Right forward through the years, nor any more
Shrink with a cringing prescience to behold
The glitter of dead summer on the grass,
Or the grown-glimmered crimson of still trees
Across the intervale where flashed along,
Black-silvered, the cold river.

## II

As has been said, Robinson's method — which on some fronts has been labeled antipoetic — would not amount to as much as it does were not the modes of thought presented in

such powerful and disturbing dramatic forms. For an "anti-
poet," Robinson was an astonishing craftsman. One has only
to read a few of his better poems in the classic French repeti-
tive forms, such as "The House on the Hill," to recognize the
part that traditional verse patterns play in his work. This much
is demonstrable. It is among those who believe the poetic essence to lie somewhere outside or beyond such considerations,
somewhere in the image-making, visual, and visionary realm,
that Robinson's position has been challenged. And it is true
that his verse is oddly bare, that there are few images in it —
though, of these, some are very fine indeed — and that most of
it is highly cerebral and often written in a scholarly or pseudo-
scholarly manner that is frequently more than a little pedantic.
Many of his poems contain an element of self-parody, and
these carry more than their share of bad, flat, stuffy writing.

> There were slaves who dragged the shackles of a
>     precedent unbroken,
> Demonstrating the fulfillment of unalterable schemes,
> Which had been, before the cradle, Time's inexorable
>     tenants
> Of what were now the dusty ruins of their fathers'
>     dreams.

Infrequently there is also a kind of belaboring-beyond-belabor-
ing of the obvious:

> The four square somber things that you see first
> Around you are four walls that go as high
> As to the ceiling.

And now and then one comes on philosophical pronounce-
ments of a remarkable unconvincingness, demonstrating a total
failure of idiom, of art:

> Too much of that
> May lead you by and by through gloomy lanes
> To a sad wilderness, where one may grope
> Alone, and always, or until he feels
> Ferocious and invisible animals
> That wait for men and eat them in the dark.

At his worst, Robinson seems to go on writing long after whatever he has had to say about the subject has been exhausted;
there is a suspicious look of automatism about his verse instrument. The reader, being made of less stern stuff, will almost always fail before Robinson's blank verse does.

Robinson certainly wrote too much. Like Wordsworth —
even more than Wordsworth, if that is possible — he is in need
of selective editing. In the present book, *The Selected Poems
of Edwin Arlington Robinson,* this is what the late Morton
Dauwen Zabel has done, and I believe with singular success.
The Robinson of this book is much more nearly the essential,
the permanently valuable Robinson than the Robinson of the
*Collected Poems,* though there are unavoidable exclusions —
particularly of the good book-length poems, such as *Lancelot*
and *Merlin* — which one might legitimately regret and to which
it is hoped that the reader will eventually have recourse. Yet
even in the present volume one is likely to be put off by the
length of many of the pieces. Then, too, if the casual reader
skims only a little of a particular poem and finds that nothing
much is happening or that event, action, and resolution are
taking place only in various persons' minds, he is also likely
to shy away. But once in the poem, committed to it, with his
mind winding among the alternative complexities of Robinson's
characters' minds — that is, winding with Robinson's mind —
the reader changes slowly, for Robinson hath his will. One is
held by the curious dry magic that seems so eminently un-
magical, that bears no resemblance to the elfin or purely verbal
or native-woodnote magic for which English verse is justly
celebrated. It is a magic for which there is very little precedent
in all literature. Though external affinities may be asserted
and even partially demonstrated with Praed and Browning,
though there are occasional distant echoes of Wordsworth,
Keats, Hardy, and Rossetti, Robinson is really like none of
them in his root qualities; his spell is cast with none of the
traditional paraphernalia, but largely through his own reading
of character and situation and fate, his adaptation of traditional poetic devices to serve these needs — an adaptation so unexpected, so revolutionary, as to seem not so much adaptation
as transformation.

Another odd thing about Robinson is that his best work

and his worst are remarkably alike. The qualities that make
the good poems good are the same qualities that make the
bad poems bad; it is only a question of how Robinson's method
works out in, "takes to," the situation he is depicting, and
often the difference between good, bad, and mediocre is thin
indeed. This difficulty is also compounded by the fact that
Robinson is equally skilled as a technician in both memorable
poems and trivial ones. In the less interesting poems, particularly the longer ones, Robinson's air of portentousness can be
tiresome. Reading these, one is tempted to say that Robinson
is the most prolific *reticent* poet in history. Though he gives
the impression that he is reluctant to write down what he is
writing, he often goes on and on, in a kind of intelligent mum-
bling, a poetical wringing of the hands, until the reader becomes restive and a little irritated. In these passages, Robinson's verse instrument has a certain kinship with the salt
maker in the fairy tale, grinding away of its own accord at the
bottom of the sea. Then there is the gray, austere landscape
of the poems, the lack of background definition. One is accustomed to finding the characters in a poem — particularly
a narrative poem — in a *place,* a location with objects and a
weather of its own, a world which the reader can enter and
in which he can, as it were, live with the characters. But there
is very little of the environmental in Robinson's work. What
few gestures and concessions he makes to the outside world
are token ones; all externality is quickly devoured by the tormented introversion of his personages. In Robinson, the mind
eats everything and converts it to part of a conflict with self;
one could say with some justification that all Robinson's
poems are about people who are unable to endure themselves
or to resolve their thoughts into some meaningful, cleansing
action. So much introversion is not only harrowing; it can
also be boring, particularly when carried on to the enormous
lengths in which it appears in "Matthias at the Door" and
"Avon's Harvest."

And yet with these strictures, the case against Robinson's
poetry has pretty much been stated, and we have on our hands
what remains after they have been acknowledged.

### III

No poet ever understood loneliness or separateness better

than Robinson or knew the self-consuming furnace that the brain can become in isolation, the suicidal hellishness of it, doomed as it is to feed on itself in answerless frustration, fated to this condition by the accident of human birth, which carries with it the hunger for certainty and the intolerable load of personal recollections. He understood loneliness in all its many forms and depths and was thus less interested in its conventional poetic aspects than he was in the loneliness of the man in the crowd, or alone with his thoughts of the dead, or feeling at some unforeseen time the metaphysical loneliness, the *angst,* of being "lost among the stars," or becoming aware of the solitude that resides in comfort and in the affection of friend and family — that desperation at the heart of what is called happiness. It is only the poet and those involved who realize the inevitability and the despair of these situations, "Although, to the serene outsider,/There still would seem to be a way."

The acceptance of the fact that there is no way, that there is nothing to do about the sadness of most human beings when they are alone or speaking to others as if to themselves, that there is nothing to offer them but recognition, sympathy, compassion, deepens Robinson's best poems until we sense in them something other than art. A thing inside us is likely to shift from where it was, and our world view to change, though perhaps only slightly, toward a darker, deeper perspective. Robinson has been called a laureate of failure and has been accused (if that is the word) of making a cult and a virtue of failure, but that assessment is not quite accurate. His subject was "the slow tragedy of haunted men," those whose "eyes are lit with a wrong light," those who believe that some earthly occurrence in the past (and now forever impossible) could have made all the difference, that some person dead or otherwise beyond reach, some life unlived and now unlivable, could have been the answer to everything. But these longings were seen by Robinson to be the delusions necessary to sustain life, for human beings, though they can live without hope, cannot live believing that no hope ever could have existed. For this reason, many of the poems deal with the unlived life, the man kept by his own nature or by circumstances from "what might have been his," but there is always the ironic Robinsonian overtone that what might have been would not have been much better than what is — and, indeed, might well have been worse; the failure would only have had its development and setting altered somewhat, but not its pain or its inevitability.

Though Robinson's dramatic sense was powerful and often profound, his narrative sense was not. His narrative devices are few, and they are used again and again. The poet is always, for example, running into somebody in the street whom he knew under other circumstances and who is now a bum, a "slowly-freezing Santa Claus," a street-corner revivalist, or something equally comical-pathetic and cut off. The story of the person's passing from his former state to this one then becomes the poem, sometimes told by the derelict, the "ruin who meant well," and sometimes puzzled out by the poet himself, either with his deep, painful probing or, as in some of the later long poems, such as "The Man Who Died Twice," with an intolerable amount of poetical hemming and hawing, backing and filling.

And yet Robinson's peculiar elliptical vision, even when it is boring, is worth the reader's time. The tone of his voice is so distinctive, his technique so varied and resourceful, and his compassion so intense that something valuable comes through even the most wasteful of his productions. Not nearly enough has been made of Robinson's skill, the chief thing about which is that it is able to create, through an astonishing number of forms and subjects, the tone of a single voice, achieving variety within a tonal unity. And it is largely in this tone, the product of outlook (or, if I may be forgiven, inlook), technique, and personality, that Robinson's particular excellence lies; thus the tone is worth examining.

Robinson's mind was not sensuously rich, if by that is meant a Keatsian or Hopkinsian outgoingness into nature as a bodily experience and the trust and delight in nature that this attitude implies. His poetic interests are psychological and philosophical; he examines the splits between what is and what might have been, what must be and what cannot be. That Robinson sees these differences to matter very little, finally, does not mean that they do not matter to the people who suffer from them; it is, in fact, in this realm of delusionary and obsessive suffering that Robinson's poems take place. Though his mind was not rich in a sensuous way, it was both powerful and hesitant, as though suspended between strong magnets. This gives his work an unparalleled sensitivity in balance; and from this balance, this desperately poised uncertainty, emanates a compassion both very personal and cosmic — a compassion that one might well see as a substitute for the compassion that God failed to supply. It is ironic at times, it is bitter and self-mocking, but it is always compassion unalloyed by sentimentality; it has been earned, as it is the burden of the poems themselves to show. This attitude, this tone, runs from gentle, rueful humor — though based, even so, on stark constants of human fate such as the aging process and death — to the most terrible hopelessness. It may appear in the tortuous working out of a long passage, or it may gleam forth for an instant in surroundings not seen until its appearance to be frightening, as in the poem below.

"Isaac and Archibald" is a New England pastoral in which a twelve-year-old boy takes a long walk with an old man, Isaac, to visit another old man at his farm. Nothing much happens, except that both Isaac and Archibald manage to reveal to the boy the signs of mental decline and approaching death in the other. The two men drink cider; the boy sits and reflects, prefiguring as he does the mature man and poet he will become. The boy's awareness of death is built up by small, affectionate touches, some of them so swift and light that they are almost sure to be passed over by the hurried reader.

> Hardly had we turned in from the main road
> When Archibald, with one hand on his back
> And the other clutching his huge-headed cane,
> Came limping down to meet us. — "Well! well! well!"
> Said he; and then he looked at my red face,
> All streaked with dust and sweat, and shook my hand,
> And said it must have been a right smart walk
> That we had had that day from Tilbury Town. —
> "Magnificent," said Isaac; and he told
> About the beautiful west wind there was
> Which cooled and clarified the atmosphere.
> "You must have made it with your legs, I guess,"
> Said Archibald; and Isaac humored him

With one of those infrequent smiles of his
Which he kept in reserve, apparently,
For Archibald alone. "But why," said he,
"Should Providence have cider in the world
If not for such an afternoon as this?"
And Archibald, with a soft light in his eyes,
Replied that if he chose to go down cellar,
There he would find eight barrels — one of which
Was newly tapped, he said, and to his taste
An honor to the fruit. Isaac approved
Most heartily of that, and guided us
Forthwith, as if his venerable feet
Were measuring the turf in his own door-yard,
Straight to the open rollway. Down we went,
Out of the fiery sunshine to the gloom,
Grateful and half sepulchral, where we found
The barrels, like eight potent sentinels,
Close ranged along the wall. From one of them
A bright pine spile stuck out alluringly,
And on the black flat stone, just under it,
Glimmered a late-spilled proof that Archibald
Had spoken from unfeigned experience.
There was a fluted antique water-glass
Close by, and in it, prisoned, or at rest,
There was a cricket, of the soft brown sort
That feeds on darkness. Isaac turned him out,
And touched him with his thumb to make him
      jump. . . .

Until the introduction of the cricket and the few words that
typify it, there is nothing startling in the passage, though it is
quite good Robinson, with the judicious adverb "alluringly"
attached to the protrusion of the pine spile and the lovely
affectionate irony of Archibald's "unfeigned experience" with
the cider. But the cricket, of the sort that feeds on darkness,
changes the poem and brings it into the central Robinsonian
orbit. Here, the insect is a more terrifying and mysterious
creature — a better symbol for the context — than a maggot
or dead louse would be, for it is normally a benign spirit of
household and hearth. This simple way of referring to it, as

though the supposition that it "feeds on darkness" were the most obvious and natural thing in the world to say about it, produces a haunting effect when encountered along with the gentle old farmers' proximity to death and the boy's budding awareness of it.

It may be inferred from the above passages that Robinson is not a writer of unremitting brilliance or a master of the more obvious technical virtuosities. He is, rather, as has been said, a poet of quick, tangential thrusts, of sallies and withdrawals, of fleeting hints and glimpsed implications. In his longer poems, particularly, the impacts build up slowly, and it is only to those who have not the sensitivity to catch the sudden, baffling, half-revealing gleams — those who are "annoyed by no such evil whim/As death, or time, or truth" — that Robinson's poems are heavy and dull. Though he has a way, particularly in the later poems, of burying his glints of meaning pretty deeply in the material that makes them possible, Robinson at his best manages to use the massiveness of discourse and the swift, elusive gleam of illumination — the momentary flashing into the open of a stark, tragic hint, a fleeting generalization — as complementaries. And when the balance between these elements is right, the effect is unforgettable.

At times it appears that Robinson not only did not seek to avoid dullness but courted it and actually used it as a device, setting up his major points by means of it and making them doubly effective by contrast, without in the least violating the unity of tone or the huge, heavy drift of the poem toward its conclusion. He is a slow and patient poet; taking his time to say a thing as he wishes to say it is one of his fundamental qualities. This has worked against him, particularly since his work has survived into an age of anything but slow and patient readers. The pedestrian movement of much of his work has made him unpopular in an era when the piling on of startling effects, the cramming of the poetic line with all the spoils it can carry, is regarded not so much as a criterion of good or superior verse of a certain kind, but as poetry itself, other kinds being relegated to inferior categories yet to be defined. But Robinson's considered, unhurried lines, as uncomplicated in syntax as they are difficult in thought, in reality are, by virtue of their enormous sincerity, conviction, and

quiet originality, a constant rebuke to those who conceive of
poetry as verbal legerdemain or as the "superior amusement"
that the late T. S. Eliot would have had it be.

The Robinson line is simple in the way that straightforward English prose is simple; the declarative sentence is made
to do most of the work. His questions, though comparatively
rare, are weighed with the agony of concern, involvement, and
uncertainty. It is the thought, rather than the expression of the
thought, that makes some of Robinson difficult, for he was
almost always at pains to write simply, and his skills were
everywhere subservient to this ideal. My personal favorite
of Robinson's effects is his extremely subtle use of the line as
a means of changing the meaning of the sentence that forms
the line, the whole poem changing direction slightly but unmistakably with each such shift.

> What is it in me that you like so much,
> And love so little?

And yet for all his skill, Robinson's technical equipment is
never obvious or obtrusive, as Hopkins', say, is. This is, of
course, a tribute to his resourcefulness, for in his best pieces
the manner of the poem is absorbed into its matter, and we
focus not on the mode of saying but on the situations and
characters into whose presence we have come.

### IV

Robinson's favorite words, because they embody his favorite way of getting at any subject, are "may" and "might."
The whole of the once-celebrated "The Man Against the Sky,"
for example, is built upon their use. When the poet sees a man
climbing Mount Monadnock, it is, for the purposes of his
poem, important that he not know who the man is or what he
is doing there, so that the poem can string together a long
series of conjectural possibilities as to who he might be, what
might happen to him, and what he might conceivably represent.

> Even he, who stood where I had found him,
> On high with fire all around him,
> Who moved along the molten west,
> And over the round hill's crest

That seemed half ready with him to go down,
Flame-bitten and flame-cleft,
As if there were to be no last thing left
Of a nameless unimaginable town —
Even he who climbed and vanished may have taken
Down to the perils of a depth not known. . . .

When he reaches the word's "may have," the reader is in true Robinson country; he lives among alternatives, possibilities, doubts, and delusionary gleams of hope. This particular poem, which not only uses this approach but virtually hounds it to death, is not successful mainly because Robinson insists on being overtly philosophical and, at the end, on committing himself to a final view. Another shortcoming is that he is not sufficiently close to the man, for his poems are much better when he knows *something* of the circumstances of a human life, tells what he knows, and *then* speculates, for the unresolved quality of his ratiocinations, coupled with the usually terrible *facts,* enables him to make powerful and haunting use of conjecture and of his typical "may have" or "might not have" presentations of alternative possibilities.

It is also true of this poem that it has very little of the leavening of Robinson's irony, and this lack is detrimental to it. This irony has been widely commented upon, but not, I think, quite as accurately as it might have been. Though it infrequently has the appearance of callousness or even cruelty, a closer examination, a more receptive *feeling* of its effect, will usually show that it is neither. It is, rather, a product of a detachment based on helplessness, on the saving grace of humor that is called into play because nothing practical can be done and because the spectator of tragedy must find some way in which to save himself emotionally from the effects of what he has witnessed.

No, no — forget your Cricket and your Ant,
For I shall never set my name to theirs
That now bespeak the very sons and heirs
Incarnate of Queen Gossip and King Cant.
The case of Leffingwell is mixed, I grant,
And futile seems the burden that he bears;

But are we sounding his forlorn affairs
Who brand him parasite and sycophant?

I tell you, Leffingwell was more than these;
And if he prove a rather sorry knight,
What quiverings in the distance of what light
May not have lured him with high promises,
And then gone down? — He may have been deceived;
He may have lied — he did; and he believed.

The irony here is not based on showing in what ridiculous and humiliating ways the self-delusion of Leffingwell made of him a parasite and sycophant; it works through and past these things to the much larger proposition that such delusion is necessary to life; that, in fact, it is the condition that enables us to function at all. The manufacture and protection of the self-image is really the one constant, the one obsessive concern, of our existence. This idea was, of course, not new with Robinson, though it may be worth mentioning that many psychiatrists, among them Alfred Adler and Harry Stack Sullivan, place a primary emphasis on such interpretations of the human mentality. What should be noted is that the lies of Leffingwell and of Uncle Ananias are in their way truths, for they have in them that portion of the truth that comes not from fact but from the ideal.

All summer long we loved him for the same
Perennial inspiration of his lies . . .

There is something more here, something more positive, than there is in the gloomy and one-dimensional use of similar themes in, say, Eugene O'Neill's The Iceman Cometh, for in Robinson's poems the necessity to lie (and, with luck, sublimely) is connected to the desire to remake the world by remaking that portion of it that is oneself. Robinson shows the relation between such lies and the realities they must struggle to stay alive among, and he shows them with the shrewdness and humor of a man who has told such lies to himself but sadly knows them for what they are. The reader is likely to smile at the absurdity — but also to be left with a new kind of admiration for certain human traits that he had theretofore believed pathetic or contemptible.

## V

These, then, are Robinson's kinds of originality, of poetic value — all of them subtle and half-hidden, muffled and disturbing, answering little but asking those questions that are unpardonable, unforgettable, and necessary.

It is curious and wonderful that this scholarly, intelligent, childlike, tormented New England stoic, "always hungry for the nameless," always putting in the reader's mouth "some word that hurts your tongue," useless for anything but his art, protected by hardier friends all his life, but enormously courageous and utterly dedicated (he once told Chard Powers Smith at the very end of his life, "I could never have done *anything* but write poetry"), should have brought off what in its quiet, searching, laborious way is one of the most remarkable accomplishments of modern poetry. Far from indulging, as his detractors have maintained, in a kind of poetical know-nothingism, he actually brought to poetry a new kind of approach, making of a refusal to pronounce definitively on his subjects a virtue and of speculation upon possibilities an instrument that allows an unparalleled fullness to his presentations, as well as endowing them with some of the mysteriousness, futility, and proneness to multiple interpretation that incidents and lives possess in the actual world.

Robinson's best poetry is exactly that kind of communication that "tells the more the more it is not told." In creating a body of major poetry with devices usually thought to be unfruitful for the creative act — irresolution, abstraction, conjecture, a dry, nearly imageless mode of address that tends always toward the general without ever supplying the resolving judgment that we expect of generalization — Robinson has done what good poets have always done: by means of his "cumulative silences" as well as by his actual lines, he has forced us to reexamine and finally to redefine what poetry is — or our notion of it — and so has enabled poetry itself to include more, to be more, than it was before he wrote.

# Frost's
# Momentary Stay

by Roy Harvey Pearce

The stir caused by Mr. Lionel Trilling's by now notorious speech at Robert Frost's eighty-fifth birthday dinner is surely an effect, not a cause, of our recent concern to resolve the problem that Frost's poetry poses for us. Reading J. Donald Adams' diatribe on the Trilling speech — issued from the ambush of his *Times Book Review* easy chair — reading this, one realized (rather wearily) that Mr. Adams just didn't want to yield Frost up to "modern criticism." The grounds were that Frost himself wouldn't want to do so, that he couldn't do so; and the letters which poured into the *Times* turned out to be not pro-Frost, but pro-Adams, therefore anti-Trilling, therefore anti-"modern."

"Frost's Momentary Stay" by Roy Harvey Pearce. From *Kenyon Review*, xxiii (Spring 1961) 258-73. Reprinted by permission of the author and the editors of *Kenyon Review*. This essay appears in different form in *Continuity of American Poetry*, Princeton University Press, 1961.

Yet modern criticism has taken over; and the cries of the anguished were those of Ordinary Readers so insecure in their ordinariness as to have no weapon against modernism except cries of anguish. Indeed, modern criticism had taken over long before Mr. Trilling announced that, even as Margaret Fuller accepted the Universe, he accepted Frost — but then, being Mr. Trilling, in effect added the bluntly ingenuous Carlylean "I damned well have to," which so infuriated Mr. Adams and his fans. For Frost's poetry, as many before Mr. Trilling have pointed out, is a "modernist" poetry, if of a special kind. And now we seem to be ready to define and assess that kind. Issues in the fuss over Frost have shifted; and we have recently been given a biography (Elizabeth Sergeant's *Robert Frost: Trial by Existence*) and two long critical studies (George Nitchie's *Human Values in the Poetry of Robert Frost* and John Lynen's *The Pastoral Art of Robert Frost*). "Accepting" Frost's work, the biographer tries to place it in the context of a heroic life, and the critics try to describe and explicate, and evaluate it in the context of a not-so-heroic culture. But I am not sure that even they have inquired fully into what it means to "accept" Frost's poetry. That is, they do not get around to asking that do-or-die post critical question: what *difference* does that poetry make? — not to Frost, but to his readers, living as and where they live. And I would suggest that its peculiar value is that it is such as to be not quite "available" to its readers. Its modernism is such as to defy — or at least, test — theirs. It does not resist criticism, but rather its readers: above all, when they would be Critics, extraordinarily Ordinary Readers. Reading Frost's poetry, we may find ourselves cast adrift, in a world that we, not Robert Frost, have made.

To say that one is cast adrift, of course, is a distinctly modernist way of saying that one is free. And Frost has recently been willing to speak explicitly about freedom in the modern world — this on the occasion of his being awarded the Emerson-Thoreau medal of the American Academy of Arts and Sciences. His speech is printed in *Daedalus* (Spring 1959) and goes, in part, like this:

> I owe more to Emerson than anyone else for troubled thoughts about freedom. I had the hurt to get over when I

first heard us made fun of by foreigners as the land of the free and the home of the brave. Haven't we won freedom? Is there no such thing as freedom? Well, Emerson says of God "Would take the sun out of the skies/Ere freedom out of a man." and there rings the freedom I choose.

I am on record as saying that freedom is nothing but departure—setting forth—leaving things behind, brave origination of the courage to be new. . . .

Now, it is most important to note that Frost allies himself with Emerson, not Whitman — thereby demonstrating that he has resisted the temptation (so fatal because so self-assuring) to take a way of poetry that only a person as tremendous as Whitman could take without losing his identity as poet. Even better than Emerson, Frost knows the dangers of too much inwardness. For this is clearly an Emersonian sentiment, and yet not quite the sort entertained by those readers who would make him "easier" than he is — a celebrant of hardheaded self-reliance, village style, a "sound" poet because somehow "traditional." Moreover, in the poems themselves, even this authentic Emersonianism is qualified — qualified by being projected always out of situations which are not quite "modern." (But then: consciousness about "modernity," antagonism toward it, is one clear symptom of modernism. "Traditionalists" flee from the modern world because they have been there before.) Frost has no interest in being a specifically "contemporary" poet — which is what Emerson felt he had to be, or perish. Moreover, in his poems Frost is master of all he surveys in a way that Emerson would never allow himself to be. Frost knows himself as a person so well, he can record the knowledge in such exacting detail, that he never has occasion to celebrate the more general and inclusive concept of self which is everywhere the efficient cause of Emerson's poetry.

The gain is one of objectivity and precision. Unlike his prose (of which there is precious little), his poetry is not at all slippery. The loss is one of that inclusiveness and sense of ever-widening possibility, characteristic of Emerson's poetry at its best. Emerson, we come to realize, *wants* his poetry to be slippery, because he is always skeptical about that which is tightly and firmly ordered; it might be too much under control.

At the heart of Frost's achievement lies his ability to consolidate the Emersonian mode, to adopt it on his own terms, and
so make it a means whereby a certain stability and certitude,
however limited, might be achieved. From his position of
strength, he bids others depart—and leave him behind. As poet,
he will not be a leader. The farthest thing from his mind is the
desire to be a culture hero. For good and for bad, this has been
the heart's desire of most men of his predecessors and contemporaries. And herein his work marks a pause—a series of
momentary stays against confusion (to use his words)—in the
continuity of American poetry. Frost is our greatest stocktaker.

The major tradition of American poetry before his time—
the "romantic" tradition—serves Frost as a limiting condition
for the making of poems. He has come to be a large poet (in a
way, our most "complete" poet) because he knows how small
man is when he acknowledges the limitations within which he
labors. Frost has been able to perfect his work as has none of
his contemporaries. Maybe we refer to this sort of thing when
we are tempted to speak of him as a "minor poet." We mean
perhaps that in his work he portrays a world, and himself in
it, that is — as I have said — not so readily available to us as
that of some of his contemporaries. In any case, he has known
quite clearly what he has been doing. As a title of one of his
later poems has it, he is "Not Quite Social." The poem begins:

> Some of you will be glad I did what I did,
> And the rest won't want to punish me too severely
> For finding a thing to do that though not forbid
> Yet wasn't enjoined and wasn't expected clearly.

The conditions which circumscribe Frost's poems are those
of a world not yet dominated by urban, industrialized, bureau-
cratized culture—the very world which, seeing its inevitable
coming, Emerson and his kind strove to confront and save for
man before it would be too late. Frost glances at this world,
only to turn to a one he knows better. In that world the proper
life style—which in turn generates the literary style—is that of
Frost's characteristic protagonists: individuals who again and
again are made to face up to the fact of their individualism as
such; who can believe that a community is no more than the
sum of the individuals who make it up; who are situated so as

to have only a dim sense, even that resisted mightily, of the transformations which the individual might have to undergo if he is to live fully in the modern world and still retain his identity as an individual. But, of course, Frost's protagonists refuse to live fully in the modern world and will have little or nothing to do with such transformations. Frost's work is in the end a series of expressions of that refusal and assessments of its cost. The cost is great, and is acknowledged unflinchingly. Reading Frost, many of us—finding ourselves in the end unable to go along with him and deny the world in which we live—must deny the world of a poet who will not live in ours with us. It is not so much that he doesn't speak our language, but that we do not, cannot, speak his. Perhaps he means for us to deny his world, so that we will be forced to live in our own, all the while knowing just how much we must pay in order to do so. This indeed would be freedom, but a dreadful freedom, generating none of the confidence in the future toward which Emerson pointed his poems. "Troubled thoughts," indeed!

And even if we cannot speak his language, we yet know what he means. We listen to him as we would listen to a sage, not daring to interrupt him because not knowing how. (Is this why we are so relieved when he shifts to his cracker-barrel podium and chats with us? He really is like one of us, we say; and then we try awkwardly to translate the poems into chat, so as to discover that we might still have a Fireside Poet living among us.) His individualism, as it comes out in his poems, is of a self which is emphatically not free to sound its barbaric yawp over the roof-tops of the world. Its freedom is a freedom to decide not what it will do unto others but rather what it will allow others to do unto it. One of the most telling expressions of this sense of solidarity by abnegation is the late poem "Directive," which begins:

> Back out of all this now too much for us,
> Back in a time made simple by the loss
> Of detail, burned, dissolved, and broken off
> Like graveyard marble sculpture in the weather,
> There is a house that is no more a house
> Upon a farm that is no more a farm
> And in a town that is no more a town.

The opening statement is marked first by a groping, hesitant, syntax, then by a series of strong parallelisms, a shifting of accents reinforces the shifting syntactic effect. Thus the poet hesitates and then confronts the modern world. Then, as he moves to describe the place—as, in fact, he *finds* a place, however foregone, to describe—the tone strengthens and the accents are regularized carrying on the effect achieved by the parallelisms which close the opening statement. The house, and its "village culture," he admits, are lost. He tells the reader:

> And if you're lost enough to find yourself
> By now, pull in your ladder road behind you
> And put a sign up CLOSED to all but me.
> Then make yourself at home. . . .

And, at the end, he bids the reader: From a brook close to the house, in a cup stolen from the deserted playhouse nearby, "Drink and be whole again beyond confusion." Frost will not, like Emerson in "Each and All," say: "I yielded myself to the perfect whole." He is, perhaps, nearer to Melville's Bartleby, with his "I prefer not to." Bartleby was driven to prison and suicide. Frost is driven to mountain and farm, to wholeness "beyond confusion," to life simplified. His act of self-assertion is an act performed in a place that is not quite a place and in a time that is no longer a time, but a memory of one. If this "Drink . . ." is sacramental, it is nonetheless he who has given the sacraments to himself. In one of his earliest poems, "The Vantage Point," he had written:

> If tired of trees I seek again mankind,
>     Well I know where to hie me—in the dawn,
>     To a slope where the cattle keep the lawn.
> There amid lolling juniper reclined,
> Myself unseen, I see in white defined
>     Far off the homes of men. . . .

Confusion is stayed, but from a distance. The distance is such that the poet could not listen to us even if we did know how to speak back to him.

But we have had a vision of "wholeness" and have been brought to acknowledge the fact that each man's wholeness is ineluctably his own. Thus the poignancy which we sense in

the poems must be for Frost more than that, tragedy and often
the bitter comedy which is beyond tragedy. We sense the poignancy too in the famous essay, delivered *ex cathedra*, from
which I have taken my title, "The Figure a Poem Makes." This
essay, written in mid-career, is a striking statement of Frost's
faith in the poem as means of filling out and realizing the substantial concerns which mark the poet's existence as man among
men: "the . . . mystery is how a poem can have wildness and
at the same time a subject that shall be fulfilled." All he wants
for the poet is "freedom."

> Political freedom is nothing to me. I bestow it right and
> left. All I would keep for myself is the freedom of my ma-
> terial—the condition of body and mind now and then to
> summons aptly from the vast chaos of all I have lived
> through.

The poet, simply enough, wants to be free to be himself. And
later:

> The artist must value himself as he snatches a thing from
> some previous order in time and space into a new order
> with not so much as a ligature clinging to it of the old
> place where it was organic.

"A new order" with new persons in it—free from the past
yet somehow defined by it. Frost's indebtedness to Emerson,
his proclamation of which has already been quoted, is clear.
Yet he puts the Emersonian doctrine of freedom to his own
special use. For Emerson, and his great contemporaries too,
conceived of the "free" person as, by internal necessity, one
who had to break through and away from substantial concerns
—the life of the workaday world, the life of the older order—so
as to *transform* himself in the breaking. Substance but fed sensibility, so that sensibility might create ever new substances
consonant with ever renewed sensibilities. Emerson broke from
the past in order to look forward. Frost does so in order to
look at the here and now, and thereby is far more loyal to the
past than Emerson could bear to be.

For Frost there is a new order, to be sure; but it is the product of a recovery and reconstitution, rather than of a rein-

vention and transformation, of the old. For the great nineteenth-century poets, life consisted of an infinite series of willed, self-generated transformations forward; the opportunity for each transformation was only that—an opportunity, its possibilities exhausted as soon as the transformation had occurred. Thus their insistent anti-formalism and their "organicism"; for the expressive form called for by one opportunity would not be that called for by another, would have to be integral to the new opportunity. Thus, in the deepest sense, the "opportunism" of their poetry. In Frost, however, this conception of the transformative opportunity has been stabilized to a point where it is not a means of advancing, but of withdrawing and consolidating. And the conception of transformation itself has atrophied and been sloughed off. Sensibility is sacrificed to substance, because so wonderfully constrained by it; achievement is possible because it is taken to be valuable only as it leads to, not as it points beyond, the specific achievement. The freedom, he might say, allows him to define, not to unleash, himself. To be sure, Frost has called freedom "departure." But, as he departs, he looks backward, not forward. He would have us enjoy our going hence because he knows so well whence we have come hither.

Frost's best poems demonstrate (at one notable point in so many words) his certainty that he is one kind of man moving down one kind of a road. The most telling of the poems are the monologues and dialogues which begin in *North of Boston,* early in his career. Again and again the subject is the failure of communication, a failure which shows just how small and delimited the effective comunity can be. As often as not it comes to be a community of one—a community which can be called such only because its existence is, as it were, authorized by the fact that all men of high sensibility who live in it will quite readily come to recognize that in the end they can communicate only the fact that they cannot communicate, that they can but find the rather limited terms in which they can communicate this fact. The terms—deriving from Frost's abiding sense of farm, mountains, and village life—are sharp enough to cut off cleanly from his fellows him who lives by them.

Moreover, Frost is honest and clear-headed enough to admit that they cut off from one another even those who do mutually live by them. This sentiment is at the heart of most of the monologues and dialogues:

> He moves in darkness as it seems to me,
> Not of woods only and the shade of trees.
> He will not go behind his father's saying. . . .
> ("Mending Wall")

> It seems to me
> I can't express my feelings any more
> Than I can raise my voice or want to lift
> My hand (oh, I can lift it when I have to).
> Did ever you feel so? I hope you never.
> It's got so I don't even know for sure
> Whether I *am* glad, sorry, or anything.
> There's nothing but a voice-like left inside
> That seems to tell me how I ought to feel,
> And would feel if I wasn't all gone wrong.
> ("A Servant to Servants")

In "Mending Wall" it is explicitly the poet who is speaking; in "A Servant to Servants" it is a character. This is Frost's range—from one who is given to observe the failure in communication, to those who fail (or think they are failing) because they are not aware that they are being made to speak greater than they know.

Always in Frost there is the desire (or a temptation so strong as to be a desire) to "go behind" something. And most always there is the failure to do so, and then a triumph in living with the failure and discovering that it is a condition of strength—the strength in discovering oneself as a person, limited by the conditions which can be made clearly to define oneself as a person. This is the subject which "shall be fulfilled." In the dramatic poems it is difficult to find precise points where this is fully realized, because the realization is not the protagonist's, but rather the poet's—as a result of the total effect of the poem. For Frost (and this is an aspect of the achievement of such poems) the failure infuses what he makes out to be a whole experience. Here, one might say, Frost is almost a novelist, because the meaning of his poems depends so much upon a minute attendance to the conditions in terms of which particular failures are portrayed. There are moments of pure, unmediated realization, however—epiphanies. Such moments are by definition private and are accordingly rendered in first-person lyrics—"Tree at My Window," "Desert Places," "The Tuft of Flowers," "The Road Not Taken," "Bereft," "Once by the Pacific," "Stopping by Woods . . ." and so many more. To name them is to recall a series of instants of awareness whose abounding clarity is gained at the expense of a certain willed irrelevance to many of the conditions in modern life. This is, one is forced to conclude, a failure which Frost wills so that he can understand it and proceed to build positively out from it.

Frost would have us feel that the failure is inevitable and therefore a means of making some sort of decision about the nature of his world, its people, and their meaning for us. He is realist enough, and delights in his realism, to recognize that many of his readers will be unable to follow him closely. Thus in the late "Lesson for Today," he at length (and in the *persona* of a medieval poet) diagnoses our malaise and justifies his way with poetry:

> Space ails us moderns: we are sick with space.
> Its contemplation makes us out as small
> As a brief epidemic of microbes
> That in a good glass may be seen to crawl
> The patina of this the least of globes.

But his belief is that we are not so different, that "One age is like another for the soul." For:

> We are all doomed to broken-off careers,
> And so's the nation, so's the total race.
> The earth itself is liable to the fate
> Of meaninglessly being broken off.
>
> . . . . . . . . . .
>
> I take my incompleteness with the rest.
> God bless himself can no one else be blessed.
>
> I hold your doctrine of Memento Mori.
> And were an epitaph to be my story
> I'd have a short one ready for my own.
> I would have written of me on my stone:
> I had a lover's quarrel with the world.

A momentary stay against the confusion of a career imminent-
ly to be broken off; an evocation, in terms of a life simpler
than that most of us can know, of the possibility, however
lonely, for the private vision of private wholeness: these are
the conditions of the quarrel which Frost has with those who
live in "the world."

What finally gives the best poems their tremendous effec-
tiveness is a sense of a local detail so sharp, so fully controlled,
so wholly the poet's own, as to make us know once and forever the gulf between his world and all others. Above all, Frost
can call up a sense of place and of the working of an individual
sensibility when limited by and therefore complementary to it:

> He thought he kept the universe alone;
> For all the voice in answer he could wake
> Was but the mocking of his own
> From some tree-hidden cliff across the lake.
> Some morning from the boulder-broken beach
> He would cry out on life, that what he wants
> Is not its own love back in copy speech,
> But counter-love, original response.
> And nothing ever came of what he cried
> Unless it was the embodiment that crashed
> In the cliff's talus on the other side,
> And then in the far distant water splashed,
> But after a time allowed for it to swim,
> Instead of proving human when it neared
> And someone else additional to him,
> As a great buck it powerfully appeared,
> Pushing the crumpled water up ahead,
> And landed pouring like a waterfall,
> And stumbled through the rocks with horny tread,
> And forced the underbrush—and that was all.

Here, in "The Most of It," the place and the occasion first
open up the hope that the protagonist is not really alone, then
close it off; or rather, they render it more ambiguous than it
was before. The book exists on a level somewhere between the
setting and the poet-protagonist in it. Where else, but in a situation like this could Frost find the substance to render his
sense of his self as an individual who can once and for all con-

front himself in all his own individuality? And the diction too
—along with the subtly insistent rhymes which serve to break
up analytically the rush of thought and insight—furnishes the
means to such a confrontation. It is the language of a man who
doubts even the echo of his own voice. Crucially, there is the
word "kept" in the first line. Although at the end the poet-
protagonist surely does not "keep" the "universe alone," still
he cannot be said to "share" it with the buck. Being a "natural"
as opposed to a "human" universe, it is neither to be kept nor
shared. This is one of Frost's major themes, in poems ranging
from "Stopping by Woods . . ." to "After Apple Picking": the
temptation of the "human" to yield wholly to his desire for
the "natural." The "natural" universe of "The Most of It"—as
that in other poems of its type—is an occasion, a situation, a
place, and therefore a means, to discover a limitation. And the
poet is grateful to have found what he sought. The occasion
is not the means of "symbolizing" the poet's relation to nature;
it *is* that relation. The poet discovers that he cannot go beyond
it. Thus: ". . . and that was all."

Frost's mountain world, as his farm world elsewhere, is
conceived of as an analogizing occasion for inner direction.
The poet cannot yield to the "natural" world; he has to *discover*
that he cannot; this is the essence of his humanity; so he turns
inward toward the "human." But it is only one man's world.
Society does not exist as an immediately conditioning factor
in Frost's poems. For him the other man is in effect part of the
"natural" world to which he must not yield.

An Emerson would have demanded much more of such an
occasion. It would have given him yet another opportunity to
move outward to define his vocation, so as Bacchus-like to
project his understanding of it. He would have declared that
the occasion had sought him, even as he had sought it; and he
would have concluded that as a man seeks, so he creates what
he seeks—the true self in a real world of other true selves. He
would not have been satisfied with Frost's ". . . and that was
all"—putting as it does poet, buck, and universe each in their
proper places. Emerson would not have been as clear as Frost
—he never was. But he would have wanted so much more—
which perhaps he never got. And that surely has made all the
difference.

Thus Frost has made his choice. He wills himself and his protagonists to choose, whereas Emerson willed himself to be chosen—unlike Frost, running the risk of losing control not only of his poems but his sense of himself. Frost has always known where he is going; or he says he has. His people are not agonized and tormented by the thought of all the possibilities they have missed. A poem like Emerson's "Days," with its account of opportunities lost, is beyond Frost's ken, because it is irrelevant to it. Frost rather makes his persons recall the days they have had. Thus in "New Hampshire":

> The glorious bards of Massachusetts seem
> To want to make New Hampshire people over.
> They taunt the lofty land with little men.
> I don't know what to say about the people.
> For art's sake one could almost wish them worse
> Rather than better. How are we to write
> The Russian novel in America
> As long as life goes so unterribly?

And later in the same poem:

> Lately in converse with a New York alec
> About the new school of the pseudo-phallic,
> I found myself in a close corner where
> I had to make an almost funny choice.
> "Choose you which you will be—a prude or puke,
> Mewling and puking in the public arms."
> "Me for the hills where I don't have to choose."

This is not retreat but strategic withdrawal, the only means whereby the poet can assess the cost to man of living in the modern world which he has shaped for himself. In "In the Home Stretch," published a few years before "New Hampshire," Frost had dramatized this strategic withdrawal from the point of view of a city couple moving to the country. They have their doubts about the wisdom of the move; the utter lack of sympathy exhibited by the men who are moving their belongings pushes their doubt to a point where it becomes fear. When the movers have left, the husband remarks,

> ". . . We puzzle them. They think —
> I don't know what they think we see in what
> They leave us to. . . ."

Husband and wife are puzzled too: Who first had the idea of moving out of the city? Is this the beginning? the middle? the end? These are the husband's questions. The wife has had the courage to say, " 'Ends and beginnings—there are no such things. There are only middles.' " In this poem, Frost's urban reader becomes his protagonist and learns that at the very least he can come to know how it might be to be able to frame such clear and coherent questions, although there is always the chance that one may "drink and be whole again beyond confusion" and learn to live with answers which are perhaps not clear and coherent. In the hills, that is to say, one is free of the burden of making irrelevant choices, freed to make those which are relevant. Frost addresses his urban reader most directly: the condition of survival is strategic withdrawal. And Frost's work is meant to occasion it.

The sense of withdrawal in Frost is intensified in the generally anti-political poems which he began to write after the publication in 1923 of "New Hampshire." And it culminates in the wry *Masque of Reason* and *Masque of Mercy,* published in 1945 and 1947. Frost has come to taunt his reader, not to challenge him as he had done formerly. In these poems Job and Jonah, seen New Englandly (the term is Emily Dickinson's), can get no satisfaction in their inquiries as to God's hard dealing with them. They have abundant wit and common sense, but little imagination. Thinking about them, one looks back at Frost's earlier work and decides that whatever weakness it has is the weakness of character—a cultivated unwillingness to be a thought-diver (the term is Melville's) for himself and his kind. But surely this is also strength; for it allows Frost to take possession fully of the little world beyond which he will not go. The two *Masques,* then, are apologies for Frost's way with the American imagination. Some of the last lines of the second serve as resolution to both:

> We . . . have lacked the courage in the heart
> To overcome the fear within the soul
> And go ahead to any accomplishment.

> Courage is what it takes and takes the more of
> Because the deeper fear is so eternal.

In such matters, absolute satisfaction is not to be got. There remains but the down-to-earth philosophizing of the *Masques*— but, after all, this is the only sort of philosophizing that the poet is capable of when he comes down out of the hills, more than ever convinced that he doesn't have to make irrelevant choices. Life did go on terribly, and therefore gloriously, for Emerson and the others. They had hoped to learn a way of facing up to it which would transform the terror to glory. Their way, they insisted, was only a way of beginning. For Frost, putting a stasis to their dialectic of the self in its world, it has been a way of living *in medias res*. No ends and beginnings, only middles.

Frost has long well known where and who he is. But more and more he has chosen to speak only to himself, albeit in public. We listen, we are delighted, we are moved and enlightened; but we are on the outside looking in at a poet who remains resolutely on the inside looking out, telling us what we are not by telling us what he and his special kind are. Emerson had written in "Experience": "It is an unhappy thing, but too late to be helped, the discovery we have made that we exist. That discovery is called The Fall of Man." Frost seems to say: "It is an unhappy thing, but too late to be helped, the discovery *I* have made that I exist. You can do it too." In his work the nineteenth-century faith in the ultimate equivalence of the "I" and the "we" has been renounced. He has no need for the after-the-fact transcendentalism toward which such a faith drove Emerson and Whitman. What is gained is a sense of the concrete, particular, bounded "I," anticipated only in the work of Emily Dickinson. Yet Frost lacks even her variety—the product of a mind which dares to be more capacious than his. That is what is lost, the expense of Frost's greatness: variety and capaciousness. Frost manages in his poems to create nothing less than an orthodoxy—as against Emerson's heterodoxy—of the self. It is, however, an orthodoxy of the one—inevitable, and in its inevitability a lesson for our day. We can learn the lesson only if we learn not to recite it. Freedom in the modern world *is* departure—departure even from Robert Frost. As Robert Frost would teach us.

# Wallace Stevens:
# The World as Meditation

*by* Louis Martz

"In an age of disbelief," says Wallace Stevens in a late essay, "it is for the poet to supply the satisfaction of belief, in his measure and in his style." It is my purpose here to explore the nature of those satisfactions, to examine the measure and the style that Stevens achieved in his later poetry, and in this way to suggest the answer that Stevens found to his own blunt question: "What, then, is the nature of poetry in a time of disbelief?" [1]

The answer is implicit in the late poem that provides my theme and title here: *The World as Meditation* (1952) seems to sum up the poetical discoveries of Stevens since that time, some thirty years earlier, when his Paltry Nude started on her Spring Voyage through the world of *Harmonium,* to become at the close of that volume a complete Nomad Exquisite, fully

"Wallace Stevens: The World as Meditation" by Louis L. Martz. From *Literature and Belief: The English Institute Essays for 1957,* ed. M. H. Abrams, pp. 139-165. Copyright © 1958 by Columbia University Press. Reprinted by permission of Columbia University Press.

[1] "Two or Three Ideas" (1951), in *Opus Posthumous,* ed. by Samuel French Morse (New York, 1957), pp. 206, 211 (cited hereafter as OP).

attuned to the harmonies of nature, creating as nature herself creates:

> As the immense dew of Florida
> Brings forth
> The big-finned palm
> And green vine angering for life,
>
> .    .    .    .    .    .    .    .
>
> So, in me, come flinging
> Forms, flames, and the flakes of flames.

The World as Meditation, on the other hand, finds its central proposition, not in any text from the surface of things, but in certain words of a human composer, Georges Enesco: "J'ai passé trop de temps à travailler mon violon, à voyager. Mais l'exercice essentiel du compositeur—la méditation—rien ne l'a jamais suspendu en moi. . . . Je vis un rêve permanent, qui ne s'arrête ni nuit ni jour." With those words as epigraph, the poem presents as its symbol of human achievement the figure of Penelope, awaiting the return of Ulysses. As the sun rises she awakens to the meditation that has composed her life:

> A form of fire approaches the cretonnes of Penelope,
> Whose mere savage presence awakens the world in which she dwells.
>
> She has composed, so long, a self with which to welcome him,
> Companion to his self for her, which she imagined,
> Two in a deep-founded sheltering, friend and dear friend
>
> .    .    .    .    .    .    .    .    .    .    .
>
> But was it Ulysses? Or was it only the warmth of the sun
> On her pillow? The thought kept beating in her like her heart.
> The two kept beating together. It was only day.
>
> It was Ulysses and it was not. Yet they had met,
> Friend and dear friend and a planet's encouragement.
> The barbarous strength within her would never fail.

There is, we see, a "savage presence" outside her, the primitive force of the sun, which arouses within her a "barbarous strength," some primitive human power that makes it possible for her to compose a self, with the sun's encouragement; and so she dwells in a world of belief created by her will. This sounds like the conception found at the close of Steven's essay "The Noble Rider" (1942), where he mentions a certain nobility of mind that constitutes "a violence from within that protects us from a violence without. It is the imagination pressing back against the pressure of reality." Thus the violence of the sun might have aroused Penelope to the violent, ugly pressure of those outward suitors; but her imagination of Ulysses, her constant meditation of reunion with the man she constantly creates in her mind, this power presses back, composes within herself a world of value and order. Thus, as Stevens concludes in that essay, imagination "seems, in the last analysis, to have something to do with our self-preservation." [2]

I have used two terms, both prominent in Stevens' writings: *imagination, meditation;* they are not synonymous. Meditation is the essential exercise which, constantly practiced, brings the imagination into play, releases creative power, enables the human being to compose a sensitive, intelligent, and generous self. It is the sort of self that Stevens has found fully represented in the person of George Santayana, as he points out in an essay of 1948. "Most men's lives," he regretfully concedes, "are thrust upon them" by the outward violence; but he insists:

> There can be lives, nevertheless, which exist by the deliberate choice of those that live them. To use a single illustration: it may be assumed that the life of Professor Santayana is a life in which the function of the imagination has had a function similar to its function in any deliberate work of art or letters. We have only to think of this present phase of it, in which, in his old age, he dwells in the head of the world, in the company of devoted women, in their convent, and in the company of familiar saints, whose presence does so much to make any con-

---

[2] *The Necessary Angel* (New York, 1951), p. 36 (cited hereafter as NA).

vent an appropriate refuge for a generous and human philosopher. [NA, 147-48]

And so in his late poem *To an Old Philosopher in Rome* (1952) he finds the fulfillment of human existence in Santayana's reconciliation of flesh and spirit on the threshold of death:

> The sounds drift in. The buildings are remembered.
> The life of the city never lets go, nor do you
> Ever want it to. It is part of the life in your room.
> Its domes are the architecture of your bed.
>
> .   .   .   .   .   .   .   .   .
>
> It is a kind of total grandeur at the end,
> With every visible thing enlarged and yet
> No more than a bed, a chair and moving nuns,
> The immensest theatre, the pillared porch,
> The book and candle in your ambered room,
>
> Total grandeur of a total edifice,
> Chosen by an inquisitor of structures
> For himself. He stops upon this threshold,
> As if the design of all his words takes form
> And frame from thinking and is realized.

Such admiration for the power of *thinking*, for the constructive power of deliberate choice—this is not the sort of values that were being attributed to Stevens fifteen or twenty years ago. The central impact of Stevens' poetry up to about 1940 has been, I think, admirably summed up by Yvor Winters in his famous essay "Wallace Stevens or the Hedonist's Progress." There Winters, basing his thesis primarily on *Harmonium,* saw in Stevens the cultivation of "the realm of emotion divorced from understanding," the commendation of "the emotions as a good in themselves." It was, he felt, a point of view that had led Stevens from the great poetry of *Harmonium* into a "rapid and tragic decay" of style, the sad, inevitable progress of the hedonist, "unable to think himself out of the situation into which he has wandered." [3]

Winters has made a brilliant diagnosis of the malady; but he underestimated the patient's will to live. Looking back now,

---

[3] *The Anatomy of Nonsense* (Norfolk, Conn., 1943), pp. 89, 91, 97.

with the immense advantage of all that Stevens has published
since Winters wrote, and with the equally great advantage of
the recent *Opus Posthumous*—looking back now, we can see
that something quite different happened. We can see something analogous to the course of Yeats's poetry. We can see a
poet, by a deliberate process of self-knowledge, rebuilding himself and his poetry, rebuilding himself through his poetry, and
achieving, in *Transport to Summer* (1947), a volume of meditative poetry that is in every way the equal of his great, first
volume of hedonist poetry. It is not a question of setting up
divisions, but of watching recessive elements in the early poetry
develop into dominance.

Let us try to sketch, now, this different progress. Stevens'
second volume, *Ideas of Order*, appeared in 1935; its slim-
ness, its dominant tone, and its title are all significant of a
change in the poet's outlook. The buoyancy that gave forth the
bounty of *Harmonium* is gone; that force within, like "the immense dew of Florida," that had brought forth "Forms, flames,
and the flakes of flames" is subsiding, although here and there
it reappears, the old gay defiance of Winters:

> But what are radiant reason and radiant will
> To warblings early in the hilarious trees
> Of summer, the drunken mother?

Or:

> What is there here but weather, what spirit
> Have I except it comes from the sun?

The trouble is that the younger Nomad Exquisite had lived
by a view that the poet of the 1930's could no longer accept,
for reasons he suggests in the late essay cited at the outset of
this discussion: "If in the minds of men creativeness was the
same thing as creation in the natural world, if a spiritual planet
matched the sun, or if without any question of a spiritual
planet, the light and warmth of spring revitalized all our faculties, as in a measure they do, all the bearings one takes, all
the propositions one formulates would be within the scope
of that particular domination"—as they were, for the most
part, in *Harmonium*. "The trouble is, however, that men in
general do not create in light and warmth alone," he continues.
"They create in darkness and coldness. They create when they

are hopeless, in the midst of antagonisms, when they are
wrong when their powers are no longer subject to their control. They create as the ministers of evil" (OP, 210). *Ideas of
Order* moves in this different world; it is filled with the tones
of evening: A *Fading of the Sun, Gray Stones and Gray Pi-
geons, Autumn Refrain, Winter Bells, Sad Strains of a Gay
Waltz.*

> There is order in neither sea nor sun.
> The shapes have lost their glistening.
> There are these sudden mobs of men.

In this new atmosphere one poem stands out to control the
chaos: the famous *Idea of Order at Key West.* Here the speaker, significantly, stands at the far edge of Florida, his back
upon that world of flame and green. The physical world now
offers none of its old "comforts of the sun," but exists here as

> The meaningless plungings of water and the wind,
> Theatrical distances, bronze shadows heaped
> On high horizons, mountainous atmospheres
> Of sky and sea.

The object of wonder and admiration is now a human figure,
that singer by the shore whose voice made

> The sky acutest at its vanishing.
> She measured to the hour its solitude.
> She was the single artificer of the world
> In which she sang.

This is more than the Palace of Hoon, the solipsist of *Harmonium;* for the idea of order here resides in more than mental
landscapes, in "More even than her voice, and ours": the idea
of order is found in a unique conjunction of landscape, singer,
and listener, a situation in which the listener's mind, exulting
in the full strength of its powers, is able to assert the controlling force of consciousness, "Fixing emblazoned zones and fiery
poles" upon the outer atmosphere, "Arranging, deepening, en-
chanting night"—while realizing fully that the outer universe
goes its inhuman way.

The fierce strength of mind in that poem, its clipped and
muted language before the final exultation, prepares the way

for a striking addition to the volume *Ideas of Order,* when it appeared in a trade edition in the next year, 1936. The volume no longer opens with the curiously fatigued poem, *Sailing after Lunch,* where Stevens truly says, "My old boat goes round on a crutch/And doesn't get under way," and where he ends with the sentimental desire:

> To expunge all people and be a pupil
> Of the gorgeous wheel and so to give
> That slight transcendence to the dirty sail.

No, the volume now opens with the stirring *Farewell to Florida,* in which Stevens renounces all that "Florida" has symbolized in his earlier poetry: that world of vivid physical apprehension, where man created within the bounds of the natural order. "Her mind had bound me round," he says, but now he cries:

> Go on, high ship, since now, upon the shore,
> The snake has left its skin upon the floor.
> Key West sank downward under massive clouds
> And silvers and greens spread over the sea. The moon
> Is at the mast-head and the past is dead.
> Her mind will never speak to me again.

And he looks forward to his engagement with a new, a tough, bitter, and turbulent subject:

> My North is leafless and lies in a wintry slime
> Both of men and clouds, a slime of men in crowds.
> The men are moving as the water moves,
> This darkened water cloven by sullen swells
> Against your sides, then shoving and slithering,
> The darkness shattered, turbulent with foam.
> To be free again, to return to the violent mind
> That is their mind, these men, and that will bind
> Me round, carry me, misty deck, carry me
> To the cold, go on, high ship, go on, plunge on.

Stevens, it is clear, has determined to take his old boat out of The Pleasures of Merely Circulating, to plunge into the turmoil of the mid-thirties, to engage it somehow in his poetry. In fact, he had already begun the effort. The year before *Farewell to Florida* appeared he had already published the first part

of what was to become his longest poetical effort, *Owl's Clover,*
which appeared in 1936 in its original version of 861 lines. It is
a poem that caused Stevens immense labor and, finally, intense
dissatisfaction. In 1937 it reappeared with nearly 200 lines cut
out; and in 1954 Stevens omitted it entirely from his *Collected
Poems,* on the grounds that it was "rhetorical," Mr. Morse tells
us (OP, xxiii). As a result of this drastic omission, the reader of
the *Collected Poems* may emerge with a sense of the poet's
steady self-possession, an ideal progress from the old gaudy
style toward a sober, muted, thoughtful, pruned, and thoroughly remade poetry: for we move from *Ideas of Order* directly
into *The Man with the Blue Guitar,* where

> The man bent over his guitar,
> A shearsman of sorts.

A shearsman indeed, a sort of tailor, cutting his cloth anew
and shearing away the excess.[4] But the effect is too neat. We
need *Owl's Clover,* preferably in its first version, to tell us all
the trouble of the change; and fortunately we have it all now
before us once again, in the new posthumous volume. It is
not a successful poem, though it contains great passages and
opens remarkably well, with the firmly controlled symbols of
*The Old Woman and the Statue.* There the magnificent statue
in the park represents the soaring, noble imagination of the
past, "leaping in the storms of light": the statue is a work of
art subtly and powerfully arranged for the human mind to
grasp and be exalted. One thing, one thing only, the sculptor
"had not foreseen": the old woman, "the bitter mind/In a flap-
ping cloak," a woman so depressed that she cannot apprehend
the statue's action:

> A woman walking in the autumn leaves,
> Thinking of heaven and earth and of herself
> And looking at the place in which she walked,
> As a place in which each thing was motionless
> Except the thing she felt but did not know.

That thing is the "harridan self," "Crying against a need that

---

[4] See Stevens' explanation of this figure in a letter to his Italian
translator, Renato Poggioli: "This refers to the posture of the speaker,
squatting like a tailor (a shearsman) as he works on his cloth." *Mattino
Domenicale ed Altre Poesie* (Turin, 1954), p. 174.

pressed like cold,/Deadly and deep." It is not simply physical poverty that tortures this suffering self: it is that she lives, as the second part tells us, amid "the immense detritus of a world"

> That is completely waste, that moves from waste
> To waste, out of the hopeless waste of the past
> Into a hopeful waste to come.

The hopeful waste of the future, I think, alludes to the sort of world proffered by Mr. Burnshaw, whose name adorns the original title of the second part: *Mr. Burnshaw and the Statue* (later altered to *The Statue at the World's End*). Stanley Burnshaw was the Marxist critic who in 1935 had reviewed *Ideas of Order* with considerable acuteness, though with a condescending tone: he had seen it as a book of "speculations, questionings, contradictions"—"the record of a man who, having lost his footing, now scrambles to stand up and keep his balance." [5] The critique, being so largely true, left the mark, as *Owl's Clover* shows in its derisive rejection of all mass-solutions that offer only "an age of concentric mobs." But what can be offered instead to the suffering self? The offering in this long second section turns out, in spite of its high rhetoric, to be surprisingly meager: it is simply the old pleasures of Florida, chanted in a weak imitation of the old hieratic style of *Sunday Morning*, as this passage (later removed) indicates:

> Dance, now, and with sharp voices cry, but cry
> Like damsels daubed and let your feet be bare
> To touch the grass and, as you circle, turn
> Your backs upon the vivid statue. Then,
> Weaving ring in radiant ring and quickly, fling
> Yourselves away and at a distance join
> Your hands held high and cry again, but cry,
> This time, like damsels captured by the sky,
> Seized by that possible blue.

But those waltzes had ended, long since. Clearly, the poet must try another way, and so, in his third section, Stevens turns to develop a contrast between two ways of life. One is the old way of religious meditation, where "each man,"

---

[5] *New Masses,* Oct. 1, 1935, p. 42.

Through long cloud-cloister-porches, walked alone,
Noble within perfecting solitude,
Like a solitude of the sun, in which the mind
Acquired tranparence and beheld itself
And beheld the source from which transparence came.

And the other is something that seems to have arisen or to be arising in place of the old religious way, something he calls Africa, a world of dense, savage, mindless animality, where

Death, only, sits upon the serpent throne:
Death, the herdsman of elephants,
To whom the jaguars cry and lions roar
Their petty dirges of fallen forest-men,
Forever hunting or hunted, rushing through
Endless pursuit or endlessly pursued,
Until each tree, each evil-blossomed vine,
Each fretful fern drops down a fear like dew.

From here on, in the middle of the poem, *Owl's Clover* provides less and less sustenance for the troubled mind trying to feed in the dark. It becomes increasingly turgid and incoherent. The old religion cannot cope with "Africa," nor can the old art of the statue; nor can the problems be met by the believers in necessity, the nostalgic admirers of the old pioneer spirit, or the worshippers of the "newest Soviet reclame." "How shall we face the edge of time?"

Where shall we find more than derisive words?
When shall lush chorals spiral through our fire
And daunt that old assassin, heart's desire?

"Lush chorals"—the backward glance toward the days of *Harmonium*—is ominous, and we are surprised to find the poem ending with a Sombre Figuration in which the poet attempts to find refuge in a vague, semi-Jungian concept of the "subman." This subman is some inner man of imagination, who lies below the torments of thought: "The man below the man below the man,/Steeped in night's opium, evading day." But the subman has a precarious tenure, for he seems to reside only in a rhetoric of empty assertion:

> And memory's lord is the lord of prophecy
> And steps forth, priestly in severity,
> Yet lord, a mask of flame, the sprawling form
> A wandering orb upon a path grown clear.

It is a relief to turn from this evasive subman to the daylight figure who shears away this outworn pomp. The sounds made by *The Man with the Blue Guitar* (1937) show that Stevens, within a year's hard thought, has taken quick, firm strides toward the position thoroughly established in his prose essays and his late poetry: that "the poet must get rid of the hieratic in everything that concerns him," that he must abolish "the false conception of the imagination as some incalculable *vates* within us, unhappy Rodomontade" (NA, 58, 61)—i.e. the opium-drugged subman must be erased, along with the style in which he had been expressed. In his place we will have something like Picasso's clear, clean image of the old Guitar Player, a product of his "blue period" (though the guitar itself happens to be tan), which was, incidentally, exhibited in Hartford in 1934. We will have an image of life explored, discovered, and developed through a language made out of "things exactly as they are," a language moving now with a tough intent toward the discovery of a self:

> Ah, but to play man number one,
> To drive the dagger in his heart,
>
> To lay his brain upon the board
> And pick the acrid colors out,
>
> To nail his thought across the door,
> Its wings spread to rain and snow,
>
> To strike his living hi and ho,
> To tick it, tock it, turn it true,
>
> To bang it from a savage blue,
> Jangling the metal of the strings.

This is as far as we can get from the puzzled, ruminative ebb and flow of *Owl's Clover,* with its dissolving, eddying, and often turbid blank verse: note here the crisp common diction, the strict driving rhythm of the short couplets, subtly bound to-

gether by irregular rhymes and half-rhymes, all focused on one
aim: a definition of the *self* as the only province of poetry:

> Ourselves in the tune as if in space,
> Yet nothing changed, except the place
>
> Of things as they are and only the place
> As you play them, on the blue guitar,
>
> Placed, so, beyond the compass of change,
> Perceived in a final atmosphere;
>
> For a moment final.

We have returned to the central position of the *Idea of Order
at Key West:* man's inner rage for order as the ultimate constructive force in man's universe, and hence the never-ending
effort of the mind to control, within the mind, that outer monster, the inhuman universe:

> That I may reduce the monster to
> Myself, and then may be myself
>
> In face of the monster, be more than part
> Of it, more than the monstrous player of
>
> One of its monstrous lutes, not be
> Alone, but reduce the monster and be,
>
> Two things, the two together as one.

From this effort, he says, "I shall evolve a man."

This sequence of thirty-three tightly argued, tightly ordered
meditations on a theme establishes the altered style of the
later Stevens. He has here, in a deliberate act of choice, sheared
away the kind of writing that he later calls "The romantic intoning, the declaimed clairvoyance," since this, he says, is the
"appropriate idiom" of apotheosis; and this is not at all his subject now. Apotheosis elevates the mortal to the stature of divinity; it glorifies; and the appropriate poetry of apotheosis is
therefore the hymn, the ode, the celebration, the chant. In a
peculiar sense, this had been the appropriate idiom of his
earlier poetry, since he was there attempting to show, as he
tells the lady in *Sunday Morning,* that "Divinity must live with-

in" the human realm: "Passions of rain, or moods in falling snow." Hence he uses the idiom of romantic intoning to glorify the satisfactions of this earth, often with deliberate irony: the Comedian speaks of his "first central hymns, the celebrants/Of rankest trivia"; and indeed the whole mock-heroic effect of the Comedian arises from the application of such grand intoning to the achievements of this "merest minuscule."

But in his new effort to evolve a man, a new idiom must be invented, since "apotheosis is not/The origin of the major man" for whom the poet is now searching. "He comes," says Stevens, "from reason,/Lighted at midnight by the studious eye,/Swaddled in revery." He is the meditative man, master of the essential exercise, student, scholar, rabbi of a new idiom, which Stevens in *Of Modern Poetry* (1940) calls "The poem of the mind in the act of finding/What will suffice." There has never been a better definition of what might be called the genre of meditative poetry. It is not, we note, a poem celebrating what suffices; nor is it any lamentation for the lack of what suffices. The difference between the true meditative poem and other poetic genres seems to be exactly this: that it alone represents "the poem of the act of the mind," the poem of the mind, in the very act of finding. One thinks of Emily Dickinson, of Hopkins, of George Herbert, and especially of Donne, in his *Divine Meditations (Holy Sonnets)*.

But further definition of the genre, if there is really such a genre, is necessary, and Stevens suggests it all in *Of Modern Poetry:*

> It has to be living, to learn the speech of the place.
> It has to face the men of the time and to meet
> The women of the time. It has to think about war
> And it has to find what will suffice. It has
> To construct a new stage. It has to be on that stage
> And, like an insatiable actor, slowly and
> With meditation, speak words that in the ear,
> In the delicatest ear of the mind, repeat,
> Exactly, that which it wants to hear, at the sound
> Of which, an invisible audience listens,
> Not to the play, but to itself, expressed
> In an emotion as of two people, as of two
> Emotions becoming one.

Let me expand, with only a little liberty, the possible implications of that text. This kind of poetry must know the common speech; it must make contact with men in their normal existence, through its language, its images, and its consideration of urgent problems, such as war, of whatever kind, whether between man and man, or between body and soul, good and evil, man and his environment—the "war between the mind and sky" that Stevens describes at the end of his "Notes toward a Supreme Fiction." It has to find what will suffice, but in order to do this, it must construct a stage on which an actor may enact the process of this finding. And as this actor speaks his meditated words, they find a growing response in a certain invisible audience, which is not simply us, the readers or listeners, but is first of all the larger, total mind of the poet himself, controlling the actor, who is some projected aspect of himself. Then, in the close, that actor and that audience, projected self and larger self, come together in a moment of emotional resolution — for a moment final. It is a process that Stevens describes thus in his *Adagia:* "When the mind is like a hall in which thought is like a voice speaking, the voice is always that of someone else." The voice is that of some projected self: the audience is the whole self. "It is necessary to propose an enigma to the mind," he says in another adage. "The mind always proposes a solution" (OP, 168). All this seems to describe something very like the action in *The Idea of Order at Key West:* the landscape is the stage, the singer by the shore is the actor, and the poet's larger mind is the audience. It is also very like the action that one finds in Donne's *Holy Sonnets,* which we may take as a prime example of pure meditative poetry, since they seem to arise directly from the rigorous meditative exercises commonly practiced by religious men of the seventeenth century. Recall how Donne projects some aspect of himself upon a stage: the deathbed, the round earth's imagined corners, the Cross; how he then allows that self to ponder the given situation; and how, at the close, the projected self makes a subtle union with the whole mind of the poet, concluding all in the finding of what will suffice.

One can only ponder the possibilities here, and pause to stress one point. In formal religious meditation, as developed during Donne's time and later practiced (certainly) by Hopkins and (presumably) by Eliot, the process of meditation consists of something akin to that just described by Stevens. It begins with the deliberate creation of a setting and the placing of an actor there: some aspect of the self; this is the famous composition of place recommended by the Jesuit exercises. This is followed by predominantly intellectual analysis of some crucial problem pertaining to that self; and it all ends in a highly emotional resolution where the projected self and the whole mind of the meditator come together in a spirit of devotion. This threefold process is related to the old division of the soul into memory, understanding, and will; the exercise of meditation integrates these facilities.

How is it that a modern poet such as Wallace Stevens, so vastly different from the seventeenth century in the objects of his belief, should come to describe the need for a kind of poetry to which Donne's *Holy Sonnets* seem to belong: a kind that we might call the genre of meditative poetry? Donne's strenuous cultivation of this kind of poetry seems to be part of his lifelong effort to transcend and resolve his grievous sense of the fickleness, the dissolution, the transiency and fragility of all physical things. In Stevens, I think, an analogous situation called forth the analogous discipline. Stevens, in mid-career, recognized the dissolution, or the inadequacy, of his old poetic self — a recognition recorded with a wry gaiety in *The Comedian as the Letter C*. His later poems represent a rigorous search for ways and means of evolving another kind of poetic self, in accord with the outlook expressed in the late essay dealing with the "time of disbelief": "There was always in every man the increasingly human self, which instead of remaining the observer, the non-participant, the delinquent, became constantly more and more all there was or so it seemed; and whether it was so or merely seemed so still left it for him to resolve life and the world in his own terms" (OP, 207).

Allusions in his prose essays indicate that in this effort Stevens engaged in broad reading among tough thinkers, while all his later poetry displays a new respect for the "radiant idea" and the "radiant will." This is clear in the first part of *Notes toward a Supreme Fiction* (1942), which insists that the fiction must be, in some sense, "abstract." Not, I think, abstract in the usual sense of a philosophical abstraction; Stevens has told us plainly what he thinks of this in his *Landscape with Boat,* where he decries the man who "wanted imperceptible air," who "wanted the eye to see"

> And not be touched by blue. He wanted to know,
> A naked man who regarded himself in the glass
> Of air, who looked for the world beneath the blue,
> Without blue, without any turquoise tint or phase,
> Any azure under-side or after-color.

By "abstract" Stevens seems rather to imply a quality of being taken out, abstracted in the root sense, from that world we call the outer universe: something concrete taken out of this and taken into the mind through a process of full, exact realization. From that "local abstraction" the turquoise tints and azure undersides can then radiate in all directions. This is the process that Stevens vividly describes in section VII of *Credences of Summer,* where he begins by scorning those who have found it too hard "to sing in face/Of the object," and have therefore fled to the woods, where they could sing "their unreal songs/Secure." In a violent reversal of mood, he advocates a fiercely opposite process:

> Three times the concentred self takes hold, three times
> The thrice concentred self, having possessed
> The object, grips it in savage scrutiny,
> Once to make captive, once to subjugate
> Or yield to subjugation, once to proclaim
> The meaning of the capture, this hard prize,
> Fully made, fully apparent, fully found.

If this bears some resemblance to the old threefold process of formal meditation, it is only because Stevens has discovered for himself the same faculties, and has taught himself a way of using them for his own meditative ends. He has, in an essay of 1943, come to define the imagination as "the sum of our faculties," and has gone on to speak of "The acute intelligence of the imagination, the illimitable resources of its memory, its power to process the moment it perceives" (NA, 61).

Indeed, it appears that Stevens has been thoroughly aware of the analogy I am suggesting, for in a newly published essay, written about 1937, we find him declaring: "The poet who wishes to contemplate the good in the midst of confusion is like the mystic who wishes to contemplate God in the midst of evil . . . Resistance to the pressure of ominous and destructive circumstance consists of its conversion, so far as possible, into a different, an explicable, an amenable circumstance." And in this search, he adds, the poets "purge themselves before reality . . . in what they intend to be saintly exercises" (OP, 225, 227).

But if we accept Stevens' use of the term *meditation* as a proper description of his own secular exercises, we may appear to be stretching the word beyond any useful signification. Cannot any poem that contains any degree of hard thinking be thus called meditative? I do not think so, if we keep in mind the careful distinctions made by the old spiritual writer, François de Sales. "Every meditation is a thought," he says, "but every thought is not a meditation; for we have thoughts, to which our mind is carried without aim or design at all, by way of a simple musing . . . And be this kind of thought as attentive as it may be, it can never bear the name of meditation." On the other hand, he says, "Sometimes we consider a thing attentively to learn its causes, effects, qualities; and this thought is named study." But "when we think of heavenly things, not to learn, but to delight in them, that is called to meditate; and the exercise thereof meditation." "So that meditation," he concludes, "is an attentive thought repeated or voluntarily maintained in the mind, to arouse the will of holy wholesome affections and resolutions." [6]

It seems valid to adapt this definition to the meditation of earthly things, since meditation is a process, not a subject. If we do this, then Stevensian meditation becomes: attentive thinking about concrete things with the aim of developing an affectionate understanding of how good it is to be alive. We can see the process working everywhere in his later poetry, but nowhere better than in *The World as Meditation*, which now needs to be read entire as an example of the full development of Stevens' meditative style. Note first how far the poem's range extends beyond the "comforts of the sun": the verbal beauty of Enesco's French draws in the cosmopolitan world of the

---

[6] Francois de Sales, *A Treatise on the Love of God* (1616), Book VI, chap. ii; adapted from the translation of 1630.

musician, as the figure of Penelope draws in the ancient world
of legend. Yet the sun exists as first cause; without it there
would be nothing. Thus the poem is phrased to allow a double
reference: the sun is Penelope's companion, along with Ulysses.
Note too how the poem fulfills all of Stevens' requirements
for this modern poetry: common speech, common images, common problems; the establishment of a stage, the placing of
Penelope as actor on that stage, the imputed working of her
meditative thoughts, along with the constant presence of the
poet's larger mind, controlling all, and concluding all with an
affectionate understanding of what will suffice.

Is it Ulysses that approaches from the east,
The interminable adventurer? The trees are mended.
That winter is washed away. Someone is moving

On the horizon and lifting himself up above it.
A form of fire approaches the cretonnes of Penelope,
Whose mere savage presence awakens the world in which she dwells.

She has composed, so long, a self with which to welcome him,
Companion to his self for her, which she imagined,
Two in a deep-founded sheltering, friend and dear friend.

The trees had been mended, as an essential exercise
In an inhuman meditation, larger than her own.
No winds like dogs watched over her at night.

She wanted nothing he could not bring her by coming alone.
She wanted no fetchings. His arms would be her necklace
And her belt, the final fortune of their desire.

But was it Ulysses? Or was it only the warmth of the sun
On her pillow? The thought kept beating in her like her heart.
The two kept beating together. It was only day.

It was Ulysses and it was not. Yet they had met,
Friend and dear friend and a planet's encouragement.
The barbarous strength within her would never fail.

She would talk a little to herself as she combed her hair,
Repeating his name with its patient syllables,
Never forgetting him that kept coming constantly so near.

The world of *Harmonium* has not been discarded here, but
its reliance on the natural force of "sensibility" has been
modified, and the pleasures of that world have been included
within a larger structure of existence. By 1951 Stevens could
strongly question "the dogma that the origins of poetry are to
be found in the sensibility," and could suggest "if one says
that a fortunate poem or a fortunate painting is a synthesis of
exceptional concentration . . . we find that the operative force
within us does not, in fact, seem to be the sensibility, that is
to say, the feelings. It seems to be a constructive faculty, that
derives its energy more from the imagination than from the
sensibility" — imagination being, as we have seen, the "sum
of our faculties." But he adds, in his cautious way, "I have
spoken of questioning, not of denying" (NA, 164). That is because the old dews of Florida have never ceased to affect him.
One of his very last poems, *Prologues to What Is Possible*, suggests that the value of existence may have resided in

A flick which added to what was real and its vocabulary,
The way some first thing coming into Northern trees
Adds to them the whole vocabulary of the South,
The way the earliest single light in the evening sky, in spring,
Creates a fresh universe out of nothingness by adding itself,
The way a look or a touch reveals its unexpected magnitudes.

There is no inconsistency here. The look, the touch, the
flick of feeling, the "times of inherent excellence," "incalculable balances," "not balances/That we achieve but balances
that happen" — these are things worth recognizing, and Stevens
never ceases to celebrate them as part of the wonder of human
consciousness. But he is quick to recognize that "the casual is
not/Enough": it does not attain the full "freshness of ourselves"; it does not satisfy the "will to make iris frettings on
the blank." Beyond the casual apprehensions there lie the
willed and reasoned structures of the mind, which Stevens
presents in two forms. One structure occurs when the mind
thoroughly and fully concentrates upon the realization of some
composition that appears to be inherent in the external scene,
as in *Credences of Summer*.

> Let's see the very thing and nothing else.
> Let's see it with the hottest fire of sight.
> Burn everything not part of it to ash.
> Trace the gold sun about the whitened sky
> Without evasion by a single metaphor.

Thus:

> One of the limits of reality
> Presents itself in Oley when the hay,
> Baked through long days, is piled in mows. It is
> A land too ripe for enigmas, too serene.

This seems to be what Stevens means by seeing things in their "first idea," their "ever-early candor"; this is the adequacy of landscape — for a moment final. It exists beyond us, it is no metaphor, and yet, Stevens insists, "the first idea is an imagined thing," since it is achieved by a calculated effort of the mind. It is part, then, "of the never-ending meditation," a poem of the mind in the act of finding what will suffice. It may be, he says, "of a man skating, a woman dancing, a woman/Combing," a Woman Looking at a Vase of Flowers, a Dish of Peaches in Russia, or a Large Red Man Reading: it may be found "in the crackling summer night,"

> In the *Duft* of towns, beside a window, beside
> A lamp, in a day of the week, the time before spring,
> A manner of walking, yellow fruit, a house,
> A street.

They are acts available to any man, a sort of poetry, "an imaginative activity that diffuses itself throughout our lives" (NA, 149). You return, say, from a long vacation with your family in the mountains, dog-tired, addle-brained, and feeling the whole expedition was a huge mistake. Two weeks later, the snapshots return, developed in full color: you are amazed at the beauty, the order, the focus; the trip is a success, after all. Such a realization would be, in Stevens' terms, a poetic action.

And finally, beyond such compositions, there lies the inexhaustible "realm of resemblance," in which the faculties of the imagination, using all their powers, "extend the object" by analogy, by metaphor. It is a realm in which the whole mind, like Stevens' Penelope, uses the world of sensory experience as a base upon which to construct a total edifice involving and demanding the whole stretch of human experience. By the use of such analogies man connects the external and the internal; the action of analogy is the mind's ultimate way of establishing its dominant, controlling position amid the "moving chaos that never ends." And this, too, is an activity that Stevens sees as available to everyone.

You sit in a chair, say, admiring the beauty of your four-year-old daughter: you call to mind certain resemblances between her and her absent mother, between her and your imagined image of yourself, between her and your memories and pictures of grandparents. You think, too, of certain painted images of children by Renoir or Romney; you think of Andrew Marvell's *Picture of Little T. C. in a Prospect of Flowers;* you think of the dogwood that bloomed last spring and of the zinnias now blooming outside. And for a moment the object toward which all these resemblances converge, or from which they infinitely extend — for a moment the object becomes a vital center through which the sense of life is composed, final: "completed in a completed scene," as Stevens says. Such is Wallace Stevens' *World as Meditation,* a world where the poet may adopt the words of Valery's Architect and say, "By dint of constructing, . . . I truly believe that I have constructed myself."

# William Carlos Williams: The True Contemporary

*by* KARL SHAPIRO

When I was twenty years old I published a little book of poems privately. It was a confused book, a mixture of Elizabethan and Modern. This volume I sent to several famous poets, only one of whom took the trouble to reply. He was William Carlos Williams. Williams did not praise my book, but his letter, the first I had ever received from a real writer, was full of sympathy and kindliness for a young man who wanted to be a poet. While he had nothing encouraging to say about my poems, he had a good deal to say about the month of March and his anger at T. S. Eliot. The month of March figures a great deal in Williams' poetry, a violent and beautiful season in Williams' New Jersey, as it was in Maryland, where I lived. The diatribe against Eliot disturbed me deeply. I was a worshiper of Eliot then and a devout reader of the *Partisan Review,* which, although a highbrow left-wing magazine, took Eliot to be the sovereign poet and critic of the twentieth century. I could not understand how any modern poet, especially Williams, who seemed of an extraordinary freshness and originality, could say unkind things about Eliot. If I had ever developed the habit of reading literary criticism I would have known what he meant. But my natural antipathy for criticism kept me away from it for many years. It was not until I began to teach in universities that I was forced to examine criticism; and it was not until I examined it carefully that I began to appreciate Williams' opinion of Eliot, the true significance of Eliot and everything he has promulgated under the name of criticism.

The radical difference between Williams and, say, Eliot, is that Williams divorces poetry from "culture," or tries to. Williams is fighting for the existence of poetry (while Eliot and Pound fought for the "uses" of poetry). Williams' entire literary career has been dedicated to the struggle to preserve spontaneity and immediacy of experience. His explanations of these aims are certainly not as impressive as Eliot's and in fact lead to such confusing theories as Objectivism. In defense of Williams one can say that his theorizing is innocent, while in the case of the Pounds and Eliots it is calculated and tricky. Williams does not stand or fall on theory; he is willing to void it at a moment's notice. But it is unfortunate for him that he must engage in theory at àll. At bottom Williams is not an intellectual, and he is too human, too sympathetic, too natural to become a symbol of the anti-intellectual. Besides, as he says in his published letters, he is illogical. He would never be able to impress the quarterly reviews or the highbrows who consider him a kind of intellectual slob. The literary quarterly follows a party line of Culture, any Culture, but Culture is a *sine qua non* for the poet, according to them.

Williams is a guinea pig of modern poetry. He lends himself to the literature of the laboratory and a thousand trials and errors of criticism. He even writes a "mythic epic" like Pound and Eliot which all the culture critics seize on as proof that Williams is not a literary imbecile but one you can practically write books about. *Paterson* is a typical culture poem, the only full-dressed one Williams ever wrote but, according to the critics, the real thing, a kind of New Jersey *The Waste Land.* Williams is so innocent that he would even do that. In writing his large bad poem Williams was perhaps trying to test the validity of works like the *Cantos* and *The Waste Land,* even to compete with them. While he carried on a lifelong fight against Eliotism—a one-sided fight, for Eliot hardly deigned to notice this gadfly—he maintained a lifelong relationship with Pound. Williams' relationship to Pound is very much like Yeats': an antimagnetic relationship. Pound leaned on Williams in the same way that Eliot and Pound leaned on each other. And Williams remained loyal to Pound because Pound seems to remain American rather than English. Williams is faithful to Pound through thick and thin, always annoyed with him, and always attempting to understand his position. Williams can see the demagoguery of Eliot but not of Pound. Somehow he identifies himself with Pound. Williams a few years ago was unseated from the poetry consultantship of the Library of Congress, with no organized protest from writers and scarcely any mention of it in the press. Pound was awarded a prize from the Library of Congress which was backed up by all the self-styled Great Poets of the English-speaking countries. Pound got his prize, was feted in the editorials of the national magazines, and was eventually freed without a trial. Williams went home and had a series of strokes. My point is that because Williams abhors fixed positions in politics as in poetics he cannot impress officialdom.

Williams is the American poet who tries to fight off Europeanism. He fights it off, singlehanded, but he cannot impress the European with his cause. Neither can he impress the American. Lacking the arrogance of an Eliot or a Pound, lacking philosophy or religion or logic, he is battered back and forth by the literati, who are always armed to the teeth with Positions and who can make anything out of him they want, except a bad poet. Eliot tried to polish him off by remarking that he had a kind of "local interest." To Eliot anything that is not of world cultural interest is "local."

Williams belongs to the generation of Modern Poetry, those poets who suddenly organized literature in 1920 or thereabouts. He was not a high-powered Modern because he lacked the political instinct, but he was aggressive and fought the distortions of Modernism throughout his life. His letters and essays and even his poems are all "local" in the sense that they are contemporary. He wanted poetry to belong to the present, not the past. This is the clue to his involvements with Ezra Pound and his hatred of Eliot.

Williams has written a good deal of literary criticism himself, but he is not a critic in any accepted sense of that word. He is a poet even in his criticism; he refuses to use terminology and everything terminology stands for. He builds up no system; he abjures "style" in his prose, except when he is not sure of his ground. (In such cases he writes a jaunty, affected lingo reminiscent of Pound or Hemingway.) A good many of his judgments seem to be affected by personal loyalty mixed with an overpowering desire to be fair. One time, because of a letter from Robert Lowell, he seemed about to revise his opinion of Eliot. In Williams' world there are no hard and fast rules; the entire literary process is fluid; the governing principle is contemporaneity—immediacy.

There are basic contradictions of judgment in Williams' appraisals. For instance, he praises Marianne Moore excessively while he sees nothing of importance in Eliot. Williams also places Gertrude Stein with Pound as an important innovator. Pound he is inclined to favor from the start, even to a slight imitation of Pound's ideas of American history and banking. But the treatment of Pound is always anguished. One is inclined to feel that Williams does not look up to Pound but is pleased by Pound's interest in *him!* Williams has little use for Stevens, but this is consistent with Williams' objections to prettified language. At the bottom of Williams' specific poetic judgments lies a theory of language, which is practically a *mystique.* Usually it is referred to as a *prosody,* and in the widest meaning of that term it is.

Compared with Pound's prose, which has the tone of the Public Address System, Williams' critical style is weak and plaintive. At times it contains a note of hysteria, frequently its shrillness gets in the way of the clarity, but on the whole there is the pervading innocence and warmth of personality, heightened by genuine excitement. But when he intellectualizes he follows in the footsteps of the Eliot-Pound faction. He praises Joyce for his clarity and his great interest in form but his basic liking for Joyce has to do with Joyce's humanity. This is not a virtue that the Joyceans usually single out. And of course Williams is attracted by the banality of subject in *Ulysses.*

His allegiances are unstable and extreme. Williams reacts sharply to the immediate political or literary event. He is as prone to follow the Right (where the politics are not too obviously putrescent) as he is to follow the Left. Extremism seems to him worth a diagnosis. His detestation of Eliot seems to be a hatred for compromise; Williams does not compromise but he veers crazily from side to side. He writes about Lorca with a political passion while clinging with one hand to the coattails of Pound. He follows Pound's admiration of Jefferson while taking a "leftist" position on Jefferson. "Let's have a revolution every ten years," is Williams' view of Jefferson. Whereas Pound would say: a solid aristocracy without hereditary rights. At the end of a stirring, almost scholarly essay on Lorca he works in a little stab at Whitman, saying that Whitman was a romantic "in a bad sense." Williams is always looking over his shoulder at Pound; in himself he feels no critical authority. Here he mimics the Modern Classical view of Whitman.

Frequently he takes off into the realm of esthetic speculation, always with a certain desperate gaiety that characterizes his criticism. "The poem alone focuses the world," he says. This pleases the Pound side of Williams. Or in an essay about E. E. Cummings: "We are inclined to forget that cummings has come *from* english to another province having escaped across a well defended border. . . ." This is about the difference between English and American, which Williams makes the center of his criticism. But he knows he is on the side of the Romantics, on the side of anyone who is opposed to "lapidary work," anyone who opposes a literary poem. Williams is always more or less on the right track, but he never comes to the point in his criticism. He does in the poems. Again he will buckle down to a first-rate piece of criticism in his bitter essay about the failure of Sandburg to continue as a poet. Here he is on safe ground. Williams is as close to Sandburg as twins but he can tell the difference between himself and the professional Americanism of Sandburg. He understands Sandburg because he has been through the same process of handling Americana. But Sandburg's soft-pedaling is to Williams the worst sort of propaganda verse. Sandburg follows the identical course Williams does in his own "formless" poetry; but Sandburg settles for a "form" and Williams still continues the search. When Williams talks about Auden he can say something as mixed-up and as *true* (reading Williams' criticism one begins to write like him, on both sides of the fence) as: "I wish I could enlist Auden in . . . a basic attack upon the whole realm of structure in the poem . . . I am sure the attack must be concentrated on the *rigidity of the poetic foot."* When Williams begins to underline something like the "rigidity of the poetic foot" he sounds even more sophomoric than his friend Ezra. It is as though Williams had reduced all the cultural viciousness of modernism to prosody—which in fact he has done. Marianne Moore seems to him to have taken recourse "to the mathematics of art." He adores her persnickety syllable snipping but he cannot abide Auden's much more fluid and graceful "feet." The point of argument seems to be British versus American. Puzzling over Dylan Thomas' poems after his death, Williams said that they smacked of the divine. But having fallen between the two stools of the "divine" Thomas and the agnostic Pound, one is not sure what *divine* is, except, as Williams says, "drunken." Clinging desperately to the only poetic he knows he cries at last: "Without measure we are lost." *Measure* is used prosodically and abstractly, as the rule, the law—one is not sure how it is used.

As a critic Williams has no credit whatever. Eliot puts up a full-scale esthetic which anticipates every question and answer. Pound bludgeons his opinions across to a few listeners. Yeats weaves over the crystal ball in a trance of culture sensibility. And poor Williams is haunted by the two specters of Whitman and Pound, the genius and the crank. All of which ends up as an unresolved internal monologue on *Prosody!* The prosody *mystique* in Williams is the center of all his prose and must be understood if the nature of Williams' poetry is to be vindicated. As my own opinion of Williams as a poet puts him over and above Pound and Eliot and Cummings and Marianne Moore, all the theorists and purveyors of sociological opinion, I will attempt to examine Williams' "prosody."

Williams has no critical reputation but he has somehow maintained the respect of the official literati. Simultaneously,

he has maintained the loyalty of the literary "underground."
(It was Williams who introduced Allen Ginsberg's *Howl*, and
dozens of similar works which only poets have ever heard of.)
He is the only modern poet who searches everywhere for new
poetry.

Imagine any of the official critics, new critics, or editors
of the highbrow quarterlies taking notice of a poem like Siegel's
*Hot Afternoons*—which Williams alone had the courage and
honesty to reintroduce as one of the best twentieth-century
poems. *Hot Afternoons* was one of the last authentically American poems, save Williams' own, before the final triumph of
Eliot's culture poetry.

The new schools of criticism have always tried to give Williams the benefit of the doubt as a poet of their persuasion.
Especially the poem *Paterson* appeals to them as a work com-
parable to *The Waste Land* and the *Cantos* or the *Anabase* of
St. John Perse. *Paterson* to these critics seems an epic in modern style, a "mythic" poem. Controversy over *Paterson* has
been considerable; but at least it is recognized by these critics
that Williams is as culturally ambitious as his contemporaries
in such an undertaking.

It is a waste of time to discuss this kind of criticism, but it
is necessary to set it aside if one is to get at a fair judgment of
Williams' poetry. There is at least one full-scale intellectual
probe of Williams. It is a quibbling book, laden with minor
points of pedantry and with a dark knowledge of "structures."
It is apparent in this work that the author is not able to read
poetry except as "comparative ideology." For instance, in speaking of a character in Williams' *Paterson* named Elsie, the critic
says: "Elsie is a kind of Yeatsian 'Crazy Jane' presented without Yeats' idealization of the desecrated woman as the authentic
guarantor of some superior wholeness, an authenticity with
which Yeats also endowed his fools and lunatics." This gib-
berish rises from the critic's intense interest in "mythic" character rather than poetry. But one of the funniest examples of
this kind of criticism is as follows. A critic takes a delightful
little poetic quip by Williams and treats it to the following ex-
position. Here is the poem, "This Is Just to Say":

I have eaten
the plums
that were in
the icebox

and which
you were probably
saving
for breakfast

Forgive me
they were delicious
so sweet
and so cold

The irony of this poem, the critic says, "was that precisely that which preserved them (the plums) and increased the deliciousness of their perfection (the refrigeration) contained in its essence the sensuous quality most closely associated with death; coldness. So the plums' death (or formal disappearance and disintegration) was symbolically anticipated in the charm of their living flesh. This is, I believe, the exact pathos of this brief poem. . . ."

Whenever I quote something like this I feel constrained to add that this is a true quotation and not a parody I have made up. Most criticism about Williams is written in this patois: in a discussion of the poem "The Yachts" we are told that "suddenly the physical referents are expanded into universals more overtly than had been Williams' earlier custom when the reader had been given the responsibility for making the concrete particulars yield the universals. . . ." etc. What the critic is trying to say is that in this poem Williams is using symbols; she cannot say anything so obvious; and she invents a way of saying the obvious to make it look profound.

A similar "explication" is published by the poetry editor of *The Nation* about the little wheelbarrow poem. This is the poem, "The Red Wheelbarrow":

so much depends
upon
a red wheel
barrow

glazed with rain
water

beside the white
chickens

Says the critic: "The poem's design is a striving for value, for significant realization, against the resistant drag of the merely habitual." This kind of highbrow marginalia is, funnily enough, *sanctioned* by Williams, who is always looking for someone to bestow critical respectability upon him.

Williams' poetry is bounded by *Kora in Hell* (1917) at the beginning of Williams' literary life and the epical *Paterson* at the other end. Pound wrote him about *Kora in Hell* and said, "The thing that saves your work is *opacity*, and don't forget it. Opacity is not an American quality." The opaque was something Pound might praise; and there is no telling how deeply influenced Williams might have been by this great literary law of Pound's. There are two books preceding *Kora* but the original preface to *Kora* is a mightily opaque and gossipy monologue in the Pound style. More important, Williams announces that the plan of *Kora* is "somewhat after the A.B.A. formula, that one may support the other, clarifying or enforcing perhaps the other's intention." This is the "form" of the *Cantos, The Waste Land,* and other "mythic structures" of the twenties. The real precedents for the book, however, are the so-called prose-poem, the *Illuminations* of Rimbaud, the poetic notes of Baudelaire, the abortive prose experiments of Eliot, etc. Probably the model of the poem was the pretty little French poem, for children perhaps, called *Aucassin et Nicolete.* Williams was charmed by this piece and evidently kept it in his mind as a form using both verse and prose. But the official precedent for *Kora,* we are told, is a book called *Varie Poesie* dell'Abate Pietro Metastasio, Venice, 1795, designedly dropped on Williams' desk by Pound.

*Kora in Hell* is a series of observations about poetry and

the stance of the poet, full of little psychological asides about our civilization, not in the Poundian political way but in the Surrealist associational manner. Williams is concerned, like all the *avant-garde* writers of his time, with the feasibility of "associations"—the random use of intellectual and personal experience. Williams simply made it his business to jot down something every night, however nonsensical, and then make a comment on it. The chief and it may be the only fact of interest about *Kora* is that *Paterson,* coming at the apex of Williams' poetry, uses the identical method. The method consists of a free use of poetic languages in various states of excitement, alternating with a free use of prose languages. Eliot, Pound, and Joyce all attempted the same technique, with varying success.

But in between *Kora* and *Paterson* we have close to a thousand pages of some of the best or most interesting American poetry in our history. Almost all of this poetry is in a style which is immediately recognizable as Williams' own; further, it is a workable style, one which permits him to write a poem almost at random. At its best, which is a good bit of the time, it is not "experimental" poetry or crank technique. Naïve it certainly is, even what some writers call primitive; it is precisely Williams' innocence of forms that frees him to respond to daily experience as a poet. Williams went on writing, day after day, year after year, losing manuscripts, not finishing them, giving them away, but never letting up. Poetry to him was a daily function of life, a means of seeing. In a sense, he is our first American poet since Whitman. It hardly matters that his counselors poisoned his mind against Whitman; Whitman is his mentor after all.

Critics and journalists tend to heroize Williams for writing poems late at night after a hard day's work at the hospital. Williams has never felt heroic about being a physician. It is pointless to try to imagine Williams ensconced in some village on the Italian Riviera brooding over the effects of the 1905 nickel on the souls of little children. Williams was a New Jersey doctor and that is that. His poetry is the poetry of a very busy man, as busy, say, as Sir Walter Raleigh or Gerard Manley Hopkins. Not that one can generalize about busy poets and poets of leisure. Williams wanted to be a doctor, have a family, live near New York City, and write poetry. As far as anyone knows, he did all these things very admirably.

But the seeming offhandedness of Williams' poems is a condition of his life. Obviously the poems would be different had Williams not been a doctor. New Jersey, New York City, Ezra Pound, the delivery room, the back alleys of charity patients, home, the little magazine, the month of March, these are all the elements in which his poetry moves. Williams accommodates himself to the brutal round of modern professsional life. It does not embitter him; it sweetens him. And the poems are "scrappy," as the critics note, but there is a method to their scrappiness. And they are not astrology or economics or theology. The element of speed in composing the poem is part of the technique of his poetry, just as speed is a factor in certain kinds of painting. There is, in fact, a definite "Oriental" tendency in his work, not cultural Orientalism like Pound's but an instinct for the work that is as natural as nature herself. And the daily life has a lot to do with it. He survives as a poet even better than his contemporaries, a consequence, perhaps, of his roots in a pedestrian world. Williams never became an "exile," how can an obstetrician be an exile?

The earliest poems are marked by the ornate imprint of Pound (the use of foreign exclamations and translation-sounding rhetoric and even the "Browning" dramatics which Pound quickly switched away from when he discovered that he could be opaque with impunity). The character of this style is that of a half-biblical, half-Victorian tone which is the quality of all of Pound's early adaptations. In Williams it sounds like:

> Eight days went by, eight days
> Comforted by no nights, until finally:
> "Would you behold yourself old, Beloved?"

Actually Pound never rose above this style, either in the *Pisan Cantos* or in the latest additions to his epic. Williams saw through it more quickly. It goes on intermittently through "So art thou broken in upon me, Apollo" and many such imitations of Style, but soon it stops abruptly. One can see the sudden transition in:

> Your thighs are apple trees
> whose blossoms touch the sky.

which is more or less phony Pound, but is followed by:

Which sky? . . .
Which shore? . . .
what/sort of man was Fragonard?

This is the beginning. Williams sheds figurative language as a snake sheds its skin; henceforth he is naked, a poet without decoration, without metaphor.

March,
      you remind me of
the pyramids, our pyramids—

There is still a lot of mincing Italian, Spanish, Latin quotation, but this falls away also.

a green truck
dragging a concrete mixer
passes
in the street—
the clatter and true sound
of verse—

*     *     *

Moral
      it looses me
Moral
      it supports me
Moral
      it has never ceased
      to flow

(through various series of data, means, signs on walls and labels on bottles). Then a descent into pure spoken idiom, the rejection of all the devices of poetry for speech, always a sign of the poet's sincerity. Where Eliot ends up snipping philosophy from textbooks, Pound cutting whole chapters from history documents and statistics, Williams dives back into the spoken tongue.

It can never be said of Williams that he writes a well-rounded poem like "Ode on a Grecian Urn" or "The Love Song of J. Alfred Prufrock" or even "my father moved through dooms of love." He loathes the *fait accompli* in poetry or in painting. On the other hand, he does not worship the "fragment" for the fragment's sake. He tries to find the center of his experience in relation to the art of poetry; and he finds it over and over again. His "discoveries" are many more than "The Red Wheelbarrow" or "The Botticellian Trees"—good poems but two of many hundreds which are not repeated in the anthologies.

Williams puts his poetry in a direct relationship with daily experience. With Eliot there is no daily experience: there are "symbols" of the quotidian (empty lots, carbuncular young men, sandwich papers along the Thames, the silence in the subway) and with Pound there are stock-market reports, the struggles of artists and war communiques. Williams tries to accommodate his poetry to what the day brings to a poet in a place like New Jersey, where there is no dazzle of the past or of the cultural present. Williams writes about an apple rotting on the porch rail.

He does not exploit his knowledge. It does not occur to him that what he happens to know as an expert might be turned to the uses of poetry. Yet he himself is the organizing center of the poem, bringing together around him the untold *disjecta membra* of the day. *Without metaphor.* This is the challenge. Hence the directness of all his poems and their somewhat shocking physical quality. Williams is like Catullus in his outspokenness and unthinking sensuality and amorality — for there is no bragging or sexual athleticism (or asceticism either) in the poems. Pound is sexless, Eliot ascetic, Yeats roaring with libidinal anguish and frustration. Williams includes the physical in the day's work; he meets it at every turn, being a doctor, and is not obsessed.

> The young doctor is dancing with happiness
> in the sparkling wind, alone
> at the prow of the ferry! He notices
> the curly barnacles and broken ice crusts . . .

or

> I bought a dishmop—
> having no daughter—

There is very little twentieth-century poetry like this except outside the English language. But Williams does not "translate" or "adapt" except infrequently. He refuses to improve upon the language — this is the whole secret of his flatness of style and the inconclusiveness of the forms. He writes in his speaking voice.

In his autobiography, Williams refers to the publication of *The Waste Land* as "the great catastrophe." Looked at from Williams' point of view and from that of all the *avant-garde* of his time, it was indeed the great catastrophe. "It wiped out our world," says Williams, "as if an atom bomb has been dropped upon it . . . I felt at once that it had set me back twenty years . . . Critically Eliot returned us to the classroom just at the moment when I felt that we were on the point of escape . . . I knew at once that in certain ways I was most defeated." Williams' recognition of the true nature of *The Waste Land* marks him as first-rate prophet in criticism. And the effects of Eliot's poem were even more far-reaching than Williams said; not only was it the poem the academy needed as a pseudomodern example; it was a poem that made poetry and criticism one and the same thing, and that provided a justification for a new critical philosophy. Williams was also right in seeing that he was more damaged by this poem than anyone else. He was left high and dry: Pound, who was virtually the co-author of Eliot's poem, and Marianne Moore were now polarized to Eliot. Williams felt all this and would feel it for another twenty years. His own poetry would have to progress against the growing orthodoxy of Eliot criticism.

At first glance, Williams' remarks about poetic form seem superficial and even inane. One thinks, well, here is a nice man who is sick and tired of effeminate poeticizing and who would like American poets to display some gusto and originality. On second glance, one thinks, the old boy is becoming a bore with his din about prosody and "the line." All that shrieking about the "language" in *Paterson* is as bad as "the precise definition" in the *Cantos* or the "way of saying it" in the *Four Quartets*. And because Williams refuses to use the standard terminology of criticism, because he has a sincere interest in an American poetry, and because he is so suggestible, at least in his early years, to the literary politics of his fellow writers, he generally sounds half unintelligible. But there is a lot more to his "prosody" than that, much more, in fact, than exists in the new criticism.

Prosody is the science of verse. In English there is not and there has never been such a science. English scholars have long since given up prosody studies as a hopeless task. Because prosody and versification have such a justifiably bad name in English literature, no reader is apt to prick up his ears when William Carlos Williams or anyone else introduces the subject. Prosody is a mare's nest. Eliot and Pound took care not to identify themselves as prosodists, even while they were quietly laying down laws for it. In public they always guffawed at the mention of the word.

By prosody Williams does not mean versification. If you examine his own poems or his own remarks about what he calls mysteriously "the line," you will see the following things: He neither preaches nor practices "foot" prosody; he does not preach or practice meters; nor syllabic versification, such as Marianne Moore adopted; nor is his prosody accentual; nor is it "typographical" or what one critic calls grandly "spatial" form; nor does he base versification on rhyme nor on the internal figurations which rhyme may produce. The prosody of Pound is based on cadence which runs close to foot prosody — an imitation of Homeric and English trisyllabic. Eliot's prosody is extremely conservative, either a copy of Laforgue, at its most daring, or of Milton's *Samson Agonistes* (though I have never examined this closely) and it degenerates easily into modified "iambic." Williams' prosody is more advanced than any of these: it consciously departs from every intonation of the past. This is also its danger, as it is its advantage.

The thing to remember about Williams' "line" is that it is not a prosodic line at all. The word "prosody" for him is a metaphor for the whole meaning of the poem. Iambics to him mean cottages all in a row: sameness, standardization of things and of lives. His refusal to write iambic is therefore the same thing as Whitman's. It means that the iambic is not a language for the American poet. Pound and Eliot maintained the same doctrine, each in a less convincing way.

A good start for understanding the significance of Williams' belief about prosody and language (they are the same thing) is to consider his contempt for the modern sonnet. The virtue of the sonnet (which is the only "set" form in the English language) is that it prescribes a kind of syllogism. A sonnet in its simplest form makes a statement, develops or contradicts it, then resolves it. It is a game; hence its popularity with lovers. Eliot began by rejecting the sonnet; Pound rejected it after a few acrobatic flops. On the other hand, a poet like Cummings has advanced the sonnet to a new fame. With him it becomes the most ironical sonnet in English literature. What Williams resents about the sonnet form, even in the hands of Cummings, is the neatness of it. That is what the sonnet is for. The sonnet "line" can lead to nothing but a trick poem or exercise. A poem, according to Williams, should not be that closed, should not click like a box (which was Yeats' way of describing his own metrical poetry). The "closed" poem — the poem that clicks like a box — is the type of poem which has lately become a standard in the twentieth century; the most recent models were made by W. H. Auden.

All the appurtenances of the closed poem, especially the stanza, become anathema to Williams from the beginning. Rhyme itself seems to him meretricious; when he uses it (and he uses it as well as anybody), it is with a slur. The poem must not be governed by meters — any meters — nor by periods and paragraphs (stanzas), nor by the figures of speech. What is left? Nothing. The raw material of the poem is all. It is the same process that Whitman went through: a rebirth.

But Williams had even rejected Whitman's line. (We must try to remember that Williams uses the word "line" in the metrical sense, and in the linguistic sense at once.) The turning away from Whitman is all but fatal in Williams, but he manages to do pretty well in his own way. Williams grew up in the day when Whitman seemed incorrigibly nineteenth century and Emersonian. How Williams could have missed the lesson of Whitman is beyond me. But Williams started over, too. No ideas, no meters, no forms, no decorations; only the search for the raw poetry of experience.

"No ideas but in things," Williams said over and over, for a time. He became an "Objectivist," a man on the search for objects instead of thoughts. But this was just a variation of Pound's Imagism; for there could be no object-poetry that would lead anywhere; any more than Imagism could stand on its own legs. Williams dropped the Objectivist idea, just as he dropped the "antipoetic." These were harmful simplifications. Williams' larger conception of poetry is based on the understanding that a thing is neither poetic not antipoetic, neither prose nor poetry: there is something else which cannot be so bound. To write a poem about a rotten apple is not "antipoetic"; people laugh at such a poem and love it precisely because it is the poetry of the thing. The poetry of the rotten apple lies outside prosody, outside what is proper for apple-poetry, and outside what is called Symbolism (if you say *apple* to a modern critic you will be pelted with religion, mythology, and Freud before you can duck — but to Williams an apple is an apple.)

As for Williams' versification, it goes entirely by ear, and luckily for him he has a good ear most of the time. It is not cadenced, not accentualized, not syllabified, not metered. It may or may not have a "typographical" form: sometimes it has, sometimes it hasn't. For certain periods Williams will print in "couplets"; at other times in tercets; he is not adverse to the single word per line nor the long line. Generally (and this is the significant thing) he accommodates the "line" — that is, the typographic or verse line — to the sense of the whole poem. Thus he is doing approximately what Hopkins did in sprung rhythm, creating a total form rather than a unit form. It was a horror to Williams to see *The Waste Land,* partly because of Eliot's use of the old "unit" forms: an iambic passage here; a trochaic passage there: an image poem here, a long rhetorical build-up there and so on, with no organic principle anywhere.

But Williams himself in his desperate moments does the same thing. *Paterson* is just as artificial as *The Waste Land* when it comes to the "line."

Williams and his contemporaries had been schooled to despise "narrative poetry." To tell a tale in verse seemed to the early modern poets of our century the weakest excuse for writing a poem. They tried to get rid of tale-telling altogether and switch to Ideas, which are much more "masculine" than narratives. There is a large residue of narration in Williams' collected poetry which for years he did not know what to do with. The wonderful episode 17 in *Paterson*, one of the most powerful passages Williams ever wrote, was without a context

until he stuck it in *Paterson*. But true to his Modernist up-
bringing, he could not even then *narrate* it, any more than he
could narrate *Paterson*. Williams' "epic" poem is thus just another example of *The Waste Land* technique. He is better when
he writes about Sacco and Vanzetti (a theme which could not
move the great culture poets to even a single word) or about
the death of D. H. Lawrence (which the culture poets also
avoided like the plague). An interesting thing about Williams'
poems is that they move from one to the next easily. The
"secret of that form," as Williams calls it somewhere, is to
make poetry natural, not literary. This is, in fact, the secret
of his "prosody," the secret of his "antipoetic" line, the secret
of his concentration upon objects as ideas. *The "secret of that
form" is the eradication of the line between poetry and prose,
between life and art.* Eliot speaks of an art emotion, an emotion reserved for the moments when one turns on the esthetic
faucet. And it is precisely this attitude toward poetry that
Williams condemns.

At the present, at the end of his long struggle with prosody,
Williams turns to something very like a "form" but so loose
that one can hardly call it a form. Perhaps it began with an admiration of a little quatrain by Byron Vazakas which resembled
typographically a toy pistol or the State of Oklahoma. Vazakas
managed this thing for speaking in his own voice. Williams hit
upon a step-down kind of typography which he has used constantly in recent years. But it is not a be-all and end-all; he may
drop it any time he likes. It is not a syllogistic sonnet or sestina
at any rate. This style differs from Williams' earlier style only
in that it appears to conform to a certain regularity. But there
is none, except the regularity of thought as it progresses in
the poem.

Had Williams been as good a theoretician as he was a poet
he would probably be the most famous American poet today.
But Williams cannot explain, fortunately for him, or he explains badly when he does. It is the poem he is after. His kind
of poem may be the chief development of the American poem
since *Leaves of Grass*. When it is successful, as it is an amazing number of times, it abolishes the dualism of form-content,
expression-artistry, and all those other dualisms which get in
the way of art. Williams' almost mystical repetitions about

"the line" (and somewhat wildly in *Paterson* about the *Language*) are a decree against critical speculation about forms. He knows that forms are not predetermined, not inherited, not traditional. He knows, too, that forms do not matter for the honest artist, whether he uses them or not. It is when form becomes a fetish that he draws back and howls.

Speaking of howling, Williams has been the sole example in twentieth-century poetry, along with Lawrence, for hundreds upon hundreds of poets, the majority of whom are Americans who oppose the Eliot "line." Williams knows too much about poetry to set up a critical shop or lay out a curriculum like Pound. He is the godfather, all the same, of nearly all the existent *avant-garde* poetry, all the free poetry that exists in the English world today. This is recognized by the young poets who long ago branched away from the cultural highway and took to the backstreets and bohemias of the land. Williams is no bohemian; he is a serious man of letters (as the stuffy expression goes) but he is closer to the life of the poet than any of his contemporaries. By the life of the poet I mean the man to whom the daily life is the poetry itself, whatever his occupation. Williams may have been trying to do the impossible in taking for granted the unity of expression and artistry in the early years of the century, but he was one of the few who accepted this high premise of the poet. When the "great catastrophe" (the publication of *The Waste Land*) occurred, most of Williams' friends dropped by the wayside or split into little groups or went over to the enemy, as Williams put it. It is curious that through all the ensuing years Williams remained loyal to Pound and could not perceive that it was Pound who was the lever for the catastrophe and would continue to be.

A newly published book by Williams serves better than anything I have ever read about him to clarify and sum up his poetry and his poetics. It is a strange and charming work called *I Wanted to Write a Poem*. The book is an informal bibliography which is also a kind of autobiography. The editor (Edith Heal) lists the books chronologically, fifty of them, and gets the poet to discuss their inception. Mrs. Williams, the poet's editor throughout his career, makes additional comments. Throughout this running commentary one can follow the fifty-year search for form which has been Williams' lifelong preoccupation. I

would like to conclude by condensing and commenting upon
his own findings after which I will give my evaluation of his
achievement.

His earliest influences, he says, are Keats and Whitman.
He would rather be a painter than a poet (his mother is an artist) but cannot because of the medical profession. He finds his
contemporaries quickly: Wallace Stevens, Marianne Moore,
Hilda Doolittle, Ezra Pound. Pound is the only one of these to
whom he feels literary loyalty. Stevens tags him with the label
"anti-poetic," which Williams resents ever after (Mrs. Williams,
curiously enough, does not understand the poet's rage over this
designation.) He abandons rhyme and meter in his second book
(1913). While he is writing *Kora*, "Prufrock" appears; Williams
says: "I had a violent feeling that Eliot had betrayed what I
believed in. He was looking backward; I was looking forward.
He was a conformist, with wit, learning which I did not possess . . . But I felt he had rejected America and I refused to
be rejected . . . I realized the responsibility I must accept. I
knew he would influence all subsequent American poets and
take them out of my sphere. I had envisioned a new form of
poetic composition, a form for the future. It was a shock to me
that he was so tremendously successful; my contemporaries
flocked to him — away from what I wanted. It forced me to be
successful . . . " He consciously rejects free verse, simultaneously rejecting metered verse. "The greatest problem [he says]
was that I didn't know how to divide a poem into what perhaps
my lyrical sense wanted." *Paterson* seems to him the answer:
he personifies a city and follows its river (the Passiac) and the
river-of-history from Paterson down to the sea. Documentary
prose breaks the flow of the poetry. Evidently it is the formless
form that he has been searching for. In *Paterson, II* he hits upon the step-down form in which all his subsequent poems are
written. The line he now refers to as the "variable foot."

What then is the "prosody" of the Williams poem? If we
can believe that every good poem ever written in form is
good despite the form, and that every formless (free verse)
poem that succeeded has suceeded despite its formlessness,
then we will be getting close to the idea of Williams' form. It is
the purest theory of poetry I have ever heard of and I take it to
be the ideal of all poets, formalists or *vers librists*. For meter

has nothing to do with it; meter is an aftereffect. Metaphor and simile have nothing to do with it. "The coining of similes is a pastime of very low order, depending as it does upon a merely vegetable coincidence . . . " Structure has nothing to do with it: you cannot remove the parts from the whole; or rather you cannot find the structure. Beautiful language has nothing to do with it any more than the antipoetic. And finally, poetry is a secular art "free from the smears of mystery."

I am not sure I understand all this (assuming I've got it down accurately) but I know in my bones it is right. It is not theory; it is the laborious explanation of an artist stammering out the reason why his poem came out the way it did. Each poem is its own form, as it must be. The poem is unique and unrepeatable; it is when you repeat that form arises, for form is imitation, as in Eliot, precedent heaped upon precedent. With Williams the poem is raw, quivering, natural, an *object trouvé*, something you look at twice before you pick it up. It is the extreme of the original, the condition of poetry which frightens off most poets, a complete breakthrough to his own language. It is the kind of poetry which it may take years to see but once seen remakes all other poetry and conceptions of poetry.

But I do not mean that Williams' works are perfection or even that he has written a score or two of poems which will set him beside Milton or Catullus or Marlowe. It is hard to judge such work comparatively; it is too new, too unlike anything else. But there is one sure sign of its value; it has already penetrated the poetry of a whole generation of American poets, not the ones we read month after month in the apple-pie-order journals of letters or the fat anthologies, but in the less-known, less-official magazines and pamphlets strewn over the countryside, which Williams has always lent his hand to. With D. H. Lawrence, Williams is the leader of what authentic American poetry is being written today. Little enough of it is up to his mark, yet the tendency is the right one. The example is there in Williams' poems, not in his criticism. And it is being followed. When I read his poems I feel I am reading a foreign language, my language. After all, there is practically no American poetry to speak of, and nearly all of it has come in the twentieth century, and a good portion of that has been written by William Carlos Williams.

I call him the true contemporary because he saw the challenge from the beginning and saw it whole: to create American poetry out of nothing, out of that which had never lent itself to poetry before. To do this without betraying the present to the past (like Eliot) and without exploiting the present (like Sandburg) and without trying to force the future (like Pound). I call him the true contemporary also because he could not resist trying to write the Great American Epic. But in Williams' case this can be overlooked: he has written enough true poetry to show the twentieth century that *American* and *poet* are not contradictions in terms.

# Ezra Pound's
# London Years

by RICHARD M. LUDWIG

I think one work of art is
worth forty prefaces and as
many apologiae.—*Pavannes
and Divisions*, 1918.

It is too early for apologiae and too late for the kinds of
prefaces Pound's fellow poets — Eliot, Aiken, Flint, Aldington,
Sandburg — were writing when "the good Ezra" was living in
London: appreciation and censure following hard upon the
publication of a new collection of poems. Ezra Pound's major
work has been on our shelves for so many decades he is in no
need of prefaces. But if we wish, by our criticism, to send
readers back to the poems, and that is all a good poet asks of
good criticism, we need to look closely at these London years,
1908-20, putting aside for the moment Pound's later work, the
*Cantos,* the economic pamphlets, and the critical writings.

"Ezra Pound's London Years" by Richard M. Ludwig. From *Aspects
of American Poetry*, ed. by Richard M. Ludwig, pp. 99-119. Copyright ©
1962 by the Ohio State University Press. Reprinted by permission of the
author and the Ohio State University Press.

By looking closely I do not mean *explication de texte.*
Pound has had more than his share of exegesis in the last ten
years. It has not, even Hugh Kenner's exhausting efforts have
not, brought him more readers. He is still the formidable
*collagiste,* compiler of an endless epic which remains largely
unread. Mr. Kenner asks early in his book "why Eliot, Joyce,
and Yeats are thoroughly assimilated" and "Pound's reputation alone remains so much a matter of inert convention." [1]
The reason is patent, but Mr. Kenner will never accept it.
F. R. Leavis spelled it out for him in 1932 in his *New Bearings
in English Poetry.* T. S. Eliot hinted at it in his contribution[2] to
*An Examination of Ezra Pound,* Peter Russell's collection of
essays published for Pound's sixty-fifth birthday. Alfred Alvarez says it more justly, and more eloquently, in his essay
on Pound in *The Shaping Spirit.* For too long, he believes, we
have been asked to accept the *Cantos* as a masterpiece of
structure, as the culminating work in Pound's stormy career,
whereas "his most expressive form is the short poem. Both
*Mauberley* and *Propertius* are a series of these; the finest parts
of the *Cantos* have the same singleness and concentration."[3]
Whether the *Cantos* are a masterpiece or a failure I shall not
argue here. We know where Mr. Kenner stands. What I
share with Mr. Alvarez is the strong feeling that "one of the
main troubles with the *Cantos* is not their obscurity but their
remoteness."[4] Pound's work from 1908 to 1920 was neither
obscure nor remote, and it consisted chiefly of short poems.
They deserve revaluation.

When Pound came up to London from Venice in 1908, he
brought with him not only his first published book but a whole
armful of poetry. With his own money he paid for the printing
of one hundred copies of *A Lume Spento,* a collection of forty-
four poems. He had been fired from Wabash College at the
age of twenty-three[5] and had left America in disgust for the
part of Europe he has loved ever since: Spain, France, and

[1] *The Poetry of Ezra Pound* (London, 1951,), p. 18.

[2] First published in *Poetry,* LXVII (September, 1946), 326-38.

[3] *The Shaping Spirit: Studies in Modern English and American Poets*
(London, 1958), p. 68; published in the United States under the title
*Stewards of Excellence.*

[4] *Ibid.,* p. 59.

[5] The details are recorded in Charles Norman's biography, *Ezra
Pound* (New York, 1960), pp. 22-24.

Italy. But he could not have chosen, even as an ex-instructor of Romance languages, a more unlikely city than Venice in which to publish poems in English. He had come to Europe, after all, to be near Yeats, and within four months he was writing from London to his old friend, William Carlos Williams. This long letter (the first of hundreds Williams received over the years) is one of the most revealing Pound has ever written. Among other things, he says:

> I am very sure that I have written a lot of stuff that would please you and a lot of my personal friends more than A L[ume] S[pento]. But, mon cher, would a collection of mild, pretty verses convince any publisher or critic that I happen to be a genius and deserve audience? I have written bushels of verse that could offend no one except a person as well read as I am who knows that it has all been said just as prettily before.[6]

During the next ten years, Pound winnowed these bushels of verse in a way that may delight a bibliographer but maddens the general reader who admires a single poem and then tries to find the rest of the volume in which it appeared. Before we can judge the London years, we need to set the publishing record straight. It is less complex than it looks at first glance.

A Lume Spento was not reprinted in London, although Yeats called the collection "charming" and Pound told Williams that "Mosher is going to reprint." Instead, a second volume, A Quinzaine for This Yule, appeared in London late in 1908. It contained only twenty-seven pages, probably for private circulation, and today it is as rare as A Lume Spento. Pound's third volume, Personae, appeared in April, 1909. He had written Williams in February that he was "by way of falling into the crowd that does things here. London, deah old Lundon, is the place for poesy.'" With this fifty-nine page volume, Pound had indeed found his place. Elkin Mathews, the Vigo Street bookseller, was the publisher. The reviews could not have been better had Mathews written them himself. In Ford Madox Ford's English Review, Edward Thomas

---

[6] The Letters of Ezra Pound: 1907-1941, ed. D. D. Paige (New York, 1950), p. 4.

[7] Letters, p. 7.

said that "from the first to the last lines of most of his poems he holds us steadily, in his own pure, grave, passionate world." Rupert Brooke praised the book in the *Cambridge Review,* R. A. Scott-James in the *Daily News. Punch,* the *Observer,* the *Bookman* nodded full approval. No one mentioned the fact that almost half of *Personae* had been first published in Venice.

Mathews issued another volume of Pound's work in the fall of the same year, 1909, twenty-seven new poems called *Exultations.* America was now ready to recognize this expatriate. In spite of his feelings about the moribund American audience, Pound did not object. He spent ten months in America (from summer, 1910, to spring, 1911) seeing his parents in Wyncote, Pennsylvania, getting to know New York City, and arguing about poetry with Williams and his wife, out in Rutherford, New Jersey. In Boston, he arranged for the publication of *Provença,* technically his fifth book but actually a collection reprinted from *Personae* and *Exultations,* plus a few new poems. His fifth and sixth volumes appeared in London: *Canzoni,* in 1911, and *Ripostes,* in 1912. He later called *Canzoni* "many false starts never reprinted." Actually, he had exhausted his experiments with Pre-Raphaelite subjects, imitations of Browning. Provençal forms, self-conscious diction ("olde-worlde" diction, it has been called), and transmogrifications of Latin and Italian poems. *Canzoni* is the end of a cycle. With *Ripostes,* Pound began the second stage of his poetic career.

*Ripostes* is dedicated to William Carlos Williams, whose approval he cherished although they quarreled over theory. One wonders if Williams recognized the sharp break Pound was making here with his past enthusiasms. The collection includes "translations," it is true, notably "The Seafarer," but it also gives us Pound's own authentic voice: sharp images, overt satire, polished epigrams, and free-verse lyrics. The last five pages of the book contain the "complete poetical works of T. E. Hulme" which Pound claimed were "reprinted here for good fellowship . . . a custom out of Tuscany and Provence." Pound owed much to Hulme, the reactionary philosopher whose career was tragically brief, and to F. S. Flint, the talented linguist. They were the instigators of the Thursday evening meetings in Soho restaurants of a poetry club at which Pound, early in 1908, discovered congenial companions and attentive ears. Moreover Hulme was a spokesman for the "new" poetry. He was certain that "images in verse are not mere decoration, but the very essence of an intuitive language."[8] In a two-page introduction to these poems by Hulme, Pound uses for the first time in print the term *Les Imagistes* to describe the poets writing what Hulme later called "dry, hard, and classical verse." The whole history of Imagism cannot detain us here,[9] but it is significant that in *Ripostes*, 1912, Pound was ready to announce the direction he and some of his friends were taking. In January, 1913, Harriet Monroe's magazine, *Poetry*, published H. D.'s first work and Pound's notes from London:

> Space forbids me to set forth the program of the
> *Imagistes* at length, but one of their watchwords is
> Precision, and they are in opposition to the numerous
> and unassembled writers who busy themselves with
> dull and interminable effusions, and who seem to
> think that a man can write a good long poem before
> he learns to write a good short one, or even before
> he learns to produce a good single line.[10]

Precision continued to be Pound's watchword long after he had lost interest in the Imagist school.

This same year his new direction was luckily bolstered by the gift of Ernest Fenollosa's notes and translations, sent to him by the widow of this former Imperial Commissioner of Arts in Japan. *Cathay*, 1915, Pound's seventh volume of verse, is the result. The title page calls the work "translations for the most part from the Chinese of Rihaku, from the notes of the late Ernest Fenollosa, and decipherings of the Professors Mori and Agira." Rihaku is the Japanese name for Li T'ai Po, the eighth-century Chinese poet. On the last page of *Cathay*, Pound appended this strange note, an early sign of what in a

---

[8] *Speculations*, ed. Herbert Read (London, 1958), p. 135.

[9] F. S. Flint published *A History of Imagism* in 1915. For a recent, detailed account of the movement, see Stanley K. Coffman, Jr., *Imagism: A Chapter for the History of Modern Poetry* (Norman. Oklahoma, 1951).

[10] "Status Rerum," *Poetry*, I (January, 1913), 126.

few years was to become a petulant dissatisfaction with literary London:

> I have not come to the end of Ernest Fenollosa's notes by a long way, nor is it entirely perplexity which causes me to cease from translation . . . . But if I give them, with the necessary breaks for explanation, and a tedium of notes, it is quite certain that the personal hatred in which I am held by many, and the *invidia* which is directed against me because I have dared openly to declare my belief in certain young artists, will be brought to bear first on the flaws of such translation, and will then be merged into depreciation of the whole book of translations. Therefore I give only these unquestionable poems.

Poems they unquestionably are; translations they are not. Sinologists have been making that clear for more than forty years. But when Eliot says "Pound is the inventor of Chinese poetry for our time," he means *"Cathay* will be a 'Windsor Translation' as Chapman and North are now 'Tudor Translations': it will be called (and justly) a 'magnificent specimen of XXth Century poetry' rather than a 'translation.' '"[11] Critics other than Eliot, Yeats among them, have acknowledged that *Cathay* is even more than that. They see it as a major influence on all modern poetry and as a seminal volume in Pound's development, for *Cathay* leads directly into *Lustra,* 1916. His competence in Romance philology did not extend to the Oriental languages; but in his insistence that Fenollosa wanted his work treated as literature, not philology, Pound took liberties with the text, saturated himself with the philosophy behind the ideogram, learned how to assume new (Oriental) *personae,* investigated the Japanese *haiku* and *tanka,* and ultimately forged for himself an idiom through which he could mirror pre-war London. The Fenollosa manuscripts were catalysts in perfecting the "dry, hard, classical" style which Hulme had prophesied and Eliot so much admired.

Elkin Mathews published *Lustra* in London, Alfred Knopf in New York. Both editions included all of *Cathay,*

---

[11] "Introduction: 1928," *Ezra Pound: Selected Poems,* ed. T. S. Eliot (London, 1928), pp. 14-15.

"some new Chinese stuff," as Pound wrote Iris Barry, "and all of my own work since *Ripostes*."[12] His work "since *Ripostes*" revealed a new, sharp-tongued, sophisticated Pound. A *lustrum*, we are reminded on the title page, is "an offering for the sins of the whole people, made by the censors at the expiration of their five years of office." His skill in *vers libre* is everywhere evident in these seventy-six new poems, and it is not enough to say, as Eliot did in his anonymous *Ezra Pound: His Metric and Poetry* (1917), that skill such as this "comes only after much work in rigid forms." Of course the pre-*Ripostes* volumes demonstrate Pound's years of practice with the sestina, the ballad, the conventional lyric. But *Lustra* is also illustration in depth of Pound's 1913 prescription for modern poetry: direct treatment of the "thing"; accuracy and economy of language; and rhythm "in sequence of the musical phrase, not in sequence of the metronome."[13] His theory of verse-as-speech is ably demonstrated here. When Eliot, in 1922, called Pound *il miglior fabbro*, it is possible he had these poems in mind as well as the first cantos. He had said as much, five years earlier, in his anonymous essay: "When anyone has studied Mr. Pound's poems in *chronological* order, and has mastered *Lustra* and *Cathay*, he is prepared for the *Cantos*—but not till then."[14]

Three more volumes followed *Lustra* before Pound left London for Paris. *Quia Pauper Amavi*, published by the Egoist Press in 1919, gave us eight more poems in the *Lustra* vein, six lyrics labeled "Langue d'Oc," three cantos (some parts of which were salvaged for the *Cantos*), and a version of certain passages in Books II and III of the Elegies of Propertius which Pound carefully titled "Homage to Sextus Propertius." He wrote A. R. Orage the next spring that "there was never any question of translation [of Propertius], let alone literal translation. My job was to bring a dead man to life, to present a living figure."[15] The academicians ignored his title and misjudged

---

[12] *Letters*, p. 81.

[13] "Imagisme" and "A Few Dont's by an Imagiste," Poetry, I (March, 1913), 198-206.

[14] *Ezra Pound: His Metric and Poetry* (New York, 1917), p. 28.

[15] *Letters*, pp. 148-49. See also W. G. Hale, "Pegasus Impounded," Poetry, XIV (April, 1919), 52-55, for violent disapproval of Pound's treatment of Propertius.

his intentions. The quarrel still continues. *Hugh Selwyn Mauberley,* published in April, 1920, is Pound's climactic achievement, not only his farewell to London but a reaffirmation of
his role as midwife to modern poetry. *Umbra: The Early Poems
of Ezra Pound,* dated June, 1920, is a gathering (and a most un-
satisfactory one at that) of "all that [the poet] now wishes to
keep in circulation from *Personae, Exultations, Ripostes,* etc.,
with translations from Guido Cavalcanti and Arnaut Daniel
and poems by the late T. E. Hulme." It was the last of Pound's
books to be printed by Elkin Mathews. In September, 1920,
Pound unburdened himself to William Carlos Williams:

> AND now that there is no longer any intellectual *life*
> in England save what centres in this eight by ten
> pentagonal room; now that Remy [de Gourmont]
> and Henry [Henri Gaudier-Brzeska] are gone and
> Yeats faded, and NO literary publications whatever ex-
> tant in England, save what "we" print (*Egoist* and
> Ovid Press), the question remains whether I have to
> give up every shred of comfort, every scrap of my per-
> sonal life, and "gravitate" to a New York which wants
> me as little now as it did ten and fifteen years ago.
> Whether, from the medical point of view it is maso-
> chism for me even to stay here, instead of shifting to
> Paris. Whether self-inflicted torture ever has the
> slightest element of dignity in it?
>
> > Or whether I am Omar.
> > Have I a country at all . . . .[16]

By the end of the year he was ready to join the expatriate
crowd in Paris, but he tired of them more quickly and five
years later left for Rapallo. Pound's country was everywhere
and nowhere.

A mere recapitulation of publishing history, however impressive, will convince no one that these twelve years of
Pound's life may well be the apex of his genius. Students of
poetry acquainted with the whole canon know the rest of the
story, the feverish activity: Imagism, Amygism, Futurism, Vor-
ticism; *Poetry, Blast,* the *Little Review,* the *Egoist,* the *Dial;* his
months with Yeats at a turning point in their careers ("To talk

[16] *Letters,* pp. 158-59.

over a poem with [Ezra] is like getting you to put a sentence into dialect. All becomes clear and natural."); his finding publishers for Joyce and Eliot and Wyndham Lewis; his letters to Chicago badgering Harriet Monroe ("Until 'we' accept what I've been insisting on for a decade, i.e., a universal standard which pays no attention to time or country—a Weltlitteratur standard —there is no hope."). Readers who come to Pound through the *Cantos,* alas, share none of this excitement, this growth of a bumptious young philogist, in love with Provence, into a perceptive critic and lyric poet. They see only the irascible old man who has turned his ideogrammic method into the logic of no logic and his ambitious epic into a deafening harangue. They say his ego has exploded; but his ego was always enormous and, if we believe Pound, it had to be.

He wrote to Alice Henderson in 1913:

> I wonder if *Poetry* really dares to devote a number to my *new* work. There'll be a *howl.* They won't like it. It's absolutely the *last* obsequies of the Victorian period. I won't permit any selection or editing. It stands now a series of 24 poems, most of them very short.

In the same letter he assured the editors:

> It's not futurism and it's not post-impressionism, but it's work contemporary with those schools and to my mind the most significant that I have yet brought off.
>
> BUTT they won't like it. They won't object as much as they did to Whitman's outrages, because the stamina of stupidity is weaker. I guarantee you *one* thing. The reader will not be *bored.* He will say ahg, ahg, ahh, ahhh, but-bu-bu-bu-but this isn't Poetry."

Yet these very poems are the breakthrough in modern poetry. If few readers were ready to recognize their quality, at least Pound knew what he has accomplished. They are what he meant when he wrote of Walt Whitman, "It was you that broke the new wood,/Now is time for carving." He was determined his audience would come to like the "carving," and he nearly exhausted himself (and made enemies in the process) imposing this "new" poetry on them. That is not to dis-

---

"*Letters,* pp. 23-24.

count Hulme or Flint or Ford Madox Ford, or even Harold
Monro. They were in London before Pound arrived, setting the
stage, founding the magazines, proclaiming the doctrine. Nor
is it to deny that Yeats and Eliot ultimately surpassed Pound
in the decade following the First World War. He was prepared
for that; his letters leave no doubt.[18] What I fear, however, is
the neglect of eleven volumes of verse—from *A Lume Spento*
to *Umbra*—which so brilliantly illustrate, in a way that the *Cantos* do not, Pound's urbane lyricism, his bold metaphors and
startling rhythms, his caustic wit, above all his contagious gusto. The individual volumes, of course, are out of print, but the
poet's own selection of the best poems is readily available.
In 1926, Horace Liveright asked Pound for a volume of collected poems. He chose two hundred, all pre-*Cantos,* and titled
the book *Personae,* not with a perverse desire to confuse but
for an obvious reason. They are the masks of his youth, re-
assembled. New Directions republished the collection in 1949,
Faber and Faber in 1952. Both the student of poetry and the
general reader will find it a textbook and a gallery.

To assume *personae* and translate other poets is to court
the label "derivative." Pound took that risk; these were his
apprentice pieces. His singing school in the London years
ranged from the Provençal lyrics of Bertrans de Born and Arnaut Daniel to Guido Calvalcanti of thirteenth-century Florence,
Swinburne and Browning, Dowson and Johnson and the Nineties crowd, some of Whitman, some of Kipling, especially
Yeats. Before he left for Paris he had also absorbed Li Po
through Fenollosa, Sappho through the Imagists, Catullus and
Propertius, Gautier and Heine, Laforge and Corbière. The barrier of language was no deterrent. When he discovered the
Chinese ideogram he was quick to see its similarity to the
Anglo-Saxon kenning and to what Hulme was propounding in
his emphasis on "the image." Being the eclectic humanist who
never looked on "tradition" as mere conventionalism, Pound
wanted to cut across the centuries and bring all Western poetry

---

[18] On receiving the manuscript of "Prufrock," he wrote Harriet Monroe that Eliot "is the only American I know of who has made what I
can call an adequate preparation for writing. He has actually trained
himself *and* modernized himself *on his own.*" And with typical emphasis,
he says of the poem: "PRAY GOD IT BE NOT A SINGLE AND UNIQUE
SUCCESS" (*Letters,* p. 40).

to life again. And so *Personae,* 1926, is among many things a
gallery of adaptations. "The Ballad of the Goodby Fere"[19] takes
a traditional verse form for an untraditional portrait: Jesus,
"the goodliest fere o' all," no "capon priest" but a "man o'
men" who "cried no cry when they drave the nails." The popular monologue, "Cino," laid in the Italian Campagna, 1309,
opens with a Browning overtone:

> Bah! I have sung women in three cities,
> But it is all the same;
> And I will sing of the sun,

and descends into diction that was certain to set some teeth
on edge. Cino's song is splendid mockery:

> 'Pollo Phoibee, old tin pan, you
> Glory to Zeus' aegis-day,
> Shield o' steel-blue, th' heaven o'er us,
> Hath for boss thy lustre gay!

Pound was never one to treat his models gently. "You, Master
Bob Browning," he shouts in the poem "Mesmerism": "Heart
that was big as the bowels of Vesuvius . . . Here's to you,
Old Hippety-Hop o' the accents." Of Whitman, he says, "I
come to you as a grown child/Who has had a pig-headed
father." Heine he loved for his daring:

> O Harry Heine, curses be
> I live too late to sup with thee!
> Who can demolish at such polished ease
> Philistia's pomp and Art's pomposities!

The Troubadours he loved even more, particularly Bertrans de
Born.[20] *Personae,* 1926, gives us his translation (i.e., adaptation)
of Bertrans' plaint for Prince Henry Plantagenet, a noble lament turned into stately English in "Planh for the Young English King." He takes half of a stanza in Bertrans' "Dompna
pois de me no us cal" and builds around it a haunting portrait,

---

[19] "Fere" is a medieval word meaning "mate" or "companion."

[20] See especially the first half of Pound's *The Spirit of Romance*
(London, 1910). For more competent discussion than I can give of Pound's
translations from Provençal originals, see Leonard Casper's informative
article "Apprenticed in Provence," *Poetry,* LXXXI (December, 1952), 203-
11.

"Na Audiart," not wholly successful in rhyme and diction but
an early exercise in rhythmic sweep. Bertrans' scorn of sloth
and peace is occasion for Pound's most impressive demonstration of his powerful rhythmic control, "Sestina: Altaforte."
Altaforte is Bertrans' castle; Papiols is his jongleur. "Dante Al-
ighieri," Pound tells us in a headnote, "put this man in hell for
that he was a stirrer up of strife. Eccovi! Judge ye! Have I
dug him up again?" He has. With bold spondees, Bertrans
bursts on the scene. We can hear Pound declaiming the lines
in Bellotti's Soho restaurant, to the delight of the poets' club
and the consternation of the other diners:

> Damn it all! all this our South stinks peace.
> You whoreson dog, Papiols, come! Let's to music!
> I have no life save when the swords clash.

Pound manipulates the demanding Provençal verse form with
appropriate harshness ("There's no sound like to swords swords
opposing") and shocking juxtaposition ("Hell grant soor we
hear again the swords clash!" followed four stanzas later by
"May God damn for ever all who cry 'Peace!' "). From the
Troubadours he learned boldness in song and subject; from
the Anglo-Saxons, exactness of image; from the English poets
of the generation before him, a colloquial diction and late-Ro-
mantic themes. "The history of art," he tells us in The Spirit
of Romance, "is the history of masterwork, not of failures, or
mediocrity . . . . The study of literature is hero-worship." He
said it another way in a letter to Margaret Anderson: "The
strength of Picasso is largely in his having chewed through and
chewed up a great mass of classicism: which, for example, the
lesser cubists, and the flabby cubists have not."[21] But the
jongleur must someday find his own voice, or he never becomes the troubadour. The apprentice, much as he learns by
translation and adaption, must make his own forms.

Personae, 1926, is replete with poems that show us Pound's
individual talent. I shall be the first to admit that they are not
profound poems. Pound's attempts at profundity are invariably faltering, and that, let us confess, is one of the troubles
with the Cantos. But these short poems, in the conciseness of
their notation, influenced twentieth-century poetry more than

[21] Letters, p. 113.

critics are willing to admit. Dated 1912–16, they set a tone and
a style which in time was imitated just as Pound imitated his
predecessors. The tone is alternately ecstatic, world-weary,
caustic, fragile. The style is precise, strongly rhythmic, frequently colloquial, a style fitted for verse-as-speech, a style
that never bores. "It is the business of the artist to prevent
ennui," Pound believed, "to relieve, refresh, revive the mind
of the reader—at reasonable intervals—with some form of ecstasy, by some splendor of thought, some presentation of sheer
beauty, some lightning turn of phrase."[22] Ecstasy can be fragile.
"The Encounter" has but five lines, yet the central image is
remarkably supple and haunting:

> All the while they were talking the new morality
> Her eyes explored me.
> And when I arose to go
> Her fingers were like the tissue
> Of a Japanese paper napkin.

Almost as briefly, and with guileless understatement, he recalls past ecstasy in "Erat Hora":

> "Thank you, whatever comes." And then she turned
> And, as the ray of sun on hanging flowers
> Fades when the wind hath lifted them aside,
> Went swiftly from me. Nay, whatever comes
> One hour was sunlit and the most high gods
> May not make boast of any better thing
> Than to have watched that hour as it passed.

Ecstasy can be visual. His familiar "L'Art, 1910" and "In a
Station of the Metro" are too often reprinted in favor of the
lesser-known but lovely "Gentildonna":

> She passed and left no quiver in the veins who
>      now
> Moving among the trees, and clinging
>      in the air she severed,
> Fanning the grass she walked on then, endures:
> Grey olive leaves beneath a rain-cold sky.

The single image of "Alba" takes the severe economy of the
Imagists as far as it can go:

[22] *The Spirit of Romance*, p. 8.

> As cool as the pale wet leaves
>     of lily-of-the valley
> She lay beside me in the dawn.

Nor is Pound afraid of humor, though his humor is usually dry. "Laughter is no mean ecstasy," he tells us. In "Tame Cat" he says that it rests him to converse with beautiful women:

> Even though we talk nothing but nonsense,
> The purring of the invisible antennae
> Is both stimulating and delightful.

"Phyllidula," on the other hand, might have shocked in 1916:

> Phyllidula is scrawny but amorous,
> Thus have the gods awarded her,
> That in pleasure she receives more than she can give;
> If she does not count this blessed
> Let her change her religion.

"The Temperaments" we know caused difficulties. Elkin Mathews marked it for deletion from *Lustra;* Alfred Knopf omitted it from the American trade edition but printed it privately in sixty copies not for sale:

> Nine adulteries, 12 liaisons, 64 fornications and
>     something approaching a rape
> Rest nightly upon the soul of our delicate friend
>     Florialis,
> And yet the man is so quiet and reserved in
>     demeanour
> That he passes for both bloodless and sexless.
> Bastidides, on the contrary, who both talks and writes
>     of nothing save copulation,
> Has become the father of twins,
> But he accomplished this feat at some cost;
> He had to be four times cuckold.

The reader unfamiliar with *Personae* may not be satisfied with these vignettes. He will want to read the more ambitious poems, reprinted in this 1926 volume, from *Ripostes, Lustra,* and *Cathay.* "Portrait d'une Femme" may have derived from Henry James; but in the opening lines we sense at once that Pound gives it his own spare diction and flat rhythm, the world-weary tone "Prufrock" made popular five years later:

Your mind and you are our Sargasso Sea,
London has swept about you this score years
And bright ships left you this or that in fee:
Ideas, old gossip, oddments of all things,
Strange spars of knowledge and dimmed wares of
    price.
Great minds have sought you—lacking someone else.
You have been second always. Tragical?
No. You preferred it to the usual thing;
One dull man, dulling and uxorious,
One average mind—with one thought less, each year.

"Provincia Deserta" and "Near Perigord" are Pound in Provence, not mere borrowings from the Troubadours. "The River-
Merchant's Wife: A Letter" and "Poem by the Bridge at Ten-
Shin" derive from Fenollosa's notes on Li Po, but they are
English syntax and idiom, dressing a universal subject. Pound
has learned not only to assume the *persona* but to inhabit it.
In "Moeurs Contemporaines," a group of eight sketches, there
is no question of Pound's intentions: scathing satire, verse-as-
speech, broken rhythms, colloquial diction. Conceivably they
lead to Auden, Cummings, MacLeish, as well as to "The Waste-
land."

    *Hugh Selwyn Mauberley* is the major work, a sequence of
dramatic lyrics. Pound keeps telling us that he is no more
Mauberley than Eliot is Prufrock, and I suppose we must take
his word. Back in 1908 he was telling Williams what the dramatic lyric meant to him:

> To me the short so-called dramatic lyric—at any rate
> the sort of thing I do—is the poetic part of a drama
> the rest of which (to me the prose part) is left to the
> reader's imagination or set in a short note. I catch the
> character I happen to be interested in at the moment
> he interests me, usually a moment of song, self-analy-
> sis, or sudden understanding or revelation. And the
> rest of the play would bore me and presumably the
> reader. I paint my man as I *conceive* him. Et voilà
> tout.[23]

Yet in preparing the poem for the New Directions reprinting,

[23] *Letters*, pp. 3-4.

in 1949, of *Personae,* 1926, he added this note in small type at
the foot of the title page: "The sequence is so distinctly a
farewell to London that the reader who chooses to regard
this as an exclusively American edition may as well omit it
and turn at once to page 205." Let us read it then as a farewell, and whether Mauberley is Pound or another *persona* is
irrelevant. He divides the poem into eighteen parts, speaking
through his own voice in the first thirteen, admittedly the poet
"out of key with his time," one who "strove to resuscitate the
dead art of poetry," in vain. The last five parts, labeled "Mauberley 1920," can be read either as a five-part coda or as a
"portrait d'un homme," that is, an imaginative projection of
one facet of Pound or merely another picture in the gallery;
but it is the poetry, not the identification, that is important.

It is impossible and unnecessary to rehearse this entire
poem here, impossible because of its length, unnecessary because John J.Espey has done it so admirably in his study, *Ezra
Pound's "Mauberley."* But I cannot end this essay without repeating, with alteration, Eliot's dictum of 1917. Not until we
have read *Lustra* and *Cathay,* he felt, are we ready for the
*Cantos.* Rather I should say, not until we have read *Personae,*
1926, are we ready for *Hugh Selwyn Mauberley.* But when we
are ready, we will discover how extraordinarily subtle, precise, and evocative this sequence is, how much it is a collage
of Pound's work from 1908 to 1920, neither obscure nor remote.
Some parts of it are derivative. The thirteenth is patently Edmund Waller, reversed:

> Go, dumb-born book,
> Tell her that sang me once that song of Lawes:
> Hadst thou but song
> As thou hast subjects known,
> Then were there cause in thee that should condone
> Even my faults that heavy upon me lie,
> And build her glories their longevity.

Some parts are bitter satire. The ninth, "Mr. Nixon," could be
a portrait of Arnold Bennett:

> In the cream gilded cabin of his steam yacht
> Mr. Nixon advised me kindly, to advance with fewer

Dangers of delay. "Consider
"Carefully the reviewer.

.    .    .    .    .    .    .    .    .

"And no one knows, at sight, a masterpiece.
"And give up verse, my boy,
"There's nothing in it."

The fourth and fifth lament the loss of the best young men "for an old bitch gone in the teeth/For a botched civilization." Pound felt that German guns had killed the best sculptor of his generation, Gaudier-Brzeska, a young critic, T. E. Hulme, a young poet, Rupert Brooke, and the liveliest mind in France, Remy de Gourmont. The second and third poems are bitter for equally personal reasons:

> The age demanded an image
> Of its accelerated grimace,
> Something for the modern stage,
> Not, at any rate, an Attic grace;
> Not, not certainly, the obscure reveries
> Of the inward gaze;
> Better mendacities
> Than the classics in paraphrase!

Other parts of the sequence are warm and sensitive portraits. Ford Madox Ford, an old friend back from the war, found London intolerable and retreated to Sussex:

> Beneath the sagging roof
> The stylist has taken shelter,
> Unpaid, uncelebrated,
> At last from the world's welter
> Nature receives him . . . .

From first to last line, in other words, Pound is in complete control, having tried out his forms, his rhythm, his diction for ten years and more. To his constant readers the sequence must have come, in 1920, as affirmation of his talent, not as baffling pastiche or willful obscurity. This talent for precise image and contrapuntal rhythms is spread in profusion over the pages of *Ripostes, Lustra,* and *Cathay. Mauberley* was his farewell; but it is, at the same time, his arrival.

# The Peaceable Kingdom
# of Marianne Moore

*by* VIVIENNE KOCH

"This is a strange fraternity."
". . . formal as the scales of a fish."
"Liking an elegance of which the source is
not bravado . . . knows by heart the antique . . ."
"Where there is personal liking we go."
"Acknowledgments seem only honest."

Elizur Wright, an American, and apparently the first comprehensive Englisher of La Fontaine's *Fables*, in a preface to the 1841 edition of his translation, wrote:

> Human nature, when fresh from the hand of God, was full of poetry. Its sociality could not be pent within the bounds of the actual. To the lower inhabitants of air, earth, and water,—and even to those elements themselves, in all parts and forms,—it gave speech and reason. The skies it peopled with beings, on the noblest model of which it could have any conception—to wit, its own!

It is precisely Marianne Moore's "sociality (which) could not be pent within the bounds of the actual." It is her entirely social shuttling from the actual to the imagined, or from what is imaginable in the actual, to its actuality, that is at once the key and the meaning to her charmed movement between the human and animal kingdom.

Historically, fable was a mere auxiliary to impassioned discourse. The great fabulists of antiquity were orators first. Marianne Moore is in the tradition of the great fabulists, for her method is the method of discourse. The differential resides in her *tone* which is conversational, rather than as with the older fabulists rhetorical. Thus, while in intention and framework she takes over the heritage of the fable, she feels quite free to ignore the stock trappings. One rigid convention of the fable is that animals are given human speech. Miss Moore's animals hardly ever speak, although she speaks to them. What remains in common with the fabulists is the descriptive element (but more closely executed than by the fabulists), the animal revealed in some characteristic action (but with Miss Moore narrated rather than *dramatized*), and the concluding sententia, which in her work is always a new and delicately stated relationship in the realm of conduct rather than, as with La Fontaine and the tradition he utilized so wittily, a brisk climax of proverbial wisdom.

But there are other differences, too. There is, in Miss Moore's work, a vast emblematic heraldry of symbols cunningly disguised in zoological, ornithological, botanical or piscatorial forms. Always her quaint animals are meant to illuminate qualities and, unlike the fabulists' practice, they are not necessarily human ones. In the oriental fable or in those of La Fontaine, one does not find the animal acting *themselves* out, as do Miss Moore's, to give us knowledge of humanity; instead, the fabulist endows the animal with human traits and attributes. With Miss Moore the animals *as* animals count for just as much as the humans they may eventually inform. In Marianne Moore's exotic cosmology it is always a real elephant, a *real* dragon, and a real man (if there is a man at all in her oddly-denuded-of-humans domain). Once we have seen them clearly, the points at which their respective spheres of conduct touch are, as it were, lit up. We see the elephant *as* (not *is*) man; the

man *as* (not *is*) elephant. Qualities are reciprocal, mutually il-
luminating, and serve to adumbrate a huge transcendental correspondence of eidolons in a pantheistic, Emersonian sense.

In the end, it is not only people we understand better, but
animals too. Whenever Marianne Moore describes *real* people,
like her imagined Swedish lady in "A Carriage From Sweden,"
she does so in terms of birds, and beasts and flowers:

> . . . And how beautiful, she
> with the natural stoop of the
> snowy egret, grey-haired and straight-haired,
> for whom it should come to the door,—
> of whom it reminds me. The split-
>
> pine hair, steady gannet-clear
> eyes and the pine-needled-path-deer
> swift step; . . .

In "The Jerboa" man and the natural universe interact in the
most casual yet effective way on the levels of culture and
morality. The poem's scheme is a lyrical notation of varieties of
*made* animal objects in early cultures and also their *real* animal
referents. The piece while notable for its music (there is a daring usage of identical words both as internal and end-rime)
also relies on assonance[1] for wit,  a risky (almost punning)
practice which Miss Moore manages gallantly:

> . . .Course
> the jerboa, or
> plunder its food store,
> and you will be cursed. . . .

In "The Frigate Pelican" the human application of this remarkable bird is overt. He is compared to Handel as he "hides / in
the height and in the majestic / display of his art . . . a true
knight." "Peter" (about a house cat) begins on an amusing domestic note and ends as a powerful plea for fidelity to one's
own nature. Peter does as he likes, doesn't "sit caged by the
rungs of a domestic chair (which) would be unprofitable—
human. What is the good of hypocrisy?"

---

[1] I am using "assonance" here to mean more inclusively imperfect
rime. This follows Saintsbury's usage. See *A History of English Prosody
I, Chapter One.*

> . . .When one is
> frank, one's very
> presence is a compliment. It is clear that he can see
>    the virtue of naturalness, that he is one of those
>       who do not regard
>    the published fact as a surrender. . . .

Sometimes, as in "Nine Nectarines and Other Porcelain" Miss Moore cannot contain her pleasure in the correspondence she finds:

> We cannot find flaws
>    in this emblematic group

Although Miss Moore always looks for (and finds!) equivalences in her close studies of the animal kingdom, she has the humility and the humour to wonder, now and then, as in "The Buffalo" if her "signifyings" are not fictive:

> . . .The
> soot-brown tail-tuft on
>    a kind of lion-
>    tail; what would that express?
>
> . . .
>
>                               . . . Yet
>    some would say the sparse-haired
> buffalo has met
>    human notions best—

And in "Snakes, Mongooses, Snakecharmers And The Like" she reproaches herself: "The passion for setting people right is itself an afflictive disease."

This reduction of people to animal-size moral scale (see "The Zoo," for example), while not a "disease" reflects a curious need: the need to manipulate, rearrange and classify like a working scientist on order-able levels. It is this need which keeps Marianne Moore from being a novelist of manners. When one solves problems in the animal kingdom, no matter how intimate and tracery-fine the observation, the problems posed by pressures of context don't exist, (at least not in the same way) as they do in the social universe. Still, Marianne Moore's direction is a will to order as all satire, criticism, grows from a will to place, to judge. Her universe is really, then, the universe of

manners but translated to the animal sphere. Is this not clever—
to have found an "objective correlative" (which first she instructs us of as in a learned travelogue) to carry the weight of
her need for judging? Basically, Miss Moore is interested in
character as are the fiction-writers. But, and this marks the difference, in spite of their particularity, her "characters" become
almost as didactically charged as the figures in a morality play.
It is well to notice how it is only the most admirable and ad-
venturous of the animals which seem to entertain her.

## II

While it may be useful to say that, as a fabulist, Marianne
Moore's first interest is conduct, this term must be further defined if its centrality to her meaning is to be understood. For,
in her ideal sense, conduct is a sort of art, and, conversely, art
is a sort of fastidious conduct. Thus there is a fiery relationship between morality and art, but in an inverted Tolstoyan
sense: that is to say, her aesthetic becomes an ethic, and not
the other way around. Like almost every significant twentieth
century writer, Henry James, Joyce, Proust, Eliot, Woolf, to
mention only a few, Miss Moore has written at some length
about the problem of the artist and of art. But in her delinea-
tion, one feels no agony, no conflict; she *knows* what art is
about and she will tell any fool who can take her delightfully
astringent asperity.  In "Novices," a stinging satire of the
novices who

> anatomize their work
>
> . . .
>
> the little assumptions of the sacred ego confusing the
> issue so that they do not know "whether it is the
> buyer or the seller
>     who gives the money"—
> an abstruse idea plain to none but the artist,
> the only seller who buys and holds on to the money.
> Because one expresses oneself and entitles it wisdom,
>     one is not a fool. What an idea!

The entire poem is built around a subtle but sharply pointed
contrast: the novices, "blind to the right word, deaf to satire . . .
(who) . . . write the sort of thing that would in their judgment
interest a lady;" are opposed, in a brilliantly onamatapoetic re-

construction, to the genius and quality of Hebrew poetry "this drama of water against rocks" which the novices have rejected as "the stuffy remarks of the Hebrews."[2] In "The Labours of Hercules," about the creative process, in "The Monkeys," a literary zoo, (one of the few places, significantly, where an animal is given speech), in "Poetry," ("I too dislike it"), that much-quoted and peppery spray of wit against those who charge "unintelligibility," in "To A Snail," on the problem of style, (clearly obligated to some of Kenneth Burke's early fore-shadowings of "the container and the thing contained"), in "Pedantic Literalist" (not successful because it imitates the qualities it seeks, obliquely, to condemn: this is the pathetic fallacy on the ideological level; the plethora of quotes and polysyllabic words in this short poem striking precisely the note of tediousness and literality which it purports to satirize), and in many other poems, the *critical* function of *art as a mode of conduct* is elaborated through Miss Moore's animal symbol-ism or through shadowy and abstract humans, usually address-ed in the plural ("Novices," "Critics and Connoisseurs," etc.).

The way in which Miss Moore's aesthetic merges almost always with the ethical sphere is effectively stated in "Critics and Connoisseurs" where she writes: "There is a great amount of poetry in unconscious fastidiousness" and then goes on to say that she likes best the imperfect human effort:

> . . . a
> mere childish attempt to make an imperfectly ballasted
>     animal stand up
> similar determination to make a pup
>     eat his meals from the plate.
>
> . . .
> . . . I have seen this swan and
> I have seen you; I have seen ambition without
> understanding in a variety of forms; . . .[3]

In "Picking And Choosing," a discourse on her contemporaries and their artistic values which seems, like many of her poems

---

[2] This reconstruction is no less brilliant because it is a mosaic of quotations from five different sources ranging from the *Decameron* to *The Expositor's Bible.*

[3] This poem is particularly rewarding to analyze for Miss Moore's associational techniques.

in this vein, to be addressed to the critics, she makes clear her
identification of creative conduct with the focus of the artist's
personality.

Literature is a phase of life.

. . .

. . . It is not Hardy
the distinguished novelist and Hardy the poet, but one man
'interpreting life through the medium of the emotions.'

"The Monkey Puzzle" ( a deliberately prosaic title) would seem
to be Miss Moore's final comment on "beauty" (art), what it is
and how it got to be that way:

this is beauty — 'a certain proportion in the skeleton
which gives the best results.'

And she concludes with modest, yet characteristically practical acceptance: "But we prove, we do not explain our birth."

### III

While, on the whole, I agree with Mr. Eliot's statement
that "Miss Moore has no immediate poetic derivations" I
should like to examine some aspects of her work which, I
think, reveal a rather striking "appreciation" (to borrow a word
Miss Moore has made quite especially her own) for qualities
she finds in other poetry and seeks to infuse in her own.

In *The Poets of the Old Testament* by A. R. Gordon, a book
to which Miss Moore refers on several occasions in her notes,
and from which she quotes extensively in the poems, we find
in an analysis of the properties of the Hebrew language:

But this very failure of the philosophical
grasp enhances the pictorial power of the
speech. The verb is the predominant element
in the sentence. And though the shades of
time-distinction are blurred, the richness of
the language in intensive forms shows the
precise complexion of the act in a clear,
strong light . . . Hebrew possesses likewise a
great wealth of synonyms, especially in descriptions of the common scenes and interests
of life, and in the region of feeling. The language is equally rich in imagery.

While the composite effect of Marianne Moore's poems is similar to that of the "little paired playthings" she so admires in ancient cultures, they are internally rather more like living, breathing miniatures of a wonderfully rich and active sort. Always, within the formal, Persian mosaic of her structure we get the realistic sensation of movement. It is instructive to notice her verbs, for it is through them that we are compelled to accept the reality of her extraordinary acquaintance with the animal kingdom. We are made to see even the most exotic beast in action and reaction. She sees swans "reconnoitering," the frigate pelican "wasting the moon," lizards "spanning the bushes," the fish "wading through black jade," a tiger "coughs," the sparrow "decoys" his decoyers, the Malay dragon "dives head-first," the pangolin "endures exhausting solitary trips"; it is always nature "mechanicked" and alerted, not nature as still-life that she gives us.[4] If this were not enough to suggest that Miss Moore has profited by her interest in the Hebrew poets, there is also a structural similarity to be noted. For Miss Moore's method is essentially additive.   To this method the "synthetic-constructive" and "climactic-ascending" types of Hebrew poetic structure are most congenial. These forms would, I think, account for the musical structure of her poems, for their design forces a kind of response.   It is this responsive element, common to all Oriental poetry, which complicates and enriches the line of her movement. Note, for example, "The Frigate Pelican" which, for all its speculative impetus, is really a song-dance arrangement, a spun joyousness, all celerity, echo, and movement.

Another qualification I would put upon Mr. Eliot's judgment of Miss Moore's lack of "immediate derivations" stems from the integral cast of her method which is, in essence, that of the librarian. Anyone who thinks a card catalogue dull will not follow my implication. In the librarian's province one finds the most brilliantly *literal* demonstration of the simultaneity

---

[4] For additional evidence of her interest in Hebrew poetry, see "The Past is the Present," a delightful discourse on free-verse, in which she threatens to revert to Habakkuk, quoting one who says:
'Hebrew poetry is
prose with a sort of heightened consciousness.'
See, too, "England" (really England versus America) for her description of "the cataclysmic torrent of emotion compressed in the verbs of the Hebrew language."

of the past with other pasts, and the simultaneity of all of the
past with the present. (To say nothing at all of the presentness
of the present!) Who, except an inspired, not to say dedicated,
librarian would read the *London Illustrated News,* along with
*What to See in America, Horary Astrology,* Xenophon's *Cyg-
neticus,* a Bell Telephone leaflet, "The World's Most Accurate
Clocks," the *Vest Pocket Manual of Printing* and a government
*Report on Introduction of Domestic Reindeer into Alaska?* And,
after all, is it not what the poet in Miss Moore makes of the
librarian's materials that is the "content" of her poetry? This
vast, librarian-like omniverousness of curiosity is what makes
Miss Moore so very much *of* her time, while at the same time,
enabling her to be unbounded by it. Her meticulousness in the
use of quotation marks is not nearly so much an affectation as
some would suggest.[5] On the contrary, it is another facet of the
librarian in Miss Moore, supporting her temperamental honesty.

Miss Moore's method, in short, is the method of "The
Monkey Puzzle" ". . . we prove, we do not explain our birth."
Her quotations are a *way* of proving, not explaining, for to her
that would seem presumptuous. It is only the "opet-prophet"
like a Milton whose egoism presumes "to justify the ways of
God to man" (not a Christian obligation, in the first place). Miss
Moore, for all her elegant morality, for all that she is a didact,
perhaps, is entirely humble.   She is not a prophet-preacher
manqué; if we think her that we misplace her vision, which is
not that of the visionary but that of the scientist, the scientist
of conduct and value. The notes appended to her poems are
meant to reaffirm the quotations acknowledged in the poems,
that is to say, to *prove* (or test) that order of knowledge which
is a poem.[6]

This sort of mind while, like La Fontaine's is one which "is
wholly at home. La Fontaine's mind was exceedingly domestic.

[5] There is a significant distinction in the precision with which Miss
Moore acknowledges quotations, and the casualness with which some
of her most distinguished contemporaries lift them. Often, in modern
poetry, the borrowing, whether acknowledged or unacknowledged, is to
get the shock of recognition, or of irony, or of both. Miss Moore's is to
get the confirmation of addition, for as I have already remarked, her
method is essentially additive.

[6] It is a nice question, indeed, to try to assign authorship for the use
of the double or single quotation mark in the poems of Ezra Pound,
T. S. Eliot, and Miss Moore.

It was nowhere but at home," is capable of the most extraordinary imaginative journeys. "No Swan So Fine," interesting for the way it dramatizes the integrality of her titles to her poems (titles often functioning as first lines) is particularly useful as an illustration — it is a short poem and the traffic is easier to follow — of the way a casual newspaper sentence can lead Miss Moore into a finely quiet elegy. In "The Plumet Basilisk," one of her most successful long poems, we are so enchanted by the beautifully observed descriptions of this exotic lizard, as well as the *tuatera* and the Malay dragon, that we accept the strange territory on terms of intimacy.   Suddenly, when we think we have completely understood the functioning of these talented animals, we get a brilliant generalization, on an entirely different level of observation:

> the plumet portrays
> mythology's wish
> to be interchangeably man and fish

If Miss Moore's reading did not furnish sufficient proof of her being very much alive to her age, her occasional echoes of her contemporaries in poetry would do so. While Mr. Eliot has noted a possible obligation to H. D. in Miss Moore's early verse, his own influence is not absent. A sentence like "The tune's illiterate footsteps fail" proves Miss Moore to have read him closely, while the cadence of her charming address to

> Small dog, going over the lawn, nipping the lines and saying
> that you have a badger — remember Xenophon;

is a remarkably Eliotic reminder of the last lines of Phlebas the Phoenician. Similarly, her use of adjectives and nouns compounded with negatives is like the practice of e. e. cummings and serves, as in his usage, to emphasize more than would an antonym the quality absent (or present): In a fairly early poem, she writes:

> . . . The college student
> named Ambrose sits on the hill-side
> with his not-native books and hat

Some of the shorter poems (see "An Egyptian Pulled Glass Bottle in the Shape of a Fish") suggest a sensitve ear for Emily Dickinson's whimsicalities of rhyme. Her romantic aesthetic in

". . . . it is a privilege to see so/much confusion . . ." reminds
me of her friend, William Carlos Williams', "It's the anarchy
of poverty delights me . . ." In "A Grave," the summaries by
which she binds together her enumerated concretia, as well as
a tendency to cement her rhetoric with connectives like "however" are devices she either takes from or shares with John
Crowe Ransom, whose particular tone is also one of address.

But once one has noted Miss Moore's possible obligations
to the poetic climate of her times, one still has to deal with the
fundamental uniqueness of her achievement. I believe insufficient attention has been given to the fact that her verse is, on
the whole, syllabic, rather than accentual. "The Fish" (one of
her most exquisitely worked-out metaphors) will serve as a
useful illustration of this practice. There are eight stanzas of
five lines, each with a recurring syllabic pattern of 1, 3, 9, 6, 8,
the final longish line of each stanza connecting with and carrying over to the first two or three short lines of the next stanza.
What this accomplishes is a run-on pattern of movement very
much like that of "prose with a heightened consciousness," or
speech. For it should be noted that contrary to the historical
confusions about the possibilities for syllabic verse in English,
in actuality, experimental studies have shown that stress and
syllabic length tend to coincide; and, in addition, both the *heard*
patterns of accent, normal to speech, as well as Miss Moore's
generous usage of end rimes (in this poem aabbc, ddeef, etc.)
set up a counterpoint against which the syllabic pattern makes
its way. The result is a very complex and rich range of metrical
possibilities within the given syllabic scheme of any poem.[7] The
first two stanzas will serve to illustrate:

THE FISH

    wade
    through black jade.
       Of the crow-blue mussel-shells, one keeps
       adjusting the ash-heaps;
          opening and shutting itself like

   an
   injured fan.

---

[7] Not all of Miss Moore's poems are syllabic. Also, it should be
noted that the syllabification is not *necessarily* quantitative (as in classical meter) but more often is arrived at by the arbitrary and fixed French
method as in "The Fish."

> The barnacles which encrust the side
> of the wave, cannot hide
>     there for the submerged shafts of the . . .

Now, as with any highly individual artist, (we need think only of Milton, Donne or Hopkins) Miss Moore's defects are an excess of her felicities. "Those Various Scalpels," for example, is almost a parody of herself with its talky, polysyllabic vocabulary, its highly qualitative and adverbialized syntax, and its rather abstract argumentation. A comparison of the antithetical values of antiquity and modernity ("The Greeks liked smoothness, distrusting what was back / of what could not be clearly seen . . ."), it obscures rather than points the differences, largely, I think, because of the diffuseness and over-inclusiveness of the argument.[8] This poem might be profitably compared with "People's Surroundings" in which Miss Moore's rather too frequent opposition of modernity and antiquity comes off with humour, grace and real point.

### IV

It might be supposed from some comments I have made that Miss Moore is dissatisfied with America. All one need do to disabuse himself of this notion is to re-read *What Are Years* (1941) and *Nevertheless* (1944). (Who else but Marianne Moore would choose a rhetorical connective for a title!) As a matter of fact from her earliest writing Miss Moore has displayed a deep concern for what seems to her the false opposition commonly seen between localism and internationalism. See her sharp and telling lecture on this subject in "England" where she says of America:

>     . . . The letter
> a in psalm and calm when
> pronounced with the sound of a in candle
>     is very noticeable, but
> why should continents of misapprehension have to be
> accounted for by the fact? . . .

"Is Your Town Nineveh" is an apotheosis to individualism, à la Américaine. *What Are Years* shows her more preoccupied

---

[8] Nevertheless, there are some individual lines in this poem among the very best Miss Moore has written.

with American materials of a seemingly antiquarian sort, but, as always, with a pointed critical objective. "Virginia Birtannica" is a most brilliant example of the way her ethicalizing temper reconstructs the meaning of another culture through a minutely documented mosaic of concrete details. "Rigorists," also about American history, follows a similar pattern. *Nevertheless* continues the interest in American materials on somewhat different levels. There is the affectionate nostalgia of "A Carriage from Sweden":

> At all events there is in Brooklyn
> something that makes me feel at home.

There is, too, on another plane the well-known "In Distrust of Merits" which, growing out of the war, as it does, seems just now doubly ironic in its high humility of generous hopes.

From *What Are Years* onward the didactic vein is stronger in Miss Moore's work, or, as it were, closer to the surface. But this should not suggest a slackening in poetic power. On the contrary, while Miss Moore here still adheres to her strict accounting of sources (a practice she only recently abandoned in *Nevertheless*), and clings to her prim quotation marks, there is also a more uniform tautness in her development of correspondences in the physical and moral universe. It isn't so much that there is *less* detail, but rather that more of the detail goes to centrally support the didacticism. Her work tends all the time in the direction of greater colloquialism and she more consistently uses compounded words. The effect of much of this is to make for a greater lyricism of mood, although it would be inaccurate to describe Miss Moore, one of the most musical poets writing today, as having become a lyric one. As a matter of fact, the musical element in Miss Moore's writing has not been enough remarked. Not only is it evident that she is a scholar of music (see her frequent use of names of composers, compositions, and even performers in the poems), but it is also clear that she aims for a *flow* in her poetic structure which can best be described as musical. For example, in "Nine Nectarines and Other Porcelain", a long poem, one's pleasure in the poem's movement is almost entirely musical, both because of the intricate pattern of internal and end-rime and the characteristically daring assonance. Yet her linear arrangements, her

dry adverbs ("although not uncommonly/the opposite is seen —
/ nine peaches on a nectarine") all tend to check, as it were,
the sonal qualities of the poem by bringing it back to the basic
speech-norm on which it is built.   In "Walking Sticks And
Paper-Weights And Water-Marks" not only is her rime ingenius
and happy but the poem itself, like the "fugue" of "the pelican's community of notes" she describes in it, has an involuting
three part structure, a "chain of interactingly / linked harmony." Interestingly, the tripartite movement is reinforced by
the three terms of the title and the mention of "the three legs
of the triskelion" which composes the second line of the poem.

In the recent verse one notes, as well, a more experimental
and dramatic use of the caesura. "Spenser's Ireland" is a splendid example of this and is, as a matter of fact, one of her most
personal and social presents to the reader. She utilizes the same
spatial and, in effect, temporal representation of the caesura in
the much-discussed "The Pangolin." Her reading gets weirder,
and she now is able to extract poetic juice from a pit. In addition, while her humour is even spritelier, if that is at all possible, there is a new note of affection for her animal and human
subjects which alters the tone of her discourse.

And, finally, the last two volumes show up Miss Moore as
increasingly the taker of unpopular stands.   "He Digesteth
Harde Yron" is a fine display of the exactitude of her diagnos-
tic moral sensibility. For Marianne Moore is essentially a protestant individualist, the intense and uncompromising exponent
of an individualism in value and belief which, like Milton's
Protestantism, is, at root, without any orthodox theological
anchorage.[9] As with Milton, it is the intensity of her protest
which raises the emotion, at times, to an almost religious
power, a white-heat of *ethical* judgment which, curiously, may
in both poets stem not only from temperamental factors but
also from their regard for the Hebrew "ideal" in poetry. Miss
Moore, like Milton, had, in an early poem, "Marriage" examined that resistant paradox at some length. It is an exceedingly clever inquiry into the actual and the potentials of

---

[9] It is interesting to notice that Miss Moore has written of herself:
"I am Presbyterian and was brought up in the home of my grandfather,
the Reverend John P. Warner . . . my brother has been a chaplain for
twenty years in the Navy. . . . And the books to which I have had access
have been, on the whole serious. . . .

> this amalgamation which can never be more
> than an interesting possibility

which she concludes with a conventionalized and tersely-stated wedding-portrait (for so I interpret the closing lines) meant to serve as final re-enforcement of the impossibility of the amalgamation:

> the Book on the writing table;
> the hand in the breast pocket.[10]

Unlike Milton, the most positive attitude she can muster toward marriage is the perceptive wit of ". . . why not be alone together?"

In "Black Earth," a study of personality as opposed to character in the sense in which Herbert Read derives that opposition from Ramon Fernandez,[11] she again touches the kernel of the paradox she drew in "Marriage," although here not specifically concerned with that "interesting possibility." An opposition is posited between "external poise" (character) and "spiritual poise" (personality):

> . . . external poise, it
> has its centre
> well-nurtured—we know
>          where—in pride; but spiritual poise, it has its
>                    centre where?
> . . .
>          . . . The I of each is to
> the I of each
> a kind of fretful speech
>          which sets a limit on itself; . . .

Elsewhere, in "In the Days of Prismatic Colour" (a remarkably suggestive title) she launches into a deeply protestant, anti-mystical study of the genesis of "morality" and "sin." She

---

[10] In this very long poem occur two lines which rank among her best. I detect in them a sly dig at Milton's solemnity:
> Unnerved by the nightingale
> and dazzled by the apple

[11] See Herbert Read, *Form in Modern Poetry*, especially pp. 12-41. "All poetry, in which I include all lyrical impulses whatsoever, is the product of the personality and therefore inhibited in character." p. 18.

declares herself against the "dismal fallacy" "that all truth must be dark."

> . . . Truth is no Apollo
> Belvidere, no formal thing. The wave may go over it
>     if it likes.
> Know that it will be there where it says
>     'I shall be there when the wave has gone by.'

When it comes to the institutional level of social experience Miss Moore is as uncompromisingly questioning as one could wish of an Émile. But her protest, unlike Rousseau's, is not motivated by a naif romanticism. It is an entirely rational, although impassioned, rejection of the academy that she makes in "The Student." [12]

<h2 style="text-align:center">V</h2>

This, then, is the "strange fraternity" of man and beast into which Miss Moore initiates us. Like La Fontaine, who missed his dinner once when observing an anthill where a funeral seemed to be under way, since "He could not in all decency leave until it was over," Marianne Moore, too, has an exquisite tact toward her ant-hills and ant-eaters. She is again like the La Fontaine who "did not philosophize over the animals; (but) sympathized with them." And as in his work, there is in her cosmology the same impeccable morality of ordering which is one way of actively accepting the world. For La Fontaine, like Marianne Moore, "took his world quietly." And while I do not wish to seem to pronounce an elegy upon Miss Moore's very presence and present achievement, I am impressed with the appropriateness to her own merits of the words La Bruyère addressed to the Academy upon La Fontaine's death in 1693: "He instructs while he sports, persuades men to virtue by means of the beasts, and exalts trifling subjects to the sublime; a man unique in his species of composition, always original, whether he invents or translates, who has gone beyond his models, himself a model hard to imitate." In essence, however, La Fontaine's aim was to instruct; Miss Moore's is to illuminate.

---

[12] On the other hand, in "Silence" she is herself guilty of an academic humour which, nevertheless, is sufficiently acid to counteract the conventionality of its satiric content.

But to all this Marianne Moore brings something, a certain plastic *extension* of the sensibility into imaginative universes of which La Fontaine, had not, I think, any perception. It is *that* imaginary animal kingdom of the soul and the intellect which is at once uniquely her possession and her gift to us. We can say of it that, like her Spenser's Ireland, it is:

> the  kindest place I've never been
> the greenest place I've never seen. [13]

---

[13] After this essay was completed I learned that Miss Moore has been working for the past year on a much-needed translation of La Fontaine's *Fables*.

# Robinson Jeffers: The Anatomy of Violence

*by* RADCLIFFE SQUIRES

The poets who sing of life without
remembering its agony
Are fools or liars.

*Hungerfield*

## 1

The single most impressive characteristics of Jeffers' mature work is his preoccupation with all manner of violent action. The origins are not simple, but one can make inroads toward an understanding by considering the perplexing split between Jeffers' dedication and its formulation. He arranges his characters so that they torture each other unbearably and then moralizes that if this is the human condition, it would be well to "break out" of it. He tries thus to solve the problem of passion through logic, but the effort augments his difficulties if only because it is man's irrational passions which most readily capture Jeffers' artistic allegiance.

This peculiar dichotomy (or should I say this common dichotomy of the twentieth century?) between the dictates of intellect and the pleas of passionate imagination gives us the portrait of a man who carefully gathers up dinner crumbs to scatter for the birds but who writes a sadistic poem about a mutilated hawk. One critic has confessed to the easy belief that Jeffers may be typed among "rigidly self-disciplined or timid persons who frequently revolt via their imaginations into the realms of violence." By a skillful misinterpretation of the poem "For Una" the same critic concludes that "Mr. Jeffers admits as much."[1] The priciple of compensation probably operates to some degree in Jeffers' work, but one ought to be fearful of a current tendency to manipulate any psychological cause toward any convenient effect; and very careful about separating the artistic from the everyday personality.

The influence of the war is complicating. No violence appears in Jeffers' verse until after 1918. And more significantly, much of the violence in the poems can be taken as a symbol for war, even though the expression is often sexual. The identification, or at least the blurring in his work, of violence, war, and the passions is not superficial: For if Jeffers despises the brutality of war, he sometimes envisions war as an agency which, by humbling and upheaving, may create benefit. Likewise, if he seeks to deprecate the passions, he nevertheless envisions regeneration as the task of a primitive sexuality.

From his inability either to compose or ignore these conflicts, Jeffers has, I think, been forced to express them in an exaggerated form. When we regard the expression as half-deliberate exaggeration, we are in a position to estimate the relationship between the man and the violence which he has created. He does not, I suggest, turn to violence because his temperament longs for violence but because it longs to be rid of it. He seeks to destroy his own passions, along with the racial "passion" of war, by deliberately exaggerating them. We are reminded of what Yeats wrote about Oscar Wilde's behavior before his tragic collapse. All that "parade of gloom" and "that elaborate playing with tragedy," Yeats believed, "was an attempt to escape from an emotion by its exaggeration."[2]

---

[1] James G. Southworth, *Some Modern American Poets* (Oxford, 1950), p. 120.

This is as far as I can go with the problem of personality as such. It may, however, be that the remaining observations essentially are a description of personality, for although I relate the problem to theology, it is difficult to know if I am describing general formulas which the human psyche repeats as religious compulsions, or if I am describing the condition of one who, in repudiating formal religion, has guiltily magnified the vestiges of a creed.

Jeffers' early religious training was doubtless thorough, and probably not narrow. In a letter (1938) to Professor H. H. Waggoner, Jeffers stated: "My father was a cleryman but also intelligent."[3] William Hamilton Jeffers was more than a clergyman; he "was a distinguished theologian, the culmination of a long line of devout Calvinists."[4] Jeffers' feeling toward his learned father indicate a mixture of reverence and remorse. When his father died, Jeffers vowed to:

> Retrace his sacred footsteps reverently,
> And dream his life back to the power it was.

Twenty-five years later, Jeffers grieved:

> I dishonored and wasted all your hopes of me,
> one by one; yet I loved you well.

Is this tension of reverence and guilt the basis for Jeffers' Nietzschean concept of Christianity as a "strain"? The answer may lie in understanding the conflict between the old religious father and the agnostic son in *Give Your Heart to the Hawks*. Lance both revolts against the father who "spooned the gospel down my throat when I was a cub" and identifies himself with the father's gospel by dismissing mankind with the doctrine of original sin. Lance Fraser's dilemma is perhaps Jeffer's own. He rejects formal dogma but seems to stagger beneath the weight of a Calvinistic belief in the depravity of man.

---

[2] William Butler Yeats, *Autobiographies* (New York, 1927), p. 353.

[3] H. H. Waggoner, "Science and the Poetry of Robinson Jeffers," *American Literature*, X (November, 1938), p. 287.

[4] Lawrence C. Powell, *Robinson Jeffers, the Man and His Work* (Pasadena, 1940), p. 6.

Behind Calvin's credo stood an absolute trust in justice
—reward by salvation or damnation in a life after death. No
such faith exists for Jeffers. "We go down into blackness,"
Lance says. There is no permanently conscious immortality.
Jeffers' idea of a hereafter is as dim and uncertain as Job's
idea of Sheol, the shadowy limbo where identity dissolves.
*Tamar* conspicuously and a number of the short poems contain
ghosts who are in the process of fading. They exist for a time,
as the stain of consciousness upon the inanimate universe, but
they must, we are told, finally disintegrate. This final release
from identity Jeffers upholds as man's great good fortune. Unlike Job, who contemplates the terrors of losing his sense of
self and remains resolute against his wife's advice to "curse
God, and die," Jeffers informs us that Madrone Bothwell in
*Solstice* "had cursed God and lived."

Since for Jeffers there is no eternal life, no heaven nor
hell, the perseverance of some sort of religious emotion demanding punishment for the original sin has had a profound
effect upon his poetry. No more than the bewildered Job could
expect reward in Sheol for his model conduct can Jeffers'
characters, riddled with guilt, expect punishment for their
crimes in an afterlife. Aware, then, of their guilt, they cry out
for a fiery cleansing. The ghost of Helen in *Tamar*, knowing
that she must dissolve into nothingness which cheats her of
expiation, hisses, "There's no hell and curse God for it." Similarly, Cawdor, discovering that his son whom he has suspected
of adultery and has murdered, is innocent of the crime, says
that he would kill himself if he could believe in hell-fire. So
terrible does his unabsolvable crime become to Cawdor that
he permits himself to speculate vainly as to whether the son
might have committed the crime if he had not watched him so
carefully. He would choose to justify his own crime on the
grounds of his son's capacity for sin, rather than dwell with
his own, knowing that he cannot be cleansed by punishment.

One may well consider if this same attitude is not one
of the reasons for the violence in Jeffers' narratives and
dramas. To use the inverse parallel of Job again, one might
judge that as Job must expect his reward in this life, so for
Jeffers, punishment for sin must develop in this life. Certainly,
the mental and physical torment which he delivers to his

characters is scarely exceeded by medieval descriptions of Satan's sadistic ingenuity. This demand for temporal punishment would seem to account for the recurrence again and again of brush and forest fires in the narratives, like the fires which mercifully terminate *Tamar*, the first part of *The Double Axe*, and *Hungerfield*.

## 2

Jeffers would appear to have taken justice into his own hands without precisely realizing his presumption. If he is induced to violence by his temperament, the inducement is reinforced by a religious intensity that demands punishment for universal guilt. We are especially aware of the violence, however, because without the purpose that a formal religion gives, all the punishment, truant and self-conscious, tends to assume the appearance of masochism: and this indictment is supported by the fundamental form—the torture of animals and of men—which punishment in Jeffers' poetry takes.

Except that a starving fawn is mentioned in *Californians*, the early poetry is free of tortured animals. As the implications, however, in Jeffers' universe intensified, his preoccupation with this motive grew. It is probably not important to erect a lurid zoo of unhappy beasts, but a few examples will not be insupportable. The most conspicuous are found in the two narratives *Cawdor* (1928) and *Give Your Heart to the Hawks* (1933). In the latter a Cooper's hawk with a broken wing is tethered by a cord to a peg and made to fight a game-cock:

> Lance pushed and freed the game-cock, that eagerly
> Staring-hackled in his battle-passion
> Leaped up and struck down; the hawk tripped by its wing
> Fell quivering under the spurs, but a long-fingered
> Lean yellow hand reaching up out of ruin
> Plucked at the red king's breast: who charged again: one
>     hawk-wing
> Waved, and the talons mysteriously accomplished
> Many quick bitter acts, whence the red king
> Reeled out of hope. He crouched beyond tether's reach,
> Propping himself on both wings, but the sinking head

> Still stretched for fight; then dull-eyed, at strength's end,
> Went staggering to it again. The yellow hands
> Easily made him what would never any more
> Chirp over bright corn to the hens or subdue a rival.
> Lance came, and the little hawk ran quickly and fell
> Onto its broken shoulder at the tether's end. Lance picked
>      up the dying game-cock;
> Red grains of wheat from the torn crop fell down with
>      the blood.

Such passages may easily seem introduced for the sake of sensationalism. But the tortured animal plays a symbolic role. This is made most clear in *Cawdor* where Michal keeps as a pet a caged eagle which her brother Hood has winged. In nearly two years of imprisonment the bird has persisted in arrogant pride:

> They stood and watched
> The dark square-shouldered prisoner, the great flight-
>      feathers
> Of the dragged wing were worn to quills, and beetles
> Crawled by the weaponed feet, yet the dark eyes
> Remembered their pride. Hood said "You ought to kill him.
> My God, nearly two years!" She answered nothing,
> But when he looked at her face the long blue eyes
> Winked and were brimmed. The grim hand took the squir-
>      rel,
> It made a whispering twitter, the bleak head tore it.

When the bird is finally put out of its misery Jeffers decribes the flight of its "phantom" in one of his most successful pieces of writing, an elegy where death becomes an affirmation of life:

> There the eagle's phantom perceived
> Its prison and its wound were not its peculiar wretched-
>      ness,
> All that lives was maimed and bleeding, caged or in blind-
>      ness,
> Lopped at the ends with death and conception, and
>      shrewd

> Cautery of pain on the stumps to stifle the blood, but not
> Refrains for all that; life was more than its functions
> And accidents, more important than its pains and plea-
>      sures,
> A torch to burn in with pride, a necessary
> Ecstasy in the run of the cold substance,
> And scape-goat of the greater world. (But as for me,
> I have heard the summer dust crying to be born
> As much as ever flesh cried to be quiet.)

Not only does this passage articulate a meaning of life, but it also suggests that the eagle and his squalid cage are intended to symbolize the state of man, trapped in pain and filth, but yet performing a "necessary" task in the universal scheme. An earlier section of the same passage makes the identification of the eagle and man more explicit, for the phantom sees its own "archetype"—its god:

> . . . according to the sight of its kind, the archetype
> Body of life a beaked carnivorous desire
> Self-upheld on storm-broad wings: but the eyes
> Were spouts of blood; the eyes were gashed out; dark
>      blood
> Ran from the ruinous eye-pits to the hook of the beak
> And rained on the waste spaces of empty heaven.

Like the eagle's god, Cawdor, too, in his cage of passions, suspicion, and violence, takes the way of Oedipus, blinding himself.

The tortured animal, then, is a symbol of man's plight. But often the symbol is dropped, and man himself is tortured, principally in two patterns—castration and crucifixion. Old Morhead in *The Women at Point Sur* may be taken as the prototype of the castrated man, but Reave in *Thurso's Landing* is the more detailed example. He receives the "hell of pain and impotence" in an accident which in itself voices the failure of mankind. In *Give Your Heart to the Hawks* Lance Fraser, only temporarily impotent and for psychological reasons, embodies both the castration motive and that of crucifixion. Suffering the pangs of conscience, he rakes his hands across a barbed wire fence so "that the barbs of the wire clicked on the bones

of his hands through the torn flesh." Obviously a simulation
of the wounds of Christ. Later these wounds become infected,
and losing his reason, he commits suicide. Bruce Ferguson too,
in *Mara,* under a different strain, cuts his hands just before he
takes his own life.

It is noteworthy that in these two narratives, where the
disease of life becomes especially painful, self-crucifixion is
the forerunner of insanity and suicide. In this way the Christ-
figure is related to the insanely self-tortured man. And Jeffers
takes the relationship one step further by relating the Christ-
figure to war. The whole process of symbolic thought whereby Jeffers moves from the tortured animal to man, thence to
Christ, and finally to war as a vast, ceaseless process of self-
torture is condensed in one passage in *Such Counsels You Gave
to Me.* Howard Howren dreams:

> That he and others in the laboratory were nailing a dog to
>     wings, driving sharp horse-shoe nails
> Between the pads of the fore-paws into the shafts of the
>     wing-frames. The dog vanished from the dream, the
>     dreamer
> Himself flying wide over the city, crucified to wings; one
>     of the spikes tore out through his palm
> And he pitched down, falling along the façade of a public
>     building.

Christ and war interweave in Jeffers' thought, but for the
moment let us consider them separately. War, to Jeffers, is the
absolute in man's folly. His statements, however, in this regard
being elusive, led Hildegarde Flanner in 1937 to observe that
". . . he has recommended war, the cruelest of man's manias,
as a way of cleansing civilization and leading life back to reality."[5] It is hard to say that the critic has been entirely misled,
yet it would be wrong to say that the insight is entirely right.
Jeffers has sometimes tried to find some meaning in war, but
the meaning has always been the long-range one, the shadowy
contours in the Spenglerian vista. War, Jeffers sometimes sees
as the inevitable trap but never as the desirable course for man
in a high state of civilization. On the contrary, war becomes

---

[5] Hildegarde Flanner, "Two Poets: Jeffers and Millay," *The New
Republic,* January 27, 1937, p. 380.

the focal point of his diatribes against mankind. It can only
end "in horror," he says. Indeed, the human body is "essentially unwarlike," and man makes a fool of himself in war. In
*The Double Axe* his invective against war reaches a culmination in the characterization of Hoult Gore, who is the epitome
of the crucified man. Killed in a Pacific (unhappy irony!) battle, by power of will he drags his corpse back to his home.
War has left him with the desire to kill needlessly, and he
murders his father as a "war monger." But Hoult must be seen,
too, as a personification of Western civilization. His "corpse,"
he says, "covers the western world and sprawls over Asia."
The characterization allows us now to reconsider Jeffers' un-
conventional conjunction of the Christ-figure and war. Hoult,
the corpse of the Western world, parodies the sacrament,
drawing an obscene caricature of a dying soldier, which he
gives to his mother and father, saying:

> Now it is comic. Take it in remembrance of me. This is my
>     body
> That was broken for nothing. Drink it: this is my blood
> That was spilled for no need. Oh, yes: for victory:
> That rat-sucked hawk-egg.

It is time to ask, why this identification of Christ and
war? The drama *Dear Judas* is the logical place to look for the
answer. Here Christ deliberately chooses crucifixion as a
means to power. To Judas his decision is one that will bring
twenty centuries of war. He says to Jesus, "To let the people
alone is mercy: all stirring is death to them." And in "The
Theory of Truth" Jeffers writes:

> The beautiful young poet found truth in the desert, but
>     found also
> Fantastic solution of hopeless anguish. The carpenter was
>     not his father? Because God was his father,
> Not a man sinning, but the pure holiness and power of
>     God.
>     His personal anguish and insane solution
> Have stained an age; nearly two thousand years are one
>     vast poem drunk with the wine of his blood.

I am anxious to confess that so far I have offered a one-sided picture of the Christ-war motive. The essential attitude is not simplex. Indeed, a deep-rooted ambivalence is hinted at in the phrasing of the passage above and openly documented in the short poem, "The Redeemer," which presents a man who thinks he is saving the world by keeping old wounds in his palms fresh; he is insane, but it is clear that Jeffers thinks him not merely harmlessly mad but also divinely so. In another poem of about the same time Jeffers admits that he once considered becoming a "savior" in order to bring "peace to the unborn children," but he concludes that it is unnecessary because death is a final savior.[6] After a brief excursion in another direction I shall return to this problem.

### 3

There are two extensions to Jeffers' religious intensity: his attitude toward the phenomenon of consciousness, and his misogyny.

In the poem "Margrave" (1932) Jeffers implies that the dissolution of consciousness is not without compensation. Of course, the oriental concept of nirvana comes to mind. Amos Wilder has written of this aspect of the poetry,[7] and Rudolph Gilbert mentions traces of Sufism.[8] My impression is that, while Jeffers has undoubtedly absorbed oriental philosophy, his aspersions about consciousness may be elucidated within the framework of Christian theology. At this point a parallel with Milton pleads for expression.

Milton's purpose in *Paradise Lost* was to preach absolute reason and a merciful God, but his preoccupation in detail was the nature of sin. The justification for bringing the humanist and the inhumanist together resides in Milton's propagation of a patristic (ultimately Saint Augustine's) reasoning to the effect that the origin of sin is pride, the conscious turning from God to self. Such is Satan's archetype sin, and it is shared by Eve. Describing her first hours on earth, she tells of wandering toward the "murmuring sound" of water and coming to a "smooth lake." Here she relates:

---

[6] "Meditation on Saviors," *The Selected Poetry of Robinson Jeffers* (New York, 1938), pp. 200-204.

[7] See *The Spiritual Aspects of the New Poetry* (1940), p. 147.

[8] *Shine, Perishing Republic; Robinson Jeffers and the Tragic Sense in Modern Poetry* (Boston, 1936), p. 50.

". . . I bent down to look, just opposite
A shape within the watery gleam appeared
Bending to look on me: I started back,
It started back, but pleased I soon returned,
Pleased it returned as soon with answering looks
Of sympathy and love; there I had fixed
Mine eyes till now, and pined with vain desire,
Had not a voice thus warned me. 'What thou seest,
What there thou seest, fair creature, is thyself . . .' "

On the reverse side of the manuscript of *The Tower Beyond Tragedy* Jeffers once copied out this passage with the comment that it was an example of "narcissism," a view which C. S. Lewis twenty years later came to hold. Jeffers, it is true, questions not merely self-consciousness, the "bosom serpent" of Hawthorne, but the whole fact of consciousness. Yet his reason—that the consciousness turns to itself rather than to God—is the patristic reason.

Milton also gives an insight into the related problem of Jeffers' misogyny. His urgency to demonstrate both God's capacity for mercy and man's capacity for sin forced Milton to show that the Adamic side of mankind is superior to Satan; otherwise, why should man be saved at all? At the same time, Milton had to account for the fall without permitting Adam to sink to the level of Satan. Hence it is Eve who, like Satan, is the narcissist; and Eve who commits the Satanic sin of self-consciousness and then disobedience. Adam's weakness is simply his love for another human being. He slides down with Eve, but it is only the female half of the race that has originated the sin.

Jeffers' heroines frequently undermine the nobility of his heroes; they are narcissistic Eves. Fawn in *Mara,* for example, strokes "herself with her hands / Lovingly." These heroines are hectic in their disregard for conventional morality. Fickle, lascivious, Tamar and Electra argue seductively for incestuous unions, as do the mothers in *Such Counsels You Gave to Me,* *The Double Axe,* and *The Cretan Woman.* Female promiscuity underlies the tragedies in *Thurso's Landing, Cawdor, Give Your Heart to the Hawks,* and *Mara.* And though his heroes are powerless to change the heroines or their world, they are aware of their own superior natures. Lance Fraser asks of

Fera, "Did y' love him? Or was it only because you're female
. . . female and drunk?"

4

I have related Jeffers' symbol of the tortured man to a
religious intensity, and I have suggested that there is a connection between his attitude toward consciousness and a theological tradition. I wish that the whole scheme were more
free of inconsistency, but to some extent the confusions are
tidied, the conflicts reconciled in Jeffers' concept of God.

During the course of Jeffers' career his God has changed
from the wild god of Nature incarnate in the roan stallion that
shakes "the red-roan mane for a flag on the bare hills," to a
more nearly intelligent God in *The Double Axe*. The later figuration is that of Heautontimoroumenos, the self-tormentor,
first hinted at in "Apology for Bad Dreams." In the image of
the self-tormenting God, Jeffers cautiously narrows the gap between man and Nature. But he does not close it entirely. For
the inevitable question arises: If God is a self-tormentor, tormenting himself for the purpose of discovery, why does Jeffers
rail at man's self-torture, his crucifixions, his wars?   The
answer lies in the disparity between divine and human intention. God's torment is not "cruel," it is necessary to knowledge.
Human perpetration of cruelty, however, is a different matter.
Jeffers would have man suffer the pangs of tragic discovery
but he would have him eschew the perversion of a pointless
sadism:

> Man's world is a tragic
> music and is not played for man's happiness,
> Its discords are not resolved but by other discords.
>
> But for each man
> There is real solution, let him turn from himself and man
> to love God. He is out of the trap then . . .
> But how could I impart
> this knowledge . . .?
>
> I know that
> all men instinctively rebel against it. But yet
> They will come to it at last.

> Then man will have come of age; he will still suffer and
> still die, but like a God, not a tortured animal.[9]

And this is the important difference: to suffer "like a God,
not a tortured animal," for this illumines the whole of Jeffers'
scheme, revealing why the tortured animals are an elemental
necessity to his negative didacticism. Man may suffer like God,
but since man cannot become God, the tragedies of life are
only a reflection of celestial tragedy; man's tortures are a
dream in Nature, while God's tortures are "in earnest,"[10] meaningful, infinite. Within these relationships Jeffers reconciles
his simultaneous love and hatred of violence: the "love" on the
grounds that violence is a divine activity, the "hate" on the
grounds that it is too often a human perversion.

On similar premises Jeffers clarifies his distrust of human
consciousness. But the distrust needs clarifying, for if pursued
to the ultimate, his doubt denies the very reasoning which
provides him with his conclusion. Yet, just as there is a divine
self-torment, so there is a divine consciousness:

> A conscious God?—The question has no importance. But
>     I am conscious: where else
> Did this consciousness come from? Nobody that I know of
>     ever poured grain from an empty sack.
> And who, I would say, but God, and a conscious one,
> Ended the chief war-makers with their war, so humor-
>     ously, such accurate timing, and such
> Appropriate ends? The man of vanity in vanity,
> Having his portrait painted; the man of violence . . . in
>     the fire and frenzy
> Of Berlin falling.[11]

Hence consciousness is only evil when it is diverted by the
man of vanity from God, and pointless human violence inevitably turns back upon the violent human being.

It remains to observe that Christ, the titan who "brought
fire to his tribe," has also a place, intellectually conceived and
reconciled, within the system. As the hanged god of Norse
mythology in *At the Birth of an Age,* Christ says:

[9] "Going to Horse Flats," *Such Counsels You Gave to Me and Other
Poems* (New York, 1937), pp. 90-91.
[10] *The Double Axe and Other Poems* (New York, 1948), p. 68.
[11] *Ibid.,* pp. 53-54.

My truth is born. It has nothing to do with the dead;  I
    loved the living and taught them to love each other.
Even now on earth my love makes war upon death and
    misery, not like a sword, like a young seed,
And not men's souls, but far down the terrible fertile
    future their children, changed and saved by love,
May build the beauty of an earthly heaven on all our dead
    anguishes, and living inherit it.

The hope thus which Christ offers is mortal happiness, not
immortal glory. Yet as an intensification of man's desire to
emulate the self-torturing God, Christ has greater understanding of the divine pattern:

                                        Every discovery
        is a broken shield, a new knife of consciousness
Whetted for its own hurt; pain rises like a red river: but
    also the heroic beauty of being,
That all experience builds higher . . .

                            These are my mercy and my
        goodness, these
My peace. Without the pain, no knowledge of peace,
    nothing. Without the peace,
No value in the pain. I have long strength.

By a devious path Christ comes to his traditional office; He
interprets and evaluates pain and experience; He connects
man and God.

A final question remains: Is life, either for God or man,
only alternations of pains and peace, a series of hot and cold
seizures? Perhaps. But I interpret Jeffers as saying that these
two states are ultimately synthesized in the dimension of God.
When the eagle in *Cawdor* released its phantom, fierce, arrogant bird that it is, it left "life behind," and

The great unreal talons took peace for prey
Exultantly, their death beyond death; stooped upward, and
    struck
Peace like a white fawn in a dell of fire.

The white fawn is Jeffers' symbol for supernatural beauty, the reality behind appearance.   One must find even this final beauty in the heart of fire. Yet this is not the fire of violence, torture, punishment, but the fire of God, which preserves rather than scourges.

# T. S. Eliot:
# Thinker and Artist[1]

### by CLEANTH BROOKS

Eliot's career is no loose bundle of unrelated activities but possesses an essential unity. Indeed, once discovered, this unity of purpose becomes increasingly evident. Few literary men in our history have so consistently related all their activities to a coherent set of principles. And the consistency of his various writings reflects the quality of the man. In a time of disorder, Eliot moved toward a restoration of order—toward the restoration of order that poetry alone, perhaps, can give.

Thus, Eliot's fundamental reassessment of the twentieth-century literary and cultural situation was not expressed in his poetry alone. The poetry arose out of a mental and spiritual activity that necessarily showed itself in literary and social criticism, not only in his brilliant essays on the Elizabethan dramatists, for example, but also in a work like *Notes towards the Definition of Culture.*

From *T. S. Eliot: The Man and His Works,* ed by Allen Tate, pp. 316-332. Copyright © 1966 by the University of the South. A Seymour Lawrence Book/Delacorte Press. Reprinted by permission of the author and the publisher.

[1]A lecture given at Eliot College, University of Kent at Canterbury, December 10, 1965.

When one discusses literature, few things are so deadly as the recital of abstract statements and wide generalizations. Moreover, it seems impertinent to treat a poet in this fashion, especially a poet who succeeded so brilliantly in giving his ideas concrete embodiment and who devoted so much of his discursive prose to this very split in the modern mind, this dissociation of sensibility, in which Eliot saw not only the distemper of literature but a symptom of a more general disease. Let me try to illustrate the essential unity of Eliot's work from a single topic, his treatment of the urban scene. In an essay written near the end of his life he has told us how he discovered that the urban scene was proper material for poetry, and specifically the special material for his own poetry. The passage I mean to quote begins with some observations on literary influences and what a poet can learn from earlier poets.

Then, among influences, there are the poets from whom one has learned some one thing, perhaps of capital importance to oneself, though not necessarily the greatest contribution these poets have made. I think that from Baudelaire I learned first, a precedent for the poetical possibilities, never developed by any poet writing in my own language, the more sordid aspects of the modern metropolis, of the possibility of fusion between the sordidly realistic and the phantasmagoric, the possibility of the juxtaposition of the matter-of-fact and the fantastic. From him, as from Laforgue, I learned that the sort of material that I had, the sort of experience that an adolescent had had, in an industrial city in America, could be the material for poetry; and that the source of new poetry might be found in what had been regarded hitherto as the impossible, the sterile, the intractably unpoetic. That, in fact, the business of the poet was to make poetry out of the unexplored resources of the unpoetical; that the poet, in fact, was committed by his profession to turn the unpoetical into poetry. A great poet can give a younger poet everything he has to give him in a few lines. It may be that I am indebted to Baudelaire chiefly for half a dozen lines out of the whole of *Fleurs du Mal;* and that his significance for me is summed up in the lines:

*Fourmillante cité, cité pleine de rêves,*
*Où le spectre en plein jour raccroche le passant!*


I knew what *that* meant, because I had lived it before I knew that I wanted to turn it into verse on my own account.


I want to consider further both Eliot's notion that the poet, by his very profession, is committed "to turn the unpoetical into poetry," and his idea that poetry is a fusion of opposites —in this instance, a fusion of "the sordidly realistic and the phantasmagoric," or "the matter-of-fact and the fantastic."

Poetry is evidently not to be thought of as a bouquet of "poetic" objects. The implication is that the materials the poet uses are not in themselves poetic. To be agreeable or pleasant or charming is not the same thing as being poetic. Poetic value is a quality of a different order. It is not a *property* of objects but a relationship among them, a relationship discovered and established by the poet. Moreover, the relationship may be one of tension in which the materials pull against each other and resist any easy reconciliation. In this instance it is the realistic and the phantasmagoric that may seem intractable, or the matter-of-fact and the fantastic.

All of this Eliot had said before, and, because he had said it before, in this rather late essay he could afford to touch upon it lightly. But when he first enunciated this view of tension in poetry, it very much needed saying—or at least needed resaying. And his statement of this conception, together with the poems that embodied it, inspired the literary revolution that is sometimes given Eliot's name.

It is useful to refer to another passage in which Eliot discusses the poet's use of what the Victorians sometimes regarded as hopelessly unpromising materials for poetry. The Victorian in this instance is Matthew Arnold commenting upon the ugliness of the world of Robert Burns. After quoting Arnold's rather prim observation to the effect that "no one can deny that it is of advantage to a poet to deal with a beautiful world," Eliot suddenly rounds on the nineteenth-century critic and quite flatly denies his basic assumption. The essential advantage for a poet, Eliot remarks, is not that of having a beautiful world with which to deal, but rather "to be able to see beneath both beauty and ugliness; to see the boredom, and the horror, and the glory." "The vision of the horror and the glory," he rather acidly concludes, "was denied to Arnold, but he knew something of the boredom."

This is excellent polemics: the hard backhand drive that rifles across the court and just dusts the opponent's back line. Yet the reader may wonder at the energy with which Eliot rejects Arnold. He may wonder too at what may seem an almost gratuitous reference to "boredom," not, surely, an obvious member of a cluster that would include "horror" and "glory." But references to boredom often come into Eliot's account of urban life, and we have in this passage mention of concerns central to his poetry.

They are indeed central to his experience of the modern metropolis where so many people find themselves caught in a world of monotonous repetition, an aimless circling without end or purpose. Eliot's early poetry is full of it:

> The morning comes to consciousness
> Of faint stale smells of beer
> From the sawdust-trampled street
> With all its muddy feet that press
> To early coffee-stands.
>
> With the other masquerades
> That time resumes,
> One thinks of all the hands
> That are raising dingy shades
> In a thousand furnished rooms.

*　　*　　*

> They are rattling breakfast plates in basement kitchens,
> And along the trampled edges of the street
> I am aware of the damp souls of housemaids
> Sprouting despondently at area gates.

*　　*　　*

> At the violet hour, the evening hour that strives
> Homeward, and brings the sailor home from sea,

The typist home at teatime, clears her breakfast, lights
Her stove, and lays out food in tins.

Let us go, through certain half-deserted streets,
The muttering retreats
Of restless nights in one-night cheap hotels
And sawdust restaurants with oyster-shells:
Streets that follow like a tedious argument
Of insidious intent. . . .

The wanderer moving through the deserted city streets long past midnight walks through a genuine nightmare in which

> the floors of memory
> And all its clear relations,
> Its divisions and precisions

are dissolved, a fantastic world in which every street lamp that one passes

> Beats like a fatalistic drum. . .

Yet when the wanderer turns to his own door, he steps out of one horror into a worse horror:

The lamp said,
'Four o'clock,
Here is the number on the door.
Memory!
You have the key,
The little lamp spreads a ring on the stair.
Mount.
The bed is open; the tooth-brush hangs on the wall,
Put your shoes at the door, sleep, prepare for life.'

The last twist of the knife.

The wound in which this knife is twisted is modern man's loss of meaning and purpose. When life to which one expects to rise after sleep—a daylight world of clear plans and purposes—turns out to be simply a kind of automatism, as absurd as the bizarre world of the nightmare streets, the knife in the wound is given a final agonizing twist.

It may be useful to remind the reader, especially the reader who finds that Eliot's Anglo-Catholicism sticks in his craw and prevents his swallowing the poetry, that in passages of the sort that I have been quoting, we are not getting sermonizing but drama, not generalizations about facts but responses to situations, not statements about what ought to be but renditions of what is.

Eliot once remarked that prose has to do with ideals; poetry, with reality. The statement has proved puzzling to many a reader who has been brought up on just the opposite set of notions, but Eliot's observation seems to me profoundly true. Discursive prose is the medium for carrying on arguments, drawing conclusions, offering solutions. Poetry is the medium *par excellence* for rendering a total situation—for letting us know what it feels like to take a particular action or hold a particular belief or simply to look at something with imaginative sympathy.

Here are some presentations of reality—an urban vignette, a winter evening in the city:

> The winter evening settles down
> With smell of steaks in passageways.
> Six o'clock.
> The burnt-out ends of smoky days.
> And now a gusty shower wraps
> The grimy scraps
> Of withered leaves about your feet
> And newspapers from vacant lots;
> The showers beat
> On broken blinds and chimney-pots,
> And at the corner of the street
> A lonely cab-horse steams and stamps.

And then the lighting of the lamps.

The Song of the third Thames-daughter:

> 'Trams and dusty trees.
> Highbury bore me. Richmond and Kew
> Undid me. By Richmond I raised my knees
> Supine on the floor of a narrow canoe.'

'My feet are at Moorgate, and my heart
Under my feet. After the event
He wept. He promised "a new start."
I made no comment. What should I resent?'

'On Margate Sands.
I can connect
Nothing with nothing.
The broken fingernails of dirty hands.
My people humble people who expect
Nothing.'

la la

Even the raffish Sweeney's recital of his philosophy—a view of life held, incidentally, by many of Sweeney's betters— is a bit of reality too; for it is a dramatic projection of a man, not an abstract formulation. Its very rhythms testify to a personality and an attitude.

Birth, and copulation, and death.
That's all the facts when you come to brass tacks:
Birth, and copulation, and death.
I've been born, and once is enough.

Readers have responded powerfully to such passages, even readers who hold very different conceptions of what the world ought to be. What is primarily at stake in all these passages is not the reader's approval or rejection of a statement, but his response to authentic reality. The only compulsion to respond is that exerted by the authority of the imagination. Perhaps the poet can never do more than exert such authority; but in any case he cannot afford to do less.

This matter of the reader's response has another and more special aspect. Eliot suggests that many of those who live in the modern world have been drugged and numbed by it. One task of the poet is to penetrate their torpor, to awaken them to full consciousness of their condition, to let them see where they are. The theme recurs throughout Eliot's poetry from the earliest poems to the latest.

The people who inhabit *The Waste Land* cling to their partial oblivion. They say:

> Winter kept us warm, covering
> Earth in forgetful snow, feeding
> A little life with dried tubers.

Or like the old women of Canterbury, they may say:

> We do not wish anything to happen.
> Seven years we have lived quietly,
> Succeeded in avoiding notice,
> Living and partly living.

The trivial daily actions, they point out, at least marked

> a limit to our suffering.
> Every horror had its definition,
> Every sorrow had a kind of end. . . .

What they dread now is the "disturbance" of the seasons, the decisive break in the numbing routine that will wake them out of their half-life.

But the partially numbed creatures may be, and usually are, people of the contemporary world. They may, for example, be like the characters in *The Family Reunion* who do not want anything to rumple their rather carefully arranged lives—who want things to be "normal"—and who cannot see that—to use their nephew's words—the event that they call normal "is merely the unreal and the unimportant."

They may be like certain well-bred inhabitants of Boston, Massachusetts:

> . . . evening quickens faintly in the street
> Wakening the appetite of life in some
> And to others bringing the *Boston Evening Transcript*. . . .

Or they may be the bored drawing-room characters in "The Love Song of J. Alfred Prufrock" whom Prufrock would like to confront with the truth about themselves. He would like to say to them:

'I am Lazarus, come from the dead,
Come back to tell you all, I shall tell you all'. . . .

But he well knows that these overcivilized and desiccated
people would not be impressed by the Lazarus of the New
Testament, much less by a self-conscious man "with a bald
spot in the middle of (his) hair," a man aware of the fact that
he wears a "necktie rich and modest, but asserted by a simple
pin." In any case, these people would not understand the talk
of a man who had experienced real death or real life.

The themes that run through so much of Eliot's poetry—
life that is only a half-life because it cannot come to terms
with death, the liberation into true living that comes from the
acceptance of death, the ecstatic moment that partakes of both
life and death:

> . . . I could not
Speak, and my eyes failed, I was neither
Living nor dead, and I knew nothing,
Looking into the heart of light, the silence.

These and the other themes that recur in Eliot's poetry bear
the closest relation to his concern with the boredom and the
horror and the glory that he finds in our contemporary metro-
politan life. They also bear the closest relationship to the sense
of unreality that pervades a world that has lost the rhythm of
the seasons, has lost any sense of community, and, most of all,
has lost a sense of purpose. Such a world is unreal: the sordid
and the matter-of-fact do not erase the phantasmagoric but
accentuate it. The spectre does indeed in broad daylight
reach out to grasp the passer-by. London, "under the brown
fog of a winter noon" as well as "under the brown fog of a
winter dawn," is seen as an "Unreal City," and the crowds
flowing across London Bridge might be in Dante's Hell:

> I had not thought death had undone so many.
Sighs, short and infrequent, were exhaled,
And each man fixed his eyes before his feet.

The echo of The Divine Comedy is not merely a flourish or an
attempt to touch up the modern scene by giving it literary

over-tones. What connects the modern scene with Dante's "Inferno" is the poet's insight into the nature of hell. The man who sees the crowds flowing over London Bridge as damned souls, if challenged for putting them thus into hell, might justify his observation by paraphrasing a line from Christopher Marlowe: "Why, this is hell, nor are they out of it."

In view of the complaint that Eliot sighs after vanished glories, sentimentalizes the past, and hates the present, one must insist on Eliot's ability to dramatize the urban reality with honesty and sensitivity. If the world about which we must write has lost the rhythm of the seasons, then the poet must be open to the new rhythms so that he can relate them to the old. Eliot once wrote that the poet must be able to use the rhythms of the gasoline engine:

> At the violet hour, when the eyes and back
> Turn upward from the desk, when the human engine waits
> Like a taxi throbbing waiting . . . .

If the modern world has lost its sense of community, the poet must present that loss not as a generalization but as a dramatic rendition, not as observed from the outside but as felt from the inside. He has done so not only in the nightmare passages of *The Waste Land*—

> There is not even solitude in the mountains
> But red sullen faces sneer and snarl
> From doors of mudcracked houses—

but also in the realistic passages:

> 'My nerves are bad to-night. Yes, bad. Stay with me.
> 'Speak to me. Why do you never speak. Speak.
>      'What are you thinking of? What thinking? What?

> 'I never know what you are thinking. Think.'

But he has also on occasion rendered the sense of community in positive terms—not as something lost but as a present reality:

O City city, I can sometimes hear
Beside a public bar in Lower Thames Street,
The pleasant whining of a mandoline
And a clatter and a chatter from within
Where fishermen lounge at noon. . . .

As for the sense of loss of purpose, that loss is never merely
asserted but always rendered concretely. It occurs so frequently in Eliot's poetry that it hardly needs illustration. Indeed, it may be best in this instance to take the illustration
from Joseph Conrad's *Heart of Darkness,* a story that lies behind so much of Eliot's early poetry. Marlow, the character
who relates the story, finds many of his experiences tinged
with unreality. As he makes his way to the African coast and
then on up the Congo to try to locate Kurtz, his sense of unreality is magnified—not merely because the jungle seems fantastic, but because the civilized characters he meets are dis-
oriented, obsessed, and thus absurd. One object stands out
sharply from this miasma of unreality. Marlow finds in an
abandoned hut "an old tattered book, entitled *An Inquiry into
Some Points of Seamanship,* by a man Tower, Towson—some
such name . . . . Not a very enthralling book; but at the first
glance you could see there a singleness of intention . . . which
made these humble pages . . . luminous with another than a professional light. . . .[The book] made me forget the jungle and the
[ivory-seeking] pilgrims in a delicious sensation of having
come upon something unmistakeably real." It seems so because it is instinct with purpose—because, to use Marlow's
words, you could see in it "an honest concern for the right
way of going to work." This is why the book shines with
the light of reality.

The sense of unreality is also associated with the vision of
a world that is disintegrating. In *The Waste Land,* the cities of
a disintegrating civilization seem unreal as if they were part of a
mirage. The parched traveler asks:

What is the city over the mountains
Cracks and reforms and bursts in the violet air
Falling towers—

but these cities are also like a mirage in that they are inverted, are seen as upside-down; and the passage that follows shows everything turned topsy-turvy:

> . . . bats with baby faces in the violet light
> Whistled, and beat their wings
> And crawled head downward down a blackened wall
> And upside down in air were towers
> Tolling reminiscent bells, that kept the hours
> And voices singing out of empty cisterns and exhausted
> wells.

Eliot also uses the empty whirl in order to suggest the break-up of civilization. Toward the end of "Gerontion" we have such a vision, people whose surnames suggest that the disintegration is international and worldwide: De Bailhache, Fresca, and Mrs. Cammel are whirled

> Beyond the circuit of the shuddering Bear
> In fractured atoms.

Though "Gerontion" was written long before the explosion of the first atomic bomb, I suppose there is some temptation now-adays to read into the passage our present unease and to regard the fractured atoms into which humankind has been vaporized as the debris of an atomic war. But I doubt that Mr. Eliot ever changed his opinion about the way the world ends.

"The Hollow Men," who know in their hollow hearts that they are not really "lost/Violent souls," but only "stuffed men," sing

> *This is the way the world ends*
> *This is the way the world ends*
> *This is the way the world ends*
> *Not with a bang but a whimper.*

The vortex in which De Bailhache, Fresca, and Mrs. Cammel are caught is essentially described in "Burnt Norton":

> Men and bits of paper, whirled by the cold wind
> That blows before and after time. . . .

With the empty whirl, the purposeless moving in a circle, we are back once more to the theme of boredom, and there is a good deal of evidence that Eliot did indeed see in such torpor and apathy the real dying out of a civilization. In 1934, for example, he wrote: "Without religion the whole human race would die, as according to W. H. R. Rivers, some Melanesian tribes have died, solely of boredom." This is a polemical passage out of a polemical essay, but we need not discount the idea merely for that reason. It is an integral part of Eliot's thinking. It is to be found everywhere in his prose and poetry —even in a poem like *Sweeney Agonistes,* where we have the following spoof on the cinematic stereotype of the golden age, life on a South Sea island:

> Where the Gauguin maids
> In the banyan shades
> Wear palmleaf drapery
> Under the bam
> Under the boo
> Under the bamboo tree.

> Tell me in what part of the wood
> Do you want to flirt with me?
> Under the breadfruit, banyan, palmleaf
> Or under the bamboo tree?
> Any old tree will do for me
> Any old wood is just as good
> Any old isle is just my style
> Any fresh egg
> Any fresh egg
> And the sound of the coral sea.

Doris protests that she doesn't like eggs and doesn't like life on "your crocodile isle." And when the singers renew their account of the delights of such a life, Doris replies:

> That's not life, that's no life
> Why I'd just as soon be dead.

Doris is a young woman who is clearly no better than she should be, but in this essential matter, she shows a great deal

more discernment than J. Alfred Prufrock's companions, the
ladies who "come and go/Talking of Michelangelo."

I have tried to suggest how the themes and images of
Eliot's poetry are related to his convictions about the nature
of our present-day civilization. But I shall have badly confused
matters if in doing so I have seemed to reduce his poetry to a
kind of thin and brittle propaganda for a particular world view.
The primary role of poetry is to give us an account of reality,
not to argue means for reshaping it. To be more specific: if a
culture is sick, the poet's primary task is to provide us with a
diagnosis, not to prescribe a specific remedy. For all of his intense interest in the problems of our culture, and in spite of
the fact that he himself was deeply committed to a doctrinal
religion, Eliot was careful never to confuse poetry with politics
or with religion. The loss of a sense of purpose, the conviction
that one is simply going round in a circle, is an experience that
many readers of Eliot's poetry have recognized as their own;
but in their decisions as to what to do about it, such readers
have differed as much as the Christian differs from the atheis-
tic existentialist. To get out of the circle, to find one's proper
end and begin to walk toward it—this is a matter of the highest
importance, work for the statesman, the sage, and the saint;
but Eliot was too modest ever to claim any of these roles for
himself, and he was as well aware as anyone of the confusion
of tongues that makes it difficult for men of our century to
agree on what the proper goal is. At any rate, he argued the
case for what he took to be the true goal, not in his poetry,
but in his prose.

In a time of grave disorder, Eliot has moved toward a
restoration of order. Not the least important part of this work
of restoration has been to clarify the role of poetry, not claiming so much for it that it is transformed into prophecy, or
Promethean politics, or an ersatz religion; but at the same time
pointing out its unique and irreplaceable function and defend-
ing its proper autonomy.

Genuine poetry, seen in its proper role, performing for us
what only it can perform, does contribute to the health of a
culture. A first step toward the recovery of the health of our
culture may well be the writing of a poetry that tells us the
truth about ourselves in our present situation, that is capable

of dealing with the present world, that does not have to leave out the boredom and the horror of our world in order to discern its true glory. More modestly still, a poetry that can deal with the clutter of language in an age of advertising and propaganda restores to that degree the health of language.

Eliot was well aware of this problem. Advertising and propaganda were for him instruments for "influencing . . . masses of men" by means other than "their intelligence." And he once went so far as to say: "You have only to examine the mass of newspaper leading articles, the mass of political exhortation, to appreciate the fact that good prose cannot be written by a people without convictions."

The difficulty of writing good prose in our era extends to other kinds of writing, including poetry. Of this, too, Eliot was aware. In *The Rock,* he has the chorus assert that "The soul of Man must quicken to creation"—not only to create new forms, colors, and music but so that

> Out of the slimy mud of words, out of the sleet and hail
> of verbal imprecisions,
> Approximate thoughts and feelings, words that have taken
> the place of thoughts and feelings,
> . . . [may] spring the perfect order of speech, and the
> beauty of incantation.

In a later and finer poem, he puts this ideal of style more precisely and more memorably still, and he makes this ideal structure of the language a model of that thing which men must try to accomplish in their lives. It is Eliot's description of the relation that obtains among the words that make up a passage luminous with meaning. In it,

> . . . every word is at home,
> Taking its place to support the others,
> The word neither diffident nor ostentatious,
> An easy commerce of the old and the new,
> The common word exact without vulgarity,
> The formal word precise but not pedantic,
> The complete consort dancing together. . . .

These beautiful lines celebrate the poet's victory over disorder, the peculiar triumph possible to a master of language. They describe what Eliot actually achieved many times in his own poetry. They provide an emblem of the kind of harmony that ought to obtain in wider realms—in the just society and in the true community.

# John Crowe Ransom:
# The Evolution of his Style

*by* Guy Owen

John Crowe Ransom, now that Robert Frost and Wallace Stevens are dead, may very well be the greatest living American poet—in spite of the fact that he himself has said that he was "deliberately minor." In fact, Allen Tate pronounced recently, with perhaps pardonable sectional pride, that Mr. Ransom is "the dean of American poetry." Although he has never been a fashionable poet, Ransom has been an important seminal influence: without any question he has, through both example and teaching, changed the shape of Southern poetry and criticism and made a profound impact on modern American letters.

And yet, curiously, there has been rather little written about him. No doubt part of the reason for this comparative neglect is that Ransom chose to write in an unfashionable mode; in addition, the body of his poetry is quite small, most of it written in a five year span in the 1920's. Except for the issues of *The Sewanee Review* and *Shenandoah* which commemorate his 60th and 75th birthdays, written and edited by

From *The Twenties: Poetry and Prose,* ed. by Richard E. Langford and William E. Taylor, pp. 46-52. Copyright © 1966 by Everett/Edwards Press, Inc.

his friends and former students, there are only scattered essays here and there that examine his poetry, such as Robert Penn Warren's brilliant study of his irony, John L. Stewart's introductory essay, *John Crowe Ransom,* and *Karl F. Knight's The Poetry of John Crowe Ransom.* However, he does come in for extended comment in the two recent books on the Fugitives, John M. Bradbury's *The Fugitives: A Critical Account* and Louise Cowin's *The Fugitive Group,* where his role as the leader of the Vanderbilt poets is made clear.[1]

Whether Ransom is a major poet or a great minor poet is debatable (I incline to the latter view), but no one can deny that he is one of the most important poets to emerge during the 20's. Certainly no study of American literature of this vital decade would be complete without a chapter devoted to him. And since Ransom's style is the most interesting, as well as influential, facet of his poetic achievement, I propose in this introductory essay to examine the dynamic development of his technique. For the sake of convenience, and since it does not impose a distortion, I have followed Richard Croom Beatty's division of his development into three stages: (1) the early and open style of *Poems About God* (1919), (2) the mature middle period of *Chills And Fever* (1924) and *Two Gentlemen in Bonds* (1927), and (3) the late, rather turgid, style of such poems as "Address to the Scholars of New England." (Perhaps there are not enough poems in this last group to speak with confidence about Ransom's final development.)

Of course, I do not wish to imply that there is a clear-cut division between these three stages; there is, inevitably, considerable overlapping in technique and themes. Nevertheless, I feel that the point is worth making that Ransom is a master of a number of styles — though he is prone to leave the work in his plain style out of his collected editions.

John Crowe Ransom made a late start as a poet; he developed rapidly in a few years during the middle 1920's, then gave up poetry for criticism. He was thirty years old when his first volume was published in 1918. Most of these poems were written during a two-year period at Vanderbilt, before the exciting days of the Fugitives. Ransom sent the poems to

---

[1] Since this essay was completed there have appeared two new books: Robert Buffington, *The Equilibrist* (1967) and Thomas Daniel Young, ed., *John Crowe Ransom: Critical Essays and a Bibliography* (1968).

Christopher Morley, a friend he had made while a Rhodes
Scholar at Oxford, and on the recommendation of Robert
Frost the volume was brought out, to a mixed reception, by
Henry Holt.

Poems About God is not a distinguished volume, though
the astringent tone must have seemed fresh in 1918. Ransom,
a severe critic of his own work, has never reprinted a single
poem from his first book, although it includes a few accomplished short pieces, such as "The Four Roses" and "Moon-
light," and is clearly a cut above the run-of-the-mill collection
of verse being published at the time. The collection, for the
most part, is unified around the theme of man's relationship
to God — though this motif is stretched at points, and abandoned in a number of poems. As Richmond Beatty noted in an
early essay on the poet, Ransom has been concerned, early
and late, with fundamental issues. No one can doubt the seriousness or the intellectual motive of the poems, nor fail to
note the awkwardness of the lines and an occasional stridency.

Poems About God reveals, perhaps inevitably, an inex-
perienced poet groping for his voice—and not quite finding it.
Perhaps the opening of "April" is closest to the mature Ransom manner:

> Savor of love is thick as the April air,
> The blunted boughs dispose their lacy bloom,
> And many sorry steeds dismissed to pasture
> Toss their old forelocks. . . .

Only a few of the poems seem derivative, a rare thing for a
first volume. "The School" is in part a reworking of a Robinson theme ("I kicked his clods for being common dirt,/ Worthy
a world which never could be Greek . . .); "Under the Locusts"
and the end of "November" owe something to Housman; and
"The Lover" seems a mixture of Donne and Housman. If
there is one main influence, the honor must go to Hardy, a poet
whom Ransom avowedly admires and has written about and
edited. Unquestionably, Hardy has had an impact, especially
in those poems where Ransom is most critical of God:

> For all his mercies God be thanked
> But for his tyrannies be blamed!

> He shall not have my love alone,
> With loathing too his name is named.

In addition, John Stewart has called attention to the influence of Browning. Later Ransom would turn to Yeats and Hopkins, even occasionally to Eliot; and as Robert Buffington has shown, a few late poems owe a good deal to Wallace Stevens.

If Ransom cannot be said to base his style on one master, neither can one discover here more than hints which point to his later mature style, which has made him famous as a craftsman, even as a poet's poet. To put it negatively, there is little in his early work of the elegance and sophistication of *Chills and Fever* and *Two Gentlemen in Bonds,* to say nothing of the perfect balance and skillful texture of the poems written in the mid 1920's. The diction of the majority of the early poems is anything but bookish: it is, on the contrary, realistic, rather simple and for the most part "unpoetic." One can readily see why the volume appealed to Robert Frost. Except for rare exceptions (*escheat, damozel*), he avoids archaic words, though he does not mind using archaic sentence structure for the sake of a rhyme—a practice which mars, at times, an early poem, as well as later ones. Similarly, he does not often use such colloquial words and phrases as *gallivanting* and *over yonder.*

On the other hand, there is a good deal of irony, much of it obvious and heavy-handed, even bitter, as in "Prayer" and "Dumb-Bells." Ransom seemed to deliberately shock his contemporaries by flaunting his criticism of God in their faces:

> What can one hope of a crazy God
> But lashings from an aimless rod?

Instead of relying on explosive or fresh imagery, he resorted more often than not to an easy irony. Finally, there is a good deal of sly humor, some of it turned against the poet himself.

In contrast to many of his contemporaries—notably Cummings, Pound and Eliot—Ransom chose not to experiment with form and meter. Instead he opted to work his innovations in tone and diction, like Robinson and Frost, within established forms, normally employing an iambic measure. As one might expect, *Poems About God* shows the poet trying his hand at sonnets—later a favorite form—quatrains, couplets and a kind of loose blank verse. His first poem, "Sunset," was an attempt at free verse; it is so clumsy and diffuse that the apprentice poet must have felt safer thereafter working within the harness of established patterns. His rhymes are also quite traditional; he seldom employed an oblique rhyme or the delightful fresh rhymes of his later witty poems. The pairing of *Jesus* and *tease us* in the satiric "A Christmas Colloquy" is a noticeable exception, pointing the way to one of Ransom's signatures in his next two volumes.

Although Ransom was a harsh critic of southern poetry, the world of his poems is unmistakably southern. However, he avoids local color for its own sake, sentimental and picturesque "nature" poems, together with the legends of the South that were the stock-in-trade of such Dixie bards as the Charleston group. Obviously from the outset, Ransom was anti-romantic, a poet who trusted the head rather than the emotions. After all, it was he who wrote later, these mischievous couplets:

> Sing a song for Percy Shelley
> Drowned in pale lemon jelly,
> And for precious John Keats,
> Dripping blood of pickled beets.

Yet, since as a poet Ransom began with "a fury against the abstract," he is driven to selecting particulars in order to give his ideas substance. The particulars and the characters, then, in these poems are Tennessee folk whom he knew well. For example, his own father in "Noonday Grace," a hired plowman in the bitter "Grace"—though few of his people come to life in the manner of Frost's or Robinson's, doubtless because Ransom was from the beginning more interested in ideas than in personalities. Always in these early poems there are other references to provide what Ransom called "the texture of the world's body": home-cured country ham, canned fruit, blackberry pie, and the sullen heat of dog days. The poet, however, seldom allows local references to weight his poems down with provincialities, a characteristic which distinguishes his verse from that of the majority of his southern contemporaries.

If Ransom's mature style is not clearly adumbrated in his first volume, his chief themes are—though naturally they are not developed with his later subtlety and impeccable craftsmanship. Nearly all of the motifs that obsess him are here; for example, the dual nature of man or the conflict between the material and the spiritual can be seen in "Morning." Since Ransom is a poet of narrow range, his later volumes do little more than elaborate on the themes he treats in his early work. From the very first, the world he creates is a thwarted one, where "in the finest flesh/ There isn't any soul" and men "who might be angels" are "fastened down with bodies . . . . " and "the whole world crumples in disease . . . . "

One gathers from the preface to *Poems About God* that the author was already a little ashamed of the first fruits of his muse. At any rate, he subjected himself to a further period of apprenticeship, and when he published *Chills and Fever* in 1924, it was obvious that his poetry had taken a great leap forward. In a few years his style underwent a change that has been called miraculous. No doubt the close study and teaching of English poetry at Vanderbilt aided Ransom in developing his mastery of technique. Perhaps too the perfection of many of the new poems owes something to the dialogue the poet carried on with the other Fugitives during the heady years between 1922 and 1925 when they were publishing their famous and influential little magazine. It was Ransom's custom to read one of his poems at their weekly meetings, absorbing the criticism of his fellow poets Donald Davidson, Merrill Moore, Robert Penn Warren and Allen Tate, as well as the lesser lights of the Nashville group. Later he would revise his poem for an issue of *The Fugitive,* often re-working it again before including it in one of his collections. (Always a fastidious craftsman, Ransom has continued to revise poems that have been often anthologized and considered modern classics.)

Whatever the reasons for the transformation, *Chills and Fever* and *Two Gentlemen in Bonds* represent Ransom's "new style," a style less open and more concerned with the subtleties of meaning and the fine nuances of sound. Here we note at once the elegant manner that has made him famous, perhaps as best exemplified in such poems as the early "Dead Boy," "Bells for John Whiteside's Daughter," "Conrad in Twi-

light," "Blue Girls," "Captain Carpenter" and "Janet Waking."
But there are a dozen other poems I could cite whose art is
near perfect, including the richly textured and more ambiguous "Antique Harvesters."

As Cleanth Brooks has said, these poems are obviously
made; the poet takes pride in calling attention to the carefully
controlled texture of his art. Clearly, nothing accidental is allowed to intrude in Ransom's work; if there is an awkwardness or harshness, then it has its contribution to make to the
total design of the poem.

These poems are brilliant examples of Ransom's cool detachment, his ironic tone, the often imitated "mixed mode," the
wit and metaphysical conceits. Most of the poems are fairly
short, for Ransom has difficulty in sustaining longer pieces.
Here are the small dramatic crises, compressed to the barest
essentials, told in a conversational voice that is often charming and brutal — poems that seem impersonal, yet release
emotional power.

Perhaps the prologue to *Chills and Fever*, "Agitato ma non
troppo," will suggest the poet's mature manner:

> I will be brief,
> Assuredly I know my grief,
> And I am shaken; but not as a leaf.

Ransom has asserted that he is not the "I" of this poem; he
has recently revised the poem to point this up. Yet he makes
clear in this classical lyric the kind of poetry he is rebelling
against in his own work: the contemporary poetry that leaned
heavily on emotion and romantic trappings, symbolized by
Shelley's reed that too often "sang tremolo."

As "Agitato" suggests, however, its creator has a "grief
in his mind," and the themes of these two volumes betray
Ransom's obsessions, many of them explored tentatively in
*Poems About God*. As one discovers in *Chills and Fever*, Ransom's world is anything but a pretty one—his is a "dwindled"
world. In it one confronts the decay of old age, death coming
to the young, the beautiful losing their beauty, the inability of
man to realize his potentials, the divided nature of the modern psyche, materialistic values triumphing, the values of the
old world perishing, evil lurking everywhere. And always

there are the lovers—parting, quarrelling, caught between passion and honor, marrying for wealth instead of love, most often dying without fulfilling themselves.

Randall Jarrell has described, in part, the world Ransom created as follows:

> In the center of everything . . . is the practical world of business and science and morality (which Ransom deplored), a vortex that is laboring to suck everything into its transforming revolutions. In the foreground there is a girl weeping for a dead pet; or simply a girl, dead; and her parents are mourning—in their dry wistful, pedantic way . . . Nearby the girl, grown up now, stands under the great hollow oak that whispers gently to its daughter—stands torn with pure love, pure pain, as she watches the "serpent's track" of the bicyclist pumping his winding way up hill.... Children are playing in the vacant lots, animals are playing in the forest. Everything that the machine at the center could not attract or transform it has forced out into the suburbs, the country, the wilderness, the past: out there are the fairy tales and nursery rhymes, chances and choices, dreams and sentiments and intrinsic aesthetic goods—everything that doesn't pay and doesn't care.

If Ransom's themes are relatively few—and some of them rather shop-worn—the kind of poem he writes is limited, too —especially when he is compared to such contemporaries as Eliot or Pound. With only a little difficulty, Howard Nemerov has reduced all of the poems included in the first *Selected Poems* to five categories: (1) elegies—a favorite with Ransom during the 20's—("Dead Boy," "Here Lies a Lady"), (2) bestiaries, or fables about animals and birds ("Lady Lost," "Dog"), (3) fables about people ("Our Two Worthies," "Judith of Bethulia"), (4) poems about lovers—which cannot be called love poems ("The Equilibrists," "Two in August"), and (5) meditative poems about art and knowledge—a type that Ransom was drawn to in his later development — ("Philomela," "Painted Head").

So much for the limited world of Ransom's themes; now to return to the style of the poetry he was writing during the middle 20's. Ransom's typical poem presents a small drama, often a dramatic crisis, usually narrated by an observer not involved in the action. As Randall Jarrell has noted, here is a modern poet who tells *stories*. But it is not the story or the characters—much less the setting—that interest the poet: it is the conflict of the *ideas* presented—for example, honor versus passion in "The Equilibrists" and the active versus the contemplative life in "Two Gentlemen in Bonds." The urbane, witty, even aristocratic narrator reveals what Robert Penn Warren calls "the kernel" of his little fables in a dry, cultivated voice in a conversational flow. The language is in the so-called mixed mode, and it is often a curious mixture of ornamentation and bluntness, of courtesy and rudeness, of the pedantic and the colloquial. As Robert Lowell, one of Ransom's students, has said, Ransom's "is the language of one of the best talkers that has ever lived in the United States":

> Autumn days in our section
> Are the most used-up thing on earth
> (Or in the waters under the earth)
> Having no more color nor predilection
> Than cornstalks too wet for the fire. . . .

It has been often noted that Ransom keeps himself out of his poems after his apprenticeship period. Perhaps he felt ashamed of having presented himself and his kinsmen so nakedly in *Poems About God;* perhaps he merely revolted against the example of sentimentality that pervaded contemporary southern verse in the 20's. No doubt his training in the classics helped to serve as a guide (he read "Greats" at Oxford). In any case, Ransom speaks for himself in only two of the poems in his new *Selected Poems*.

It follows, then, that Ransom is almost always careful to keep an aesthetic distance from his subjects. As critics have observed, his dramas are set in the past, his lovers are already dead, often his world is drawn from books, as in "Armageddon," and thus twice removed from life. If there is an "I" involved in the poem, Ransom characteristically keeps this hidden until the action is over, or almost over. Cleanth Brooks has compared this strategy to the technique employed by Milton; he suggests that "it is in this control of perspective that constitutes Ransom's special claim to a kind of classical decorum."

This is another way of approaching tone. As John Bradbury writes in *The Fugitives*, "various critics have described the peculiar attitude or tone which constitutes the essential Ransom as 'wrinkled laughter' (Morley), 'acid gayety' (Van Doren), 'detached, mock-pedantic, wittily complicated' (Jarrell), 'ambiguous and unhappy' (Winters), 'suave,' 'mixed,' or simply 'ironic'." Whatever it is labeled, it can be seen that Ransom's style depends on his being detached from the subject which he is presenting.

One of the most striking qualities of Ransom's new style was his reliance on a diction that seems "old-fashioned," language that harks back to Caxton and Malory. There was a mere suggestion of this in *Poems About God*, but with *Chills and Fever* the poet's style became heavily flavored — perhaps even weighted down at times — with medieval words and the latinate language of the Renaissance. As Stewart has observed, Ransom taught Milton at Vanderbilt and was fascinated by his latinism, as well as by the diction of Sir Thomas Browne and Jeremy Taylor. And since his father was a Methodist minister, the influence of the King James Bible was inevitable.

Whatever the reason for the change from a simple, realistic vocabulary to a more learned and bookish one, the change is obvious and dramatic. Perhaps a short list of such words will suggest this aspect of the poet's style: *bruit, lissome, thole, chevelure, diuturnity, estranger, transmogrifying, saeculum, stuprate, perdure* and *pernoctated*. What other American poet would risk such language in the 1920's? In one poem alone, "Necrological," Ransom employs *albeit, ogive, leman* and *wight*. Furthermore, at this stage in his development he seems drawn to such "poetic" words as *fabulous, casement, dolorous, vaunting,* and *hyacinthine*, to cite a few examples at random.

This use of medieval and renaissance diction is a trademark of Ransom's style, and, in my opinion, it became at times a mannerism. The poet has often been twitted for his use of *escheat*, etc. Yet, to be fair, the justification for such language in Ransom's poetry is easily found. Perhaps his penchant for an almost Spenserian vocabulary can be explained in part by the fact that Southerners take an unusual interest in the trappings of chivalry and often seem fascinated by rhetoric —

witness southern political oratory or southern sermons of the old school. More important, Ransom is often dealing with medieval subjects, wherein archaic language is not only fitting but inevitable. "Armageddon" and "Necrological" are two examples. Elsewhere the poet is employing such medieval forms as the ballad, as in "Captain Carpenter." But there is a more significant reason for his use of an outrageously poetic and archaic diction. Ransom's language is often deliberately over-inflated, over pedantic, for ironic effect; that is, to call attention to the contrast between the language and the subject of a poem, or to help puncture a threatening sentimentality. The *transmogrifying* bee of "Janet Waking" is a famous example of this strategy.

There is a danger here, of course, in singling out Ransom's polysyllabic and antiquarian language. It must be remembered that he continued to write in the 20's poems that were as much in the "plain style" as most of the work included in *Poems About God*. In fact, some of his best poems — "Blue Girls," "Piazza Piece" and "Vision by Sweetwater" — are written in a language that is classical in absolute purity and lucidity. And there are other poems written as simply as a Wordsworthian ballad — "Jack's Letter" and "Little Boy Blue" — though Ransom, as a rule, has not bothered to revise such poems for the editions of his selected poems.

In addition to the archaic diction emphasized in the poems of the 20's, one might also note in passing Ransom's use of archaic word order, which becomes more obvious, and deliberate, in his second and third volumes. Ransom's is a conversational voice, not a singing one. Yet, unlike Frost, he does not always employ the natural word order of ordinary speech; the structure of his lines is more formal. For example, he seems deliberately to make use of inversions for the sake of a rhyme, as well as for emphasis: "But strange apparatus was it for a Carmelite" and "But with much riddling his head became unruly" are two lines from "Necrological." "Alone in the press of people travelled he" appears in "The Equilibrists." There are numerous examples of such inversions, some of them too obviously calling attention to themselves, scattered throughout *Selected Poems*. Perhaps Ransom would cite the example of his old master Thomas Hardy to justify the use of such a poetic device. However, in his latest poems he seems to take care to achieve a more natural word order.

I have said enough to indicate that Ransom is given to writing witty poems. His wit is not only seen in the content of such poems as the saucy and irreverent "Survey of Literature" and the satiric "Amphibious Crocodile," it also manifests itself in his oblique rhymes, for which he has a special fondness. Ransom seems to have been one of the first southern poets to experiment with this device; in fact, he is the only one to do so in Addison Hibbard's anthology, *The Lyric South* (1928). No doubt he saw this as one way to avoid poems that jingle, as well as a way to work innovations within fixed stanzaic patterns. At any rate, he became a master of slanted rhymes in his middle period — though his latest poems avoid rhyme altogether. For example, in "Bells for John Whiteside's Daughter" we note his use of such rhyming pairs as *body-study, window-shadow, little-scuttle* and *ready-study*. In the rather late "Of Margaret" he continues the practice, rhyming *hung* with *mothering* and *grass* with *gentleness*. Like T. S. Eliot, Ransom often uses rhyme as an aid to his ironic tone.

As I have observed, Ransom is a militant traditionalist in some matters, although to many of his southern contemporaries he was a dangerous modernist. It is well known that he quarrelled with his pupil Allen Tate over the merits of T. S. Eliot. To Ransom, Eliot's *The Waste Land* was undisciplined and fragmentary. It is not surprising, then, to discover that Ransom is no innovator in metrics or stanzaic patterns — though he is not a slave to any tradition. As Bradbury has written, Ransom, like Donne, fails "of keeping of accent"; he thinks nothing of varying his rhythm and the length of his lines when it suits his purpose. Normally he works in an iambic beat and feels most at home in fixed forms such as the quatrain and sonnet, where, despite his variations, the final effect is one of formality and control. Ransom is also a master of the skeltonic line and dipodic nursery line patterns such as those in "Our Two Worthies":

> Kneaded it and caked it
> And buttered it and baked it . . . .

For his lighter fables he often resorts to a loose blank verse or to couplets. His favorite form, however, is his expertly controlled variations of the ballad stanza, which he had begun to master in the early *Poems About God.*

Now for a brief comment on the final stage of Ransom's poetic development. Perhaps there are not enough poems here to make a case for development, yet I feel that a few suggestions might be offered — if it is remembered that there is, obviously, no very sharp break with Ransom's mature style.

It is possible, I think, to detect a decline in power and freshness in *Two Gentlemen in Bonds,* especially in the sonnet sequence built around the contrast of the active mind and the appreciative, contemplative mind. The lines of these sonnets tend to become mannered, too heavily freighted with archaisms and pedantry; and the "story" of the two brothers is rather tedious, perhaps because Ransom cannot interest the reader in his characters as real characters.

Be that as it may, Ransom has published very few poems since his last book — though he has continued to revise his best work for the editions of his selected poems. As Richmond Beatty observed in 1944, "the luxuriant stream of Ransom's poetry has dried up, during the last fifteen years, into a thin and turgid trickle. The incisive wit and brilliant diction . . . have disappeared. The poet, in short, has been swallowed up by the critic."

Of the half dozen or so poems of this late period, only three require comment. "What Ducks Require" seems to be a rather obscure Agrarian fable belonging to the late 20's; two experimental "extended" sonnets have not been reprinted. "Of Margaret" is a memorable reworking of a Hopkins theme. However, in 1934 Ransom produced three ambitious poems: "Prelude to an Evening," "Painted Head" and "The Address to the Scholars of New England." Although these poems do not represent any new themes, their manner is different: the last two poems especially tend to be more metaphysical, more dense and concentrated in imagery, less accessible to the reader. It is almost as though Ransom had set out to write poems in the fashionable hard manner of the early Tate and Warren — a far cry from the lucidity of *Poems About God.*

At the same time, Ransom abandons rhyme, and his lines move with a more natural conversational flow. These three late poems are written in unrhymed stanzas, in metrics that are unusually free for Ransom. More important, he leaves be-

hind the archaic diction that had often degenerated into mannerism and, except for "Prelude," does not employ his usual
dramatic method. What drama there is in "Prelude" takes
place in the husband's mind. All three of these poems are highly intellectual; one cannot help feeling that they are "made"
by a learned professor. They are, in short, examples of what
the enemies of Ransom have labelled Academic verse.  Of
course, there are earlier poems — "Armageddon" and "Necrological," to cite only two examples — that also read very much
like set pieces.

A brief look at these three important poems will suggest
Ransom's late style. Bradbury has called "Painted Head" "a
brilliant metaphysical 'conceit' poem; its theme is based on one
of Ransom's obsessions: the war between head and heart,
intellect and body. The painting of the head causes the poet to
brood over the "dark severance" of mind and body in the
twentieth century and represents his old "fury against the abstract." The head on the canvas

> Stirs up an old illusion of grandeur
> By tickling the instinct of heads to be
> Absolute and to try decapitation
> And to play truant from the body bush.

"The Address to the Scholars of New England" is an occasional poem, a poetic essay unified by the repetition of key
words. Ransom's metaphysical wit and irony are much in evidence as he attacks our New England forefathers for their
over-simplification of life, for perpetrating Plato's "scandal-
mongering" and for keeping their heads in "the always clouds"
and "giddying with transcendent clouds." The imagery here is
less dense, and as one might expect in a polemical poem, the
language tends to became dry and abstract. No doubt "Address" is a brilliant example of verse satire, but one cannot
help noting that we are a long way here from such favorites
of Ransom's as "Captain Carpenter" and "Bells for John Whiteside's Daughter."

Finally, "Prelude to an Evening" has often been called one
of Ransom's best poems. It presents a small family crisis, as
so many of his poems do, in a little drama that takes place in
a husband's mind as he returns to his wife and family after
dealings with "the nations of disorder." He imagines that since

he is haunted by the world's evil that he will infect his wife's mind, too, until she will become aware of "uncertain spirits" in their home. "Prelude" is one of Ransom's most personal poems; it is one of the two or three poems in which the author appears as himself. Nevertheless, it is rather obscure, so much so that it has been often misinterpreted. Perhaps that is why Ransom recently revised and extended "Prelude," adding five stanzas and giving the poem a "happy ending," wherein the wife does not become victimized by her husband's furies and the husband settles down for an evening of baby-sitting. Ransom realized that the poem might still be baffling; consequently, he added an eleven page explication, explaining that his married couple are really Adam and Eve, and referring to Milton's theology, an article in *ELH* and *The Origin and Development of the Moral Ideas*! As accomplished as this late poem is, one cannot help noting that Ransom's best poems — no doubt all really first-rate poetry — can stand alone without being propped up by prose explications.

Perhaps no summary of the growth of Ransom's style could be more effective than citing what I believe are typical lines from the three stages of development that I have sketched in this brief essay. The following quotations are from "One Who Rejected Christ," "Here Lies a Lady" and "Painted Head."

> I'm not like other farmers,
> I make my farming pay;
> I never go in for sentiment,
> And seeing that roses yield no rent
> I cut the stuff away.

> Sweet Ladies, long may ye bloom, and toughly I hope
>         ye may thole,
> But was she not lucky? In flowers and lace and
>         mourning,
> In love and great honor we bade God rest her soul
> After six little spaces of chill, and six of burning.

> The big birds sitting and sea-shell flats
> And caves, and on the iron acropolis
> To spread the hyacinthine hair and rear
> The olive gardens for the nightingales.

As I write this it is known that Ransom, after a lapse of nearly twenty years, is writing poetry again. No doubt it is useless to speculate on what his new manner will be, but one can certainly expect poems in which one finds a classical control and an intellect of a high order. In any event, Ransom's new poems will be interesting to any one interested in poetic technique. For Ransom is one of the greatest stylists America has yet produced.

# The Poetics of
# E. E. Cummings

*by* HASKELL S. SPRINGER

It is not what E. E. Cummings has to say, but the way in which he says it that has established for him a secure position in the history of modern American poetry. His ideas are not trite, but are, for the most part, unexceptional, and derivative rather than original. He is concerned primarily with the importance of sex, the hypocrisy of society, the sterility of science, philosophy, and theology, the crassness of American "unculture," the love of a man and a woman, the idiocy of war, the beauty, strength, and timelessness of nature, the delights of childhood, and the all-importance of the present moment. These are most of his major themes, and even his best poetry does little more than explore their more obvious possibilities. But although his ideas are not particularly exciting, his medium is.

The deliberate use of experimental stylistic techniques whose peculiarities draw attention from the ideas expressed in the poem characterizes Cummings' work. The main constituents of his language are words scattered across the page (often in

"The Poetics of E. E. Cummings" by Haskell S. Springer. From *South Atlantic Bulletin,* xxxii (Nov. 1967) 8-10. Copyright © 1967 by South Atlantic Modern Language Association. Reprinted by permission of the author and the publisher.

pieces), punctuation and capitalization erratically tossed in, syntax that seems to make a mockery of meaning. These idiosyncrasies shout from the page, and the attention of his audience cannot help but be drawn by that shout. However, the reader who condemns the formlessness of an otherwise fine poet, or who laughingly dismisses the eccentric and childish versifier, or who even shrugs resignedly and reads Cummings despite his flaws, has been caught in the snare intentionally set for him by the poet.

Cummings is most commonly thought of in relation to those wild, typographical eccentricities so vulnerable to ridicule and parody; but although he does sometimes indulge in experiment or rebellion for its own sake, much more often his seemingly capricious use of punctuation, line division, spelling, and page format is directly related to traditional prosodic principles. They constitute an extension of, rather than an attack on, the historical basis of English-language poetry. Typical is the opening sentence of "o sweet spontaneous earth":

> o sweet spontaneous
> earth how often have
> the
> doting
>     fingers of
> prurient philosophers pinched
> and
> poked
> thee
> , has the naughty thumb
> of science prodded
> thy
>     beauty          .[1]

A close look at the sentence as a whole reveals that the placement of its elements on the page has rhythmic and semantic functions. Pace, emphasis, and meaning are directly controlled by the positioning of words, and by both the inclusion

---

[1] E. E. Cummings, *Poems, 1923-1954* (New York, 1954), p. 39. All subsequent page references are to this edition.

and omission of punctuation marks. Behind this rhythm of placement and omission, however, is a more common measure: the basic, underlying meter is standard iambic pentameter. Furthermore, the two sentence-halves rhyme.

Both Cummings' use of traditional poetics and his attempt to disguise them are evident in this first sentence of "o sweet spontaneous earth." His sonnets, though, more clearly show his desire to make the formal appear deceptively free and irregular. Although "it is at moments after i have dreamed" (p. 62), and "all ignorance toboggans into know" (p. 412) are Shakespearean in form, most of Cummings' sonnets do not adhere to the commonly recognized sonnet meter, rhyme, and structure as do these two. "Next to of course god" (p. 93), for example, exhibits a mixed form resembling the Italian. "The Cambridge ladies" (p. 58), "you shall above all things be glad and young" (p. 345), "a salesman is an it that stinks Excuse" (p. 394), and "pity this busy monster manunkind" (p. 397) are all lyric, fourteen-line poems either in iambic pentameter, or having a five-stress line. Though differing in various degrees from the sonnet of tradition, they can be recognized as containing the essence of the sonnet, including the form's virtues: economy, unity of effect, concentration, and precision. But whether these poems are strictly Shakespearean, or just within the bounds of sonnet resemblance, Cummings intentionally makes them appear less formal than they are. "The Cambridge ladies" frustrates the sonnet-expectation of the casual reader by being rhymed *abcd dcba efg gfe*, and others appear totally unsonnet-like on the page, including the Shakespearean "it is at moments after i have dreamed," in which line spacing works to disguise quatrain structure and sense.

The sonnets reveal an important element in Cummings' practice of poetry. As a general principle, he intentionally makes it diffcult for a reader to comprehend his verse; and his obstacles to even moderately-paced reading are usually quite effective. "I'm sorry, but a sonnet will not be a sonnet," say most of the poems just dealt with, "until you, dear reader, put enough of yourself into them to make them sonnets." The purpose of Cummings' deliberate obscurantism, then, is to force the reader to take part in the poetic process. This principle applies to his poetry in general whether the poem employs a recognizable stanzaic-metrical base, or is relatively free of such restraint.

Cummings' experimentalism, however, does not equally affect every element of his language. In sound effects, for one, his verse is relatively conventional. He employs, in traditional fashion, alliteration, onomatopoeia, and cacaphony, as well as assonance, consonance, and full rhyme. Regard for sound, though, is sometimes involved in experimental techniques, as in "she being Brand" (p. 178), where "brought all of her tremB/   -ling" employs "B" as a unifying element recalling "Bothatonce" and "Brand." Usually the aural function is evident in the device, as is the case with the onomatopoeia of "B." Here as in other places, however, Cummings makes the sound effect dependent on visual as well as aural perception.

Concern for the esthetics of the whole printed poem as it is visually perceived is a logical extension of the use of individual visual techniques in poetic structure; but the reader's response to the poem's appearance on the page is such a highly subjective matter, and one for which there is no adequate critical vocabulary, that discussion of it seems almost futile. Yet Cummings appears to have seriously considered visual esthetics and tried to elicit such a response to certain poems. "She being Brand" is pleasing to the eye; the definite but not rigidly patterned rhythm of line length fits well with the poem's internal development. "The hours rise up" (p. 42) also seems right in appearance. Its visual feel acts in support of the strength and frailty alternately treated in the poem.[2]

The poem, then, can itself be a visual image. At the same time Cummings' imagery, in the more conventional sense of the word, exhibits the diversity and complexity common to twentieth-century poetry. Its range of reference is wide, and it seems to appeal equally to all the senses but smell. In addition, the images sometimes bypass sensation to make a direct emotional statement comprehended intellectually, so that "my father moved through dooms of love" (p. 373), although suggesting the visual or tactile with "moved," really presents its image in terms of love" plus whatever "dooms" (a nonsensual word) is taken to mean.

---

[2] In these and other poems, line length appears to grow directly out of the sense of the poet's statement, and is thus an organic element in his poetry.

Cummings' imagery ranges from the grotesque to the ordinary, and displays the unabashed use of conceits. His figures of speech in general boast the flexibility of his imagery; moreover, they seldom are merely decorative, but are structurally integral to the poem, while the whole poem itself — as in the case of "she being Brand"—is sometimes a sustained metaphor.

As might be expected, the scope of Cummings' figures of speech is matched by his variegated diction. "Give her the juice," "what the hell," "greased lightning," says "she being Brand"; "in the street of the sky night walks scattering poems," says "the hours rise up." Cummings' diction is even more far-reaching than these examples suggest. Within a single poem it will often run the gamut from the most sentimental, romantic speech to the most prosaic formal or classical diction, from archaism to slang, from colloquialism to inkhorn terminology. While seeming to negate the traditional concept of appropriateness in diction, Cummings really expands it by demonstrating that multileveled language can be integral to an unquestionably "poetic" poem, and therefore appropriate.

Cummings excels in the combination of disparate types of diction. His sensitivity to the effect of such combination is evident in the poem beginning "spring omnipotent goddess thou dost" (p. 51). This stylized line is immediately countered with "inveigle," and the iconoclastic tone of the piece is suggested. "Hangest" and "stuffest" indicate the varying use to which Cummings puts his archaisms, as he goes on to mix "slattern," "brought to bed of," "Hollers," "slobber," "dissonant," and "canary-birds" (a term familiar to those acquainted with sweet old ladies and little children); to join "pimply" to "cavaliers"; and to end with "ragging" (U. S. slang, now somewhat archaic). In poems where even this wide range of diction is insufficient, Cummings supplements it with his well-known word coinages used in a myriad of ways, depending on his immediate needs.

Another significant facet of Cummings' diction is his use of quotation and allusion, but this aspect of his language is usually limited to satire or outright attack. The material which he alludes to or quotes directly is of several types, and, as with the imagery, its use is always integral to the concerns of the poem in which it appears. Most commonly used are words and phrases in the public consciousness: advertising slogans, children's rhymes, popular and patriotic songs, and sayings from prose and verse. These words are most often easily identified, but sometimes they are disguised by the disarming Cummings manner. "Early to bed and early to rise . . . " for example, is hidden in "early to better is wiser for worse" ("buy me an ounce and i'll sell you a pound," p. 936). In addition, he seems to delight in using phrases familiar to the public memory but whose original force has decayed, or whose source has been forgotten. The former intent appears in "next to of course god" (p. 193), which employs the hollow phrases of Fourth-of-July oratory to make a statement about the emptiness of overly-familiar sentiments. Emerson's "When Duty whispers low, *Thou must,/* The youth replies, *I can,*" echoed in "come gaze with me upon this dome" (p. 195), illustrates the latter use. The opening lines of the same poem themselves incorporate Shelley's "life, like a dome of many-coloured glass . . ."; and in this case the elegiac suggestion of the line from *Adonais* iron-ically sets the stage for the satire of Cummings' poem.

Cummings' experiments, though, do not hide the fact that he is a poet of the American vernacular. Obvious exceptions are, of course, easy to find, but the dominant quality of his diction is its colloquialism. While manipulating language in an attempt to make it true to reality, he remains within the spoken idiom. His vocabulary is fairly simple (allowing for an occasional "anent" or "merde"); the notable difficulties presented by his language lie in the way the words are employed, in the manner in which they are combined — in syntax.

Because the English language depends so heavily on word order for meaning, the disruption of normal order is an obvious syntactical device. It can serve to draw attention to, and so indicate the relative significance of, certain sentence elements, as in the line "all in green went my love riding," or "four lean hounds crouched low and smiling/ the merry deer ran before" (p. 11), where the inverse order of the clauses not only indi-cates their relative importance in the medieval tapestry being woven by the poem, but also makes "crouched" an active verb.

The emphasis on verbs is characteristic of Cummings. In fact, the verb is the most common element in his frequent grammatical dislocations. Most often seen in his remodeling of the concept of parts of speech are verbs used as other parts of speech, or nouns and adjectives serving as verbs; but a complete catalogue of such syntactical inversions would no doubt reveal that almost every part of speech is used as every other. What Cummings accomplishes with his verbals is a sense of movement, of process, in his poetry. His fondness for the "-ing" form contributes to this sense. However, the employment of disordered syntax in general has wider implications.

Beyond forcing the reader into a close relationship with the poem, these syntactical devices succeed in placing an extraordinary burden of meaning on the word itself as divorced from standard associations with certain language functions. At the same time, the re-action of the word accomplished by syntactical disjunction enables it to sustain the weight of new and expanded meaning. The resulting focus on individual words creates a wide range of suggestiveness in the poetry, a close relationship between language and experience. In this connection it is relevant to note the single-letter distinction between "word" and "world." The implications of the resemblance surely did not escape Cummings, whose eye was sharp enough to see that only an "r" separated "friend" and "fiend" in "what if a much of a which of a wind." (p. 401).

Cummings' evident dissatisfaction with the limited ability of the language of literature to represent reality, and his extreme attempt to make it do so, mark him as a Romantic, and as an American in the tradition of Mark Twain, Walt Whitman, and Hart Crane in that he expresses the American experience in a specially American way. But unlike Twain and Whitman, and in common with Crane, he evidences no particular desire to speak to the mass of his fellow Americans. His work demands a fit and therefore limited audience, because his unusual sensitivity to the subtleties of language, in addition to his experimentation with it and other aspects of his medium, make him an exacting poet. Although the voice of a Cummings poem is usually that of an "i" who directly addresses an audience, that audience is often not the reader. And, of course, the "i" is not necessarily Cummings. The syntactic-typographical barrier constructed by the poet only adds to the difficulty of coming to grips with his work, while a final obstacle is the impossibility of approaching Cummings wholly on a plane of high seriousness because the reader can never trust him. He may seem to be writing a serious poem when, whoosh, a wind blows the "r" out of "friend" to make it "fiend," and seriousness is undercut. His puckishness can be exasperating, especially since it most often is not a characteristic of the poem's persona.

What could seem more personal than Cummings' poetry and yet create such a wall between poet and reader? T. S. Eliot removed himself from his work and depended on an identified persona and the objective correlative. But Cummings says, "take it from me kiddo," "listen," "come, gaze with me upon this dome," yet he remains the aloof iconoclast scorning personal contact with "manunkind," which, like it or not, includes us, his readers.

# The Lyric of
# Hart Crane

*by* A. ALVAREZ

*Ah çâ! voici qui est plaisant: depuis que je dois mourir tous les
vers que j'ai jamais sus en ma vie me reviennent à la mémoire.
Ce sera un signe de décadence . . . .*

STENDHAL, "Le Rouge et le Noir"

The myth of tortured genius and the related cult of exacer-
bated sensibility have done Crane's reputation great harm.
Those who believe in it have loaded Crane with a greatness
which weighs down his real, and more slender talent. Those
who resist it accuse Crane of inflated, rhetorical effusions and
more than his fair share of poetic luck. Either way, he comes
out badly. He is clearly not a great epic genius; equally clearly,
he wrote some good and original poems. It was Crane himself
who believed blindly in genius. There seems no reason to think
that he knew very precisely what sort of genius he had.

For the main element of his life was confusion. There was
the artistic confusion of his tradition: he thought of himself
as decending from both Whitman *and* Poe; he was "influenced"
in the dangerous, superficial way by all the reading Eliot made

fashionable: the Meta-physicals, the French Symbolists, the Jacobean dramatists, Blake. From them he took hints about language, but missed their intellectual taste. He wrote, when he was not working at advertising copy, during the confusion of the most pretentious Greenwich Village experimentation. From all this he tried to forge an epic style. He lived out his confusions personally: his parents were constantly quarrelling, viciously possessive and finally divorced; his father, a candy manufacturer from Ohio, thought poetry hateful, soft and unsafe; Crane never completed his education; he was an alcoholic and a homosexual. He committed suicide in 1932, when he was in his early 30s.

Against this, he had on his side a superb ear, great sensitivity to language and an awareness which, though it lacked breadth, went deep. His sensibility was restricted to the minutiae of his reactions. It left little room for reason and not much more for observation. He worked above all by spontaneity; constriction, or whatever we would call the rational part of communication, he disregarded.

Yet he tried to write an epic. Crane seems to have been a man of few ideas but strong beliefs. He believed intensely in the absolute quality of poetic language, that the poet, inspired, could do no wrong. Which is not to say that he was careless; he revised and rewrote a great deal. But his standard was always richness of texture and concentration, never plainness. I will return to this. What matters here is that an epic in this style would be difficult to maintain and even harder to orientate. Crane's other riding belief was more common and more pernicious. He got into his head the idea of the great American poem, the poem which should create the myth of the U.S.A. from its legends, history and its present scene. He thought he could do this by spanning all his topics by his single imaginative symbol, the Bridge. The Bridge, however, is coherent only in its theory. It is a symbol of the poem Crane wanted to write; it has no real life apart from his creative will. Crane's tragedy is that he was never able to let be. He never really got over the idea of the great American poem. The feeling that he was written out, which is said to have driven him into suicide, was, I believe, brought about by the failure of The Bridge as an epic. It was praised far more highly than his earlier volume, White Buildings, but it was praised as a collection of lyrics. Even his friend Allen Tate complained of its "fragmentary and often unintelligible framework." And Crane was haunted by this sense of limited greatness. Yet it was precisely because he belonged so much to his age and place that he failed to write the great long American poem, yet always, whatever his theme, wrote American poetry. For he inherited the chaos of his time; he reacted violently and, in the end, tragically, against Middle West philistinism; he thought of himself as moving along an opposite and more native path than the one Eliot's cosmopolitan intelligence followed; he held his own ground and his own themes when all his friends were deserting to the exiled cliques of Paris. His Americanism was a central part of his genius; greatness was not. In this way he is like Scott Fitzgerald: he responded so fully to his time that he could never go beyond its limitations. His isolation itself and that sense he gives of someone always swimming against the tide helps to define the area of his work. It is nearly always a matter of effort; which is not necessarily a mark of excellence, but it has helped create that effect of dusty grandeur which has encouraged so many critics to call him "a great failure."

Towards the end of his life Crane, too, came to think of himself in this way. His suicide was almost his mark until the poet himself steps forward in the third stanza, "I think of cinemas . . . And Thee . . .". "I think": if there is any theme to Crane's epic it is not the Bridge, nor America, nor the machine age; the theme is Crane himself. The Proem ends "descend And of the curveship lend a myth to God." His myth is not to be built up in a steady self-revealing pattern. It comes from something far more transistory and less definable: the *aesthetic impulse* which his Bridge or bits of American history have for him. It is always about the poet. The impulse, however, seems a very real one. Those opening stanzas have a strong inner rhythm which is unmistakably Crane's. There is clearly something happening; he is writing with all his sensibility alive to the inner disturbance. In fact, these strange inner rhythms of Crane seem to me his greatest contribution to poetry. At times they come through almost despite the sense. In the first stanza, for instance, the movement is far subtler than that declamatory moral, "Liberty," to which it leads.

Crane, in short, is something of a poetic spellbinder. His poetry imposes itself on you for all its apparent lack of dis-

cipline. Yet it does so without wooing you as the poets of the
'nineties wooed their audience, by the specious charms of
stock responses. Crane's poetry is original and it moves carefully and steadily on its way, but without any clear argument.
As lyric poetry, everything depends on the force of his spontaneous reactions. It demands a kind of receptive suspension.
You must be sensitive to the flow of the poet's emotional response rather than to any logical train of thought. But this has,
at its best, nothing to do with the unfelt rhetoric and automatic word-association which is often felt to be the outcome
of the lyric impulse. Crane rarely uses inspiration as an excuse
for slip-shod writing. His method may be unrational; it is not
anti-rational. His best writing is guided by a purity of response
which is his own equivalent of "tough reasonableness." (This
applies to Crane only when he is writing well. He often wrote
very badly indeed. But my object here is to see what is fresh
and worth-while in his verse, not to show what everyone
knows: that he had moments of inflated sentimentality which
makes some of his work almost unreadable. In these places he
is not at all a "great failure"; he is merely a failure.)

The queer, unreasoned element in Crane's verse has made
a number of critics write of him as though he were less poetic-
ally skillful than immensely lucky; as though, beyond the initial
impulse, things just happened of themselves. This is not true.
The rhetorical sections of The Bridge apart, his method was
from the start pre-eminently careful; in his most original and
mature poems it was almost miscroscopic. Throughout his
work he moved steadily in one direction. His adolescent poems
are thin, but their thinness comes from too much literary tact,
too much care:

> Out in the late amber afternoon,
> Confused among chrysanthemums,
> Her parasol, a pale balloon,
> Like a waiting moon, in shadow swims.
>
> Her furtive lace and misty hair
> Over the garden dial distill
> The sunlight,—then withdrawing, wear
> Again the shadows at her will.

The hesitating delicacy of movement is almost too delicate
and refined. It has the thinness of an inturned aesthetic contemplation, as though the poet were in love with his own skill
(you get it also in A. E. Housman). His business is with a mood
which withdraws from contact; a mood controlled by words
like "confused," "pale," "waiting," shadow," "furtive,"
"misty," "withdrawing." For all the scene-setting and the little
speech with which the poem ends, it is the opposite of dramatic. No one and nothing except the poet is involved.

Crane did not remain long with these slightly precious
arabesques. By the time he was 21 the pausing aesthetic precision of his early verse was brought down to earth by a more
matter-of-fact conversational tone. These two elements worked
on each other to produce something more original, a sort of
open-structure, translucent language:

> Walk now, and note the lover's death.
> Henceforth her memory is more
> Than yours, in cries, in ecstasies
> You cannot ever reach to share.

Up until this last stanza the poem, "Stark Major," explores the
situation — the girl dead, the lover departing — in a number of
rather oblique suggestions, difficult to pin down. Here the focus
seems to sharpen. There is a subtle tension in the grouping of
the phrases, a richness in the possibilities of which qualifies
which. On one side is the meaning enforced grammatically by
the punctuation, where the stress falls on "her," "yours,"
"you." It focuses the poem unflatteringly on the lover. And
then there is the other emphasis which comes when you read
with the natural pause at the end of each line. Then it is
"more," "cries," "ecstasies," "ever" and "share" which take
the weight. The lover is no longer so important. It is the girl
who moves into the centre; her memory takes on a grandeur
which is wholly out of the lover's ken. These are neither para-
phrasable meanings; it is a matter of stress. But the poem has
none of that blurred inadequacy Crane is often charged with.
He uses the possibilities of the language to the fullest whilst
remaining strictly within the limits of a slight lyric.

Certainly, "Stark Major" is no very remarkable poem. Although Crane is building on more than an evasive mood, the foundation is still slender. Perhaps it is a type of writing that any clever, accomplished amateur could, with a little luck, have done. Yet though Crane was young when he wrote this, it does not seem to me to have the usual young man's literariness. He seems too well aware of what he is about for it to be a fluke. The poem has the same sensitivity to the minutiae of language as all his maturest poems. It is a long way from the legend of Crane as the inspired but slipshod genius. The more obvious charge might be aesthetic dandyism, if it weren't that the rhythm carries the verse with considerable subtlety. It seems to have more disturbance than a mere impulse to pleasant verse-making would account for. Without that earlier, rather self-conscious hesitation, the poem has enough movement to begin to seem new and personal in a delicate, exploratory way.

But it is not fully grown poetry. Crane's most significant and original verse lies between this early, more or less aesthetic style and the coarser rhetoric of his late work. It is to be found in the poems written in about 1924 and 1925, published in *White Buildings*. They are still lyrics in the sense in which I used the term earlier: they spring from the poet's direct responses before these are mixed up with a rationalizing organization. But there is a toughening and a growing complexity in the way in which the response is realized which is as though parallel to a highly developed intellectual complexity.

> And yet this great wink of eternity,
> Of rimless floods, unfettered leewardings,
> Samite sheeted and processioned where
> Her undinal vast belly moonward bends,
> Laughing the wrapt inflections of our love; . . .
>
> > (Voyages, II)

There is nothing obviously lyrical about this, it is not easy, it is not even very clear. But it works in the manner of a lyric and demands the same openness and attention. This is the opening stanza; there is no main verb until the second, "Take this sea . . . . " So there is an impression — spurious, I think — that this poem follows from the end of the first of the series,

"The bottom of the sea is cruel." Without a verb the action of
the verse is difficult to plot; indeed, at first sight it seems to
be made up only of a number of questionably connected
phrases describing the sea. But seen from closer up it becomes
clearer how the connections were made: how "wink" brought
"rimless," which moved, with a jump, into "unfettered"; how
there is a connection between the curve of the sea's eye and
the curve of her "belly"; how "sheeted," "belly" and "love"
interact, and how the "great wink" turns into "laughing." The
closer, in fact, that you look, the subtler and more deliberate
becomes the interaction between the freedom and vast impersonal yearning of the sea for the moon and the limited
human desires of the lovers. The progression of the poem is a
series of checks and balances which work upon the reader
without logical paraphernalia. Yet they work surely enough
for the poet to end by drawing his morals with no great sense
of strain.

I would hesitate to put a specific interpretation on the
poem. It has no clear-cut meaning. It acts as a sort of mixer:
it stirs up and holds together a number of related feelings
about the sea and about love, but does little to separate them
out. Perhaps the poetic phrase is given too absolute a value;
perhaps the reader is expected to believe with too great an
intensity in the uniqueness of poetic expression. Yet I don't
find the atmosphere oppressive with poetic fury. There seems
more to it than inflated word-association. It has a perceptive
tightness of texture and a characteristic movement which could
not have been wilfully imposed on a rhetorical pattern. The
language, in short, does not cover up a failure in perception,
nor is it, as Professor Blackmur has suggested, a perception
only of linguistic qualities. On the other hand, whatever you
can make of it by analysis, the method is clearly not logical.
Some other way into the poem is needed.

Crane himself partly explained his way of writing in an
essay which was written to accompany White Buildings, but
not published until after his death. He talks there of "a logic
of metaphor," of the "emotional dynamics of the materials
used" that are "selected less for their logical (literal) significance than for their associational meanings." He then goes on
to give an example from a later stanza of the poem I have just
been discussing:

When . . . I speak of "adagios of islands," the reference
is to the motion of a boat moving through the islands
clustered thickly, the rhythm of the motion, etc. And it
seems a much more direct and creative statement than
any more logical employment of words such as "coasting
slowly through the islands," besides ushering in a whole
world of music.

Crane is giving a truth about his method, but a partial, a self-
conscious truth; the outline, not the whole story. The real
point, I think, is the self-centredness of this explanation. The
aura of suggestiveness of Crane's metaphors is first and fore-
most *subjective*. What is important is the perceiver, not the
thing perceived; Crane moving through the islands, not the
islands themselves; he imposes his own reactions on them. And
this, of course, is precisely the lyric technique I described
earlier. But instead of being allowed a whole poem to itself
the lyric reaction is concentrated into a phrase or a sentence.
These are like tributaries to a river, all of them are made sub-
sidiary to the ruling impulse, the theme of the poem. The complexity of these poems, in short, lies in the fact that they are
whole lyrics deepened by a number of smaller lyric impulses.

Earlier I said that Crane's subject matter was always, in
one way or another, himself. This does not mean that his work
has much self-dramatization in it. Nor is it dramatic in the
more usual sense. In fact, he and Stevens, for all their differences, are probably the least dramatic poets of the century.
And all this is true although Crane thought he was influenced
by Marlowe, although he modelled himself at times on the
fashionable bits of the Jacobean dramatists and although sections of *The Bridge*, "The Tunnel" for example, are cast in a
dramatic, soliloquizing form. Crane's method is less active. He
once wrote that poetry of the machine age "demands . . . along
with the traditional qualifications of the poet, an extraordinary
capacity for surrender, at least temporarily, to the sensations
of urban life." I think that all his most original poetry is made
up of continual acts of surrender to sensations. But these are
less often immediate physical sensations translated into words
than sensations about themes, about the sea, love, death, and
so on. Crane doesn't "feel his thought"; he feels instead of
thinking. The instantaneous reactions of a moment are har-

monized with a steady feeling for the whole theme. This is
why he can seem to draw conclusions; they are not rational;
they are instead his completed reaction to the subject. His
poems begin with a surrender to sensations; they end with a
kind of digestion of the whole subject.

Crane seems to have known very well what he was about.
In most of his best poems he chose themes to suit his method;
they are records of minute fractions of time so small that they
begin to seem almost timeless. They are records, in short, of
"this great wink of eternity," "Of a steady winking beat between systole, diastole . . . " in "Paraphrase"; of the "breaking
second" in "Recitative." In this last poem he sounds the theme
of them all:

> In alternating bells have you not heard
> All hours clapped dense into a single stride?

Crane's most original work is something quite new in English
or American poetry: he writes with an awareness so heightened
that he makes into whole poems those sharp but transitory
states from which other people's poems usually start.

I would not wish to claim too much for him. It seems only
proportionate to list his weaknesses. They come mostly from
the oddness of his approach. It needed a freshness and precision well-nigh impossible to maintain long. By leaning so
heavily on poetic intelligence and hardly at all on common
sense, Crane had very little to fall back on when his spontaneity failed. At best he trod a delicate path on the edge of
rhetoric; he slipped time and again. His ambition to write great
epic verse helped in this. He is invariably at his worst when
his creative impulse fails to match his desire to write. The
later sections of The Bridge, written when he was acutely
aware of his failing ability, are often mawkish, rhetorical,
exhibitionistic and, in places, brutal. Nearly all his long poems,
in fact, are patchy. He can move effortlessly from the noisiest
rhetoric to a powerful simplicity:

> Spears and assemblies: black drums thrusting on—
> O yelling battlements,—I, too, was liege
> To rainbows currying each pulsant bone:
> Surpassed the circumstance, danced out the siege!

And buzzard-circleted, screamed from the stake;
I could not pick the arrows from my side . . . .

It was Yvor Winters who first remarked that that last line
sounded like Racine. It is written with the sort of poetic conviction which it takes genius to attain and which makes the
gesticulations around it seem all the more unnecessary.

There are other moments when Crane does not seem to
have fully assimilated his reading:

Whose head is swinging from the swollen strap?
Whose body smokes along the bitten rails,
Bursts from a smouldering bundle far behind
In back forks of the chasms of the brain,—
Puffs from a riven stump far out behind
In interborough fissures of the mind . . . ?
("The Tunnel")

For all the modern odds and ends — the play, for instance, on
the name of a subway system in the last line — this seems still
too firmly attached to Jacobean dramatic verse, in a way in
which the Middleton passage in *Gerontion*, say, is not. Crane's
verse has not broken away into an independent life.

Lastly, starting with the rejection of straightforward
thinking, Crane finished too often with an approximation to
what he wanted. Even when he is writing well the rhythm of
the verse is sometimes more precise and carries more weight
than the meaning of the words:

Distinctly praise the years, whose volatile
Blamed bleeding hands extend and thresh the height
The imagination spans beyond despair,
Outpacing bargain, vocable and prayer.
("For the Marriage of Faustus and Helen," III)

This is different from the excesses of Dylan Thomas's verbaliz-
ing; Crane is not running on merely for the sake of the words.
But I feel he would have been hard put to it to explain at all
precisely what he meant.

Wit, of the type found in Eliot and Pound, was never
within Crane's range. Only in "Paraphrase," his finest poem,

is there an ironic check on an intensely serious subject. Without that sort of intellectual defense he was left in his off-
moments with shuffling exaggerations. But almost never, despite the wretched turmoil of his life, is there any self-pity in his
poetry. What saved him was the gift that made his best verse,
the fullness of his responses. It brought him not to self-pity
but to a genuine compassion and human feeling. Perhaps this
is why he saw himself, flatteringly, as an opponent of T. S.
Eliot. In 1922, after the publication of *The Waste Land,* he
wrote in a letter:

> There is no one writing in English who can command so
> much respect, to my mind, as Eliot. However, I take Eliot
> as a point of departure towards an almost complete re-
> verse or direction. His pessimism is amply justified, in his
> own case. But I would apply as much of his erudition and
> technique as I can absorb and assemble towards a more
> positive, or (if I must put it so in a sceptical age) ecstatic
> goal. I feel that Eliot ignores certain spiritual events and
> possibilities as real and powerful now as, say, in the time
> of Blake. Certainly the man has dug the ground and buried
> hope as deep and direfully as it can ever be done . . . .
> After this perfection of death — nothing is possible in mo-
> tion but a resurrection of some kind . . . . All I know
> through very much suffering and dullness . . . is that it
> interests me still to affirm certain things.

Crane's affirmation had nothing like the weight of Eliot's
denial. His poetic talent was erratic where Eliot's was highly
disciplined. He had nothing at all of Eliot's intellectual distinction. But he did have a free and easy emotional generosity.
The workings of his poems are minute. Yet, in contrast, his
own personal reactions are spontaneous or they are nothing.
It is, I believe, this openness and acceptance of emotions and
of the facts of the place which constitute Crane's particularly
American strength. In this he is like Whitman. The sections of
*The Bridge* called "Van Winkel" and "The River" seem to follow fairly directly from *The Leaves of Grass.* Crane is more
sensitive to language and far more sophisticated in his performance. But I think his sophistication is largely of the surface. Underneath is the same inclusive bonhomie, the same

strength which is never complex and the same ability, when he writes badly, to exaggerate and embarrass. But Crane lived at a period when complexity seems to have been peculiarly sought after. Partly because of the technical revolution which was taking place in poetry, partly because the pressures of his time and particular circumstances were more overwhelming and deadly than Whitman's, his final achievement was more difficult, more involuted and less assured. But at his best Crane did write from what he knew: his spontaneous and highly individual reactions. And so his "affimation" is not in the great American epic, but in a handful of obscure, powerful lyric poems. It is quite as original but altogether slighter than he wanted.

# Theodore Roethke

## by RALPH MILLS, JR.

Looking back to the early poetry of Theodore Roethke, whose premature death in August 1963 was an incalculable loss to American literature, we can see there the source of many of his constant thematic interests and of the restless exploratory impulse in technique that resulted from them. Roethke wished continually to plumb new areas of experience and to alter his style to match his discoveries. This impulse and his considerable lyric gifts give to the body of his writing a strong cumulative effect, for each successive stage of the work grows quite naturally from its predecessors. Reading his late poems, we feel the weight of earlier ones as an actual presence. By means of this closely woven pattern there is built up a universe of discourse, a poetic world of recurring themes and preoccupations into which the individual poems fit and within which they are comprehended.

Roethke's first book *Open House* (1941), impresses the reader at the start with this poet's ability to sing, with his sharp, compact lines and his fundamental rhythmic sense.

"Theodore Roethke" by Ralph J. Mills, Jr. From *Contemporary American Poetry*, pp. 48-70. Copyright © 1965 by Random House. An earlier version of this essay appeared in *Poets in Progress*, ed. by Edward Hungerford, copyright © 1962 by Northwestern University Press. Reprinted by permission of the author, Random House and Northwestern University Press.

One is sure after seeing the best of these short lyrics and descriptive poems that Roethke could never have stopped with
them; flexibility and the promise of real development lurk
everywhere under the surface of his language and in the materials of his experience. In the title poem he announces the
major theme that will influence nearly all of his future work
and the artistic personality inseparable from it:

> My secrets cry aloud.
> I have no need for tongue.
> My heart keeps open house,
> My doors are widely swung.
> An epic of the eyes
> My love, with no disguise.
>
> My truths are all foreknown,
> This anguish self-revealed.
> I'm naked to the bone,
> With nakedness my shield.
> Myself is what I wear:
> I keep the spirit spare.
>
> The anger will endure,
> The deed will speak the truth
> In language strict and pure.
> I stop my lying mouth:
> Rage warps my clearest cry
> To witless agony.

The art proposed in these stanzas is peculiarly personal,
"naked to the bone," and, we might say, resembles a journal,
kept with great pain, which traces the path of a sensitive mind
from bondage to freedom. Such is the course Roethke follows
through a substantial part of his poetry. It appears too that this
interest in the self as poetic theme evolves from a kind of
curative effort by the poet — the exorcism of a demon, T. S.
Eliot would call it. A progressive movement that takes place
in his writing falls into stages ranging from the psychological
to the visionary and mystical. This classification necessarily
slights some excellent light verse and children's poems that are
peripheral to the poet's main purposes and so will not be dis-
cussed here. Roethke sets out upon a journey in his work, a

research into the hidden corners of the psyche; through his labors he seeks to secure the liberation and integration of the self. The poet must relive his own personal history and once more find his way back into the world in order to discover himself and his ties with creation anew. The developing body of Roethke's poetry over the length of his career creates a record of the self's mutations, its final relationship to nature, and the expansion into love and illumination, its last, anagogical disposition.

The series of brief poems opening *The Lost Son* (1948), Roethke's second collection, serves as an introduction to longer and more radical pieces in the same book. Roethke has stressed the eye as the most important organ (see his "Prayer," from *Open House*); and it is an eye of microscopic powers trained on the minute, thriving vegetable and mineral realms of the earth that determines the character of sensibility here. These poems remind us somewhat of Rimbaud's *Illuminations* and Whitman's *Leaves of Grass,* not so much in subject matter or method as in their bold affront to our habitual forms of perception. We are forced to see things differently, or to reject the poetry altogether. We are urged to strip away those winding cloths of category and convention in which we bury our sense of life, and to regain a simplicity of vision, a belief in human possibility. Lying flat on the soil, as we appear to do while reading these poems, our eyes level with the ground, we begin again with the elements of the natural world. Our origins are linked by correspondences with those elements. If this procedure of close attention to budding plants and tiny creatures clashes with our pretensions to adult dignity, Roethke shows us in "Cuttings (Later)" that such observation has a surprising relevance to our own estate:

> This urge, wrestle, resurrection of dry sticks,
> Cut stems struggling to put down feet,
> What saint strained so much,
> Rose on such lopped limbs to new life?

Should we disclaim recognition of this struggle, we either have failed to admit to ourselves the truth or have not risen to meet life. Roethke always succeeds in putting before us the images of grace and defection.

As he often remarked in commenting upon his writing, Roethke spent his youth around the greenhouses in Michigan owned by his father and uncle, who had a large flower business, and he absorbed the atmosphere and the minutiae of plant life with an intensity of interest and a sympathy that transformed them into both literal facts and dominant metaphors of his poetry. Early influenced by his reading of Wordsworth, John Clare, and Whitman, and later by Léonie Adams, he quickly found poetic examples to spur his personal fascination with the details and processes of nature. There is a human lesson to be learned that starts with a humble attitude toward the lower orders of creation and the knowledge of our connections with them. True growth requires us to return along the way we came and to touch once more the roots from which we sprang:

> When sprouts break out,
> Slippery as fish,
> I quail, lean to beginnings, sheath-wet.

Such imagery identifies man with a process in the natural world and relates him to its stubborn fecundity. This assertion of existence is evident in a poem such as "Root Cellar," where

> Nothing would give up life:
> Even the dirt kept breathing a small breath.

The shorter poems of this period are generally devoted to what Roethke calls "the minimal." Their repeated themes and metaphors furnish a basis for more ambitious efforts and point to new departures. In a poem entitled "Transplanting" we watch young plants being set down in fresh soil and, as if through the lens of a camera equipped with a timing device, we see them unfurl and bloom:

> Watching hands transplanting,
> Turning and tamping,
> Lifting the young plants with two fingers,
> Sifting in a palm-full of fresh loam,—
> One swift movement,—
> Then plumping in the bunched roots,
> A single twist of the thumbs, a tamping and turning,
> All in one,

Quick on the wooden bench,
A shaking down while the stem stays straight,
Once, twice, and a faint third thump,—
Into the flat-box it goes,
Ready for the long days under the sloped glass:

The sun warming the fine loam,
The young horns winding and unwinding,
Creaking their thin spines,
The underleaves, the smallest buds
Breaking into nakedness,
The blossoms extending
Out into the sweet air,
The whole flower extending outward,
Stretching and reaching.

Roethke has realized how the same striving upward into life (suggested by the continuous movement of participles in the second stanza of this one-sentence poem) is an essential activity of the human spirit. His perception leads him to examine in a series of longer poems the relationships between the developing inner world of the self and the objects and forces of physical nature. What is merely a proposed analogy between psychic and natural processes in earlier poems approaches an identification of the two in work that follows.

The longer poems, which extend and deepen Roethke's previous concerns, finally appear as a full sequence in *The Waking* (1953). In a feat of imaginative re-creation and poetic skill he dramatizes, by means of a technique that sometimes seems close to the novelist's method of interior monologue, the borderline regions of the conscious and the preconscious in a child as he slowly, and often painfully, ascends from the mysterious center of his origins toward selfhood and a communion with the external cosmos. As the body grows the spirit grows with it, and the exchange between them, with the added consideration of lives and things outside which impose upon the forming self, creates the drama of these poems. Intimate attachments to the animal, vegetable, and mineral levels of creation are disclosed, and along with them, a tension in the child-protagonist between the desire for his whole existence and a contrary attraction for death and the inanimate. In order

to embody the immediacy of this evolution of self in the
poems, Roethke turns away from the stricter conventions of
his previous work to looser and more eclectic forms suitable
for rendering this complicated interior drama. The poems
register the impression of sensations from without on a rapidly
shifting psychic life until we sense a dialectical arrangement
between them. Passages contain abrupt changes:

> Tell me, great lords of sting,
> Is it time to think?
> When I say things fond,
> I hear singing.
>   ("O Lull Me, Lull Me")

conflict and isolation:

> A worm has a mouth.
> Who keeps me last?
> Fish me out.
> Please.
>   ("Where Knock Is Open Wide")

and unexpected juxtapositions everywhere:

> Such music in a skin!
> A bird sings in the bush of your bones.
> Tufty, the water's loose.
> Bring me a finger. This dirt's lonesome for grass.
>   ("Give Way, Ye Gates")

In spite of the difficulties caused by such associative and
prelogical techniques, some of which should disappear once
the reader surrenders himself to the purpose and rhythm of
the poet's undertaking, we still find the same precise diction
and familiar musical ease that distinguish Roethke's art. If the
poems lack the rational order we found in *Open House,* this
lack must be attributed to the fluid reality the poet tries to
capture here. The adjustments demanded of us are more extreme than before. Entering the child-protagonist's mind, we
must adopt a literalness of apprehension and discard the
adult's acquired skepticism—though we must not, on the other
hand, forget the sophisticated craftsmanship in these poems.
The world, from the new point of view Roethke provides, is

transformed into a densely populated, because animistic, universe where normal distinctions of subject and object, consciousness and unconsciousness, will and instinct are abolished and synesthesia is an accepted mode of perception. Perhaps the license for such a departure in poetry can best be explained by a remark the poet made in a recent essay (Poetry, October 1960). "We must permit poetry to extend consciousness," Roethke says, "as far, as deeply, as particularly as it can, to recapture, in Stanley Kunitz' phrase, what it has lost to some extent in prose. We must realize, I think, that the writer in freer forms must have an even greater fidelity to his subject matter than the poet who has the support of form." Roethke, as a reading of his collected verse will prove, has worked in both manners; many of his late poems display his wish to experiment with "freer forms," as do the poems of the childhood sequence.

These poems are, then, composed on a rationale wholly their own, a logic nearer that of the dream or some ellipsis of thought and sensation than the calculating intelligence. We can say of them, as T. S. Eliot says in the preface to his translation of St. John Perse's Anabase, that "there is a logic of the imagination as well as a logic of concepts." Individually, the poems constitute portions of a journey into the psyche, the memories and experiences beneath everyday conscious thought, and so they participate in different temporal dimensions by disturbing the dormant past within the self. Roethke's poetic enterprise at this juncture involves him in something resembling the interpretation of the many layers of writing on a palimpsest; each one draws him further back in time and into more obscure circumstances. But the journey is made with direction and, we feel, even with urgency. It is an attempt to win a perspective on the general plan of personal existence from its remote beginnings by finding the "lost son" and recovering the moments of that life already lived. Only a simple-minded view would discount these poems as clinical materials or the raw stuff of psychoanalysis; they are nothing of the sort. However private the resources on which Roethke has called, the problem of understanding details of separate poems seldom comes from faults of privacy. The problem may be our own carelessness or impatience. A statement Roethke wrote for Twentieth Century Authors helps to clarify his intentions:

> I have tried to transmute and purify my "life," the
> sense of being defiled by it, in both small and formal
> and somewhat blunt short poems, and latterly, in
> longer poems which try in their rhythms to catch the
> very movement of the mind itself, to trace the spirit-
> ual history of a protagonist (not "I," personally), of all
> haunted and harried men; to make in this series . . .
> a true and not arbitrary order which will permit
> many ranges of feeling, including humor.

The universal character of Roethke's protagonist compels our
participation in these inner travels. By association we are
turned into partial actors of the drama his poems relate.

The journey back into childhood exposes old sores; and
anxiety over questions about death. God, isolation, sexuality,
and parental bonds loom large in the sequence. A desire to
get out of the morass of such disturbances is the most pronounced feature of the protagonist, but he can attain his release only by facing directly all the hazards and powers —
usually psychic ones — that endanger the gradually developing
self. "The Lost Son" is probably the most representative poem
of the group for our purposes because it holds within its careful design the prominent themes of the other poems and so
forms a paradigm of the interior journey. The plan of the poem
falls into several sections tracing the narrator/protagonist's
progress: the setting forth, the quest (with its accompanying
ordeals), the discovery of a new harmony and integrity, the
protagonist's expectation of another phase, and his speculation
on what has occurred.

"The Lost Son" follows the trials and decided advance of
the self or, to use a Jungian term, charts a process of individu-
ation. Beginning, ominously enough, with suggestions of death,
gloom, and ugliness, the poem drops us into the middle of the
child-protagonist's pursuit of freedom and singular identity, a
pursuit frustrated by the shocks experience continues to ad-
minister to the frail equilibrium of his phychic life:

> At Woodlawn I heard the dead cry:
> I was lulled by the slamming of iron,
> A slow drip over stones,
> Toads brooding in wells.

The proximity of destruction and the riddle of his own nature lure the protagonist into action, and he engages himself in the search for liberation:

> Which is the way I take;
> Out of what door do I go,
> Where and to whom?

But confusion dogs his tracks, for the animistic universe where each thing has an independent and ambiguous character is nothing if not deceptive; like the magical forests of fairy tales it presents more false leads than true paths. The creatures, plants, and other entities filling this world, even the friendliest ones, haunt him, and yet he must inquire of them the way out. He looks among the smallest creatures for some reliable guides, though not always with happy results:

> All the leaves stuck out their tongues;
> I shook the softening chalk of my bones,
> Saying, Snail, snail, glister me forward,
> Bird, soft-sigh me home.

Under prevailing conditions movement offers the sole relief to the agonized protagonist, who is also heir to complaints of the flesh. His search brings him at last to "the pit," in the section of that title, and there he reaches the lowest and most dangerous point in the journey. In fact, the pit — clearly a female symbol — signifies the womb or place of his origins, and return to it indicates the risk of defeat, even of death. As the protagonist nears there to ask a fundamental question about life — "Who stunned the dirt into noise?" — he is answered with images of the womb and birth, "the slime of a wet nest." A harsh music of warning jangles his nerves, accompanied in section three, "The Gibber," by further alienation from his surroundings, sexual dilemmas, and shrill discord:

> Dogs of the groin
> Barked and howled,
> The sun was against me,
> The moon would not have me.

> The weeds whined,
> The snakes cried,
> The cows and briars
> Said to me: Die.

At the edge of annihilation the protagonist passes through the "storm's heart" and glides beyond it into a state of calm, another plane of being. The self, having survived the threats to its growth, breaks forth in a mood of spiritual exultation at the sheer pleasure of its attainment:

> These sweeps of light undo me.
> Look, look, the ditch is running white!
> I've more veins than a tree!
> Kiss me, ashes, I'm falling through a dark swirl.

Body and spirit revel in their newly won harmony. The freed self, no longer desperately struggling for independence, dissolves its conflicts with the physical world and, indeed, brings the things of that world into communion with it. The greenhouse, with its rich store of life, to which the young protagonist comes home after the quest within himself, becomes a scene of revelation and symbolizes both the unity and the potentiality of existence. This regenerative cycle is caught in the images of flowers:

> The rose, the chrysanthemum turned toward the light.
> Even the hushed forms, the bent yellowy weeds
> Moved in a slow up-sway.

In the poem's last section the protagonist meditates on his experience. This is "an in-between time" when he can merely await further motions of the spirit. The imagery of the passage recalls T. S. Eliot's "Ash Wednesday" and Four Quartets, and the resemblance is doubtless intentional, as it is also in the later "Meditations of an Old Woman." But Eliot's poems treat spiritual development as the product of individual effort in prayer and contemplation and faith, whereas Roethke sees it as the outcome of a natural process. The latter's religious vision is intuitive and remains far from orthodox Christianity. The narrator of "The Lost Son" hesitates to classify his experience; he will admit of no more than a strange visitation:

> Was it light?
> Was it light within?
> Was it light within light?
> Stillness becoming alive,
> Yet still?

The allusion to Eliot's "still point of the turning world" may be obvious, but the meaning in Roethke's poem should prevent us from taking it as a literal echo. Whatever generates the spiritual odyssey in "The Lost Son" derives from within the protagonist himself and is not based upon a definite external creed:

> A lively understandable spirit
> Once entertained you.
> It will come again.
> Be still
> Wait.

That spirit does "come again" in Roethke's writings. Though he will long be occupied with the progress of the self, the conclusion of this poetic sequence enables him to proceed in different directions.

Roethke's love poems, which began to appear in *The Waking* and have their own section in *Words for the Wind* (1958), manifest certain sharp deviations from earlier self-examination. The amatory verse blends considerations of self with qualities of eroticism and sensuality; but more importantly, the poems introduce and maintain a fascination with something beyond the self, that is, with the figure of the other, or the beloved woman.

The beloved woman of these poems takes various forms. Sometimes she assumes the figure of a wraith, an entrancing specter; sometimes she is purely physical. Her role in the poems can be called that of the female principle or the opposite or the other and frequently involves metamorphosis. Observation of her beauties by the poet leads him to rapport with creation:

> The breath of a long root,
> The shy perimeter
> Of the unfolding rose,

> The green, the altered leaf,
> The oyster's weeping foot,
> And the incipient star—
> Are part of what she is.
> She wakes the ends of life.
>       ("Words for the Wind")

In some way this loved one possesses the elusive secrets of life and its potentialities; she partakes of all that is. The style of the love poems returns to a more formal order after the experimentation of the sequence pieces, but Roethke has obviously learned a new disciplined richness of language and music from that venture.

Fulfillment in love is the theme of a quartet of lyrics, "Four for Sir John Davies," which extends the search for unity and harmony so visible in "The Lost Son" from an internal, psychological probing to a vision of the relationship between the self and the beloved. Drawing its basic metaphor of dancing from Davies' sixteenth-century poem *Orchestra,* which explains the hierarchical plan of the universe through that figure, and from Yeats, who saw in the dance an image of sexual and spiritual reconciliation, the poem leaves the poet's isolated dance at the beginning to discover a transcendent completion in which both lover and beloved share. At the start the poet celebrates the vital energies of the cosmos and of his own rhythmic movements, but the latter are occasionally humorous and lack agility and purpose:

> I tried to fling my shadow at the moon,
> The while my blood leaped with a wordless song.
> Though dancing needs a master, I had none
> To teach my toes to listen to my tongue.

In spite of the pleasures of his single dance, which gives him the feeling of kinship with *things,* the poet seeks a deeper human bond. Attraction to his newly found partner begins between "animal and human heat," but we soon realize that the meeting of the lovers physically has created a corresponding spiritual engagement:

> Incomprehensible gaiety and dread
> Attend all we did. Behind, before,

Lay all the lonely pastures of the dead;
The spirit and the flesh cried out for more.
We two, together, on a darkening day
Took arms against our own obscurity.

As traditionally befits such lovers, they receive, in the poem's third part, one identity. They recall that pair in Donne's "The Canonization" whose pure devotion to one another divorces them from the profane public world and invests them with a sacred or mystical quality, for here also, Roethke writes, "the flesh can make the spirit visible." So this dance, though it originates in human love, is anything but simply ordinary and mundane. The vertical motion of these dancers and the successive alterations they undergo in their ascent establish something close to a religious dimension in this experience. We cannot fail to see how love at its most intense, which the poems portray, is described by the poet as a spiritual event of such magnitude and significance that the lovers' connection with the universe is completely revised. In "The Vigil," the concluding poem, Dante's paradisaical vision is introduced to set off Roethke's own version of an encounter with the eternal; but this moment seems, as it did in "The Lost Son," a condition of inner blessedness the cause of which—outside of human love—is not fully known. Yet there is no doubt that the moment is one of visionary perception rendering creation, as it were, transparent and mysteriously transfiguring the couple.

The world is for the living. Who are they?
We dared the dark to reach the white and warm.
She was the wind when wind was in my way;
Alive at noon, I perished in her form.
Who rise from flesh to spirit know the fall:
The word outleaps the world, and light is all.

Roethke dedicates himself much of the time, particularly in his later work, to the accomplishment of poetic moments such as the one above, and in his Sequence, Sometimes Metaphysical (1963) openly searches for God in poems clearly written from a firsthand knowledge of the soul's dark night. But neither the ecstatic assertions of being nor the often tormented mystical visions hide from Roethke the realities of human life, indeed they are seen as the expression of that life at its zenith, when the self reaches in every direction to the heart of things. The concluding "Meditations of an Old Woman" from *Words for the Wind*, the visionary pieces of *Sequence, Sometimes Metaphysical*, and many other poems that have been published in various journals and are collected in *The Far Field* (1964) amply demonstrate the poet's repeated realization of these moments and his contemplation of the extremes of mortal experience.

"Meditations of an Old Woman," the group of five poems at the end of *Words for the Wind*, is a noteworthy achievement looking toward more recent experiments with a long, prose-style line in "Meditation at Oyster River," "The Rose," and other poems. Composed freely, the "Meditations" are sometimes said to be derivative from *Four Quartets*, but actually they owe, as Roethke confirmed, a larger debt to Whitman in both style and attitude, a debt that becomes even more plain in work that follows. Yet a limited confusion is understandable when we acknowledge that the poems are to a degree an answer to Eliot's mature view. The old woman who is the speaker of these reflective monologues serves as an opposite to Eliot, whose voice we hear throughout *Four Quartets*; and the conclusion at which she arrives in the course of the meditations about herself and the meaning of her existence have little in common with Eliot's. In fact, some passages like the following from "What Can I Tell My Bones?" can only be read as a direct reply to him—with slight overtones of parody:

> It is difficult to say all things are well,
> When the worst is about to arrive;
> It is fatal to woo yourself,
> However graceful the posture.
> Loved heart, what can I say?
> When I was a lark, I sang;
> When I was a worm, I devoured.
>
> The self says, I am;
> The heart says, I am less;
> The spirit says, you are nothing.

Old age, a retrospective look at life, and the approach of death are themes of both Roethke's and Eliot's poems, though their final visions diverge widely. In contrast to the prayer

and asceticism and renunciation of the world on which *Four
Quartets* is founded Roethke's elderly lady embraces in memory and imagination the entire spectrum of her experience,
its joys and delights, its sufferings and disappointments included. These meditations at last do more than just affirm
the precious unevenness of life; they celebrate with religious
exaltation its multitude of beauties and the horizons of possibility in evidence even at its close.

While the narrator of the poems was inspired by Roethke's
mother, she is a mask for the poet too. The poems move with
the changes of her thought, touching on incidents and ideas
of a long lifetime that revolve in her mind with many of
Roethke's favorite images and metaphors from the natural
world: the sun, the wind, the tiny creatures of earth, flowers
and seeds and grass, water, and so on. But the poems turn to
other matters as well; there is a brilliant and savage passage
on modern forms of self-destruction in women, which leads
also to suffering or destruction in those about them:

> I think of the self-involved:
> The ritualists of the mirror, the lonely drinkers,
> The minions of benzedrine and paraldehyde,
> And those who submerge themselves deliberately in trivia,
> Women who become their possessions,
> Shapes stiffening into metal,
> Match-makers, arrangers of picnics—
> What do their lives mean,
> And the lives of their children?—
> The young, brow-beaten early into a baleful silence,
> Frozen by a father's lip, a mother's failure to answer.
> Have they seen, ever, the sharp bones of the poor?
> Or known, once, the soul's authentic hunger,
> Those cat-like immaculate creatures
> For whom the world works?

These lines expose graphically the failure of the self to
rise toward completion, a warping and perversion that contrast
with the stalwart openness to surrounding reality so noticeable
in the old woman. Though she is not always serene and knows
fear, hesitation, and loneliness at certain times, the narrator
can declare, in the last two stanzas of the final poem, her faith

in the durable splendor of the world and in the miraculous transformation or rebirth the spirit works in the individual:

> The sun! The sun! And all we can become!
> And the time ripe for running to the moon!
> In the long fields, I leave my father's eye;
> And shake the secrets from my deepest bones;
> My spirit rises with the rising wind;
> I'm thick with leaves and tender as a dove,
> I take the liberties a short life permits—
> I seek my own meekness;
> I recover my tenderness by long looking.
> By midnight I love everything alive.
> Who took the darkness from the air?
> I'm wet with another life.
> Yea, I have gone and stayed.
>
> What came to me vaguely is now clear,
> As if released by a spirit,
> Or agency outside me.
> Unprayed-for,
> And final.

Though Roethke again chooses to keep his ultimate view somewhat indefinite, his later poetry has in general become more religious and mystical. In other poems from *Words for the Wind,* as well as in his last writings, he addresses himself solely to the presentation of his visionary experience. Some of these poems focus on the negative aspects of this experience, on the dilemmas in which the self is trapped, on psychic and spiritual torments, in a style that is musical but also terse and epigrammatic, with rapidly changing imagery. Roethke's concerns have progressed from those of the earlier childhood sequence poems, but we can still observe his extremely moving evocations of irrational, dreamlike perception. "The Exorcism" is a poem of spiritual pursuit and of the agony of purification that is the necessary preparation for experience or knowledge of the Divine. The poet is brought face to face with his soul's imperfections and must undergo the pain of being parted from them:

1

The gray sheep came. I ran,
My body half in flame.
(Father of flowers, who
Dares face the thing he is?)

As if pure being woke,
The dust rose and spoke;
A shape cried from a cloud,
Cried to my flesh out loud.

(And yet I was not there,
But down long corridors,
My own, my secret lips
Babbling in urinals.)

2

In a dark wood I saw—
I saw my several selves
Come running from the leaves,
Lewd, tiny, careless lives
That scuttled under stones,
Or broke, but would not go.
I turned upon my spine,
I turned and turned again,
A cold God-furious man
Writhing until the last
Forms of his secret life
Lay with the dross of death.

I was myself, alone.

I broke from that low place
Breathing a slower breath,
Cold, in my own dead salt.

Two lines from anther poem, "Elegy," might serve as a
helpful gloss on the theme of "The Exorcism":

I have myself, and bear its weight of woe
That God that God leans down His heart to hear.

Yet "The Exorcism" and "Elegy" show us only the darker
side of Roethke's religious imagination, which is more than

counterbalanced by his positive insight, the gift of a sudden and joyful revelation:

> Dry bones! Dry bones! I find my loving heart,
> Illumination brought to such a pitch
> I see the rubblestones begin to stretch
> As if reality had split apart
> And the whole motion of the soul bare:
> I find that love, and I am everywhere.
>
> ("The Renewal")

Here the poet, at the peak of vision, feels himself entering into the very essence of created things: knower and known are no longer separated by barriers of physical solidity or by appearances. The ordinary rubblestones that break open and disclose their hidden being to the poet do so only as he sees himself in the same undisguised way. Extraordinary as such a revelation is, and it is merely one of a number, we find, especially in some of Roethke's newest and most unusual poems, a profound sense of communion with this reality, though it is set forth in a more relaxed and detailed manner. These poems are freed of regular meters, and use long lines and an approach to reality previously seen in the "Meditations of an Old Woman." Roethke says (Poetry, October 1960); "There are areas of experience in modern life that simply cannot be rendered by either the formal lyric or straight prose. We need the catalogue in our time. We need the eye close on the object, and the poem about the single incident—the animal, the child." That is precisely what we get from Roethke—"the catalogue," "the eye close on the object"—in "Meditation at Oyster River," "Journey to the Interior," "The Rose," "The Long Waters," and other poems. He has named for us, one way or another, his predecessors in this mode as he went along; they are Christopher Smart, Walt Whitman, and D. H. Lawrence. To catch the feeling of this sort of poem, so rare in modern literature, we have to read more than two or three lines; here, then, are sections four and five of "The Long Waters":

### IV

> In the vaporous gray of early morning,
> Over the thin, feathery ripples breaking lightly against the
>     irregular shoreline —

Feathers of the long swell, burnished, almost oily —
A single wave comes in like the neck of a great swan
Swimming slowly, its back ruffled by the light cross-winds,

To a tree lying flat, its crown half broken.
I remember a stone breaking the eddying current,
Neither white nor red, in the dead middle way,
Where impulse no longer dictates, nor the darkening
    shadow,
A vulnerable place,
Surrounded by sand, broken shells, the wreckage of water.

## V

As light reflects from a lake, in late evening,
When bats fly, close to slightly tilting brownish water,
And the low ripples run over a pebbly shoreline,
As a fire, seemingly long dead, flares up from a down-
    draft of air in a chimney,
Or the breeze moves over the knees from a low hill,
So the sea wind wakes desire.
My body shimmers with a light flame.

I see in the advancing and retreating waters
The shape that came from my sleep, weeping:
The eternal one, the child, the swaying vine branch,
The numinous ring around the opening flower,
The friend that runs before me on the windy headlands,
Neither voice nor vision.

I, who came back from the depths laughing too loudly,
Become another thing;
My eyes extend beyond the farthest bloom of the waves;
I lose and find myself in the long waters;
I am gathered together once more;
I embrace the world.


This poem, like the other "catalogue" poems of this last
phase of Roethke's work, enumerates objects and details of
the world fondly remembered and treasured as parts of the
poet's spiritual odyssey. Thus the contemplation of external
details in the universe never takes complete precedence over

the consciousness of the poet; a relationship always exists between what has been seen in nature and the interior state of the observer. It seems clear from the end of "The Long Waters" that Roethke experiences a cycle of dispersal and reunification somewhat similar to the pattern in "The Exorcism" or "The Renewal," though the "embrace" of the final line here does not come with a blinding flash of mystical intuition but rather as a condition of the poet's soul gradually reached through the entire slow movement of the poem.

"The Long Waters" and the visionary lyrics of *Sequence, Sometimes Metaphysical* exemplify the last stage in the long metamorphosis of the self that Roethke attained in his poetry. This fundamental theme gave his work unity and yet never restricted the astonishing variety, invention, and artistry of which he was capable. Other modern poets have taken the self as theme, but no one has so fruitfully sounded his own subjective depths. Nor have any of his contemporaries been granted such an intimate communion with nature. (Eberhart grows ecstatic over the mystical suggestiveness of natural things on occasion, but he does not penetrate so deeply into it as Roethke, and he does not have the latter's vision of a profound evolutionary pattern.) Roethke's uncanny sensibilities led him to comprehend and to incorporate in his writing the continuous but nearly imperceptible communication that goes on among all living things, as well as to know moments of heightened awareness in which his relation and that of the created world to the Divine were suggested. He once said (in *New World Writing* 4) that the poet "may be lucky enough, on occasion, to create a complete reality in a single poem." Few poets of modern times have known this luck as often as Theodore Roethke.

# The Lost World of
# Randall Jarrell

*by* DENIS DONOGHUE

One of Randall Jarrell's favorite poems was "During Wind and Rain." Hardy's poem invokes the lost worlds, the songs of *Under the Greenwood Tree,* the English villages, the gallantry of bright things on the lawn. In each stanza there are seven lines, five to bring back the old images, two to concede their loss; but these two have the last word, the "sick leaves," the "white storm-birds," the "rotten rose," and the rain cutting the names on the gravestone. "Ah, no; the years, the years." It is a noble poem, keeping up appearances when there is nothing else to be done. The stanzas begin with a lift of feeling; to every dog his day of remembered ease. The loss is held at memory's length, but in the last two lines the years break in upon reverie. It is easy to guess that the poem pleased Jarrell because of its gallantry, the bravery of its tone in defeat. Gallantry: as in *King Lear* when Edgar says:

> Men must endure
> Their going hence, even as their coming hither:
> Ripeness is all. Come on.

and Gloucester answers

> And that's true too.

This is the burden of Jarrell's poems: "And that's true too."
The poems begin with loss. The lost world is, to use Eliot's phrase, "the ground of our beseeching," Act I. An entire book is called *Losses*. In "When I Was Home Last Christmas . . ." the poet says:

> There is no one left to care
> For all we said, and did, and thought—
> The world we were.

"Never again," the voice in "Moving" says, recalling dear dead schooldays, "Never again/Will Augusta be the capital of Maine." "Children's Arms" calls to "this first Rome/Of childhood," and several poems are elegies for the penny world of Pop, Mama, and Dandeen "in her black/Silk." In "The Lost Children" a mother, observing that her daughter has grown up and that the air of home is thin, reflects:

> She makes few demands; you are grateful for the few.

In "Woman":

> A girl hesitates a moment in mid-air
> And settles to the ground a wife, a mother.

There is more to be said, and the poet says it in the same poem, but this is Act I, the cause of all. The figure the feeling makes is given in "Thinking of the Lost World":

> Back in Los Angeles, we missed
> Los Angeles.

The terms of loss are the inveterate relationships: father, mother, child, wife, husband. Jarrell's poetry is a sequence of Mutability Cantos, tracing the crucial situations back to the point at which, changing, they withered into a new and darker truth. The tracing is done, mostly, in fear. In "The Märchen," "the darkness quakes with blood." Sometimes the tone tries to hold itself well back from the edge. There is a time for speaking of the woe that is in marriage, but Jarrell tries to postpone that speech; meanwhile, keep the cry muted. In "Next Day" a woman at the supermarket, her pilgrim's progress confined to a choice of Cheer, Joy, and All, is troubled by what she has become, "commonplace and solitary." Life makes few demands upon her and perhaps, like the other mother, she is grateful for those few. The demands she makes upon life are not exorbitant:

> Now that I'm old, my wish
> Is womanish:
> That the boy putting groceries in my car
> See me. It bewilders me he doesn't see me.

Not "enrages" or even "annoys"; just "bewilders." In this first act there is bound to be a moment in which the bewilderment is complete and fixed. In Jarrell's poetry it occurs when the voice says something and then, since the something said is disconsolate, says the opposite, hoping that this is the trick, the key; and finds that it makes no difference.

> The husband answers, "Life is life,"
> And when his wife calls to him from the kitchen
> He tells her who it was, and what he wanted.
> Beating the whites of seven eggs, the beater
> Asks her her own opinion; she says, "Life
> Is life." "See how it sounds to say it isn't,"
> The beater tempts her. "Life is not life,"
> She says. It sounds the same. Putting her cake
> Into the oven, she is satisfied
> Or else dissatisfied: it sounds the same.

I have spoken of this as Act I, where the dramatist gives the first hints. With the wisdom of hindsight we can say, looking at Jarrell's poetry: there, there is where it began. The poems in *Blood for a Stranger* and *Little Friend, Little Friend* are not his choice work. In these the feeling is raw, and Jarrell was not good with raw wounds. He needed, for the good of the poetry, a wound not quite healed and yet as close to healing as

it would ever come. He needed to be able to go a little way off,
far enough to talk about the experience. He was not a dramatic
poet. Reading his poems is not like seeing *King Lear*: it is like
the relief of breaking a wounded silence, letting the pain drain
away in words, in companionable talk. When we say that his
idiom is conversational, we mean that it is like the conversation that helps, in trouble; balm to hurt minds.

Meanwhile there is Act II, since we cannot live forever in
loss even if the loss lives forever in us. As Gloucester says,
"O cruel! O you Gods!" Act II is the place for blame, recrim-
ination, fighting back. As Jarrell says, "Oh, it's not *right*," the
italics the fury in the words of "The Night before the Night
before Christmas," heard again in "The Face." Some of Jarrell's
most celebrated poems come from this second act: cadences
of protest, as in "The Prince." "A man dies like a rabbit, for a
use"; followed by: "What will they pay me, when I die, to
die?" The war poems are here, and poems like "Jews at Haifa"
about the war after the War. Some years later we hear the
protest, rueful now, *diminuendo,* in the prose of *A Sad Heart
at the Supermarket* and many of the poems in *The Woman
at the Washington Zoo.* Perhaps it is the residue of the war
feeling which, turning sour, sets the cruel moments astir in
*Pictures from an Institution.* In "The Snow-Leopard" Jarrell
speaks of "the brute and geometrical necessity." In "Siegfried"
this necessity is reported as dull fact:

> It happens as it does because it does.
> It is necessary to understand; if you are still
> In this year of our warfare, indispensable
> In general, and in particular dispensable
> As a cartridge, a life

This is the "murderous/Dull will" invoked in "1945: The Death
of the Gods," arranging, as in "The Sick Nought," that the
soldier is "something there are millions of." "The book is finished. I tell you you're not in it," the poet says to the men in
the Overseas Replacement Depot. Reading the protest poems
again when another protest is in the air, I find that those which
have not survived intact are dead in their public manner. They
sound as if, for a proper reading, they need a megaphone and
Hyde Park, a public-address system and Madison Square Garden:

Man is born in chains, and everywhere we see him dead.
On your earth they sell nothing but our lives.
You knew that what you died for was our deaths?

There is nothing wrong with these lines, in principle, except
that they come from a poetic world that Jarrell never owned.
He did not lose it, because he never had it. The lines witness
a failure of the feeling to secure its proper voice, its proper
form. In an early poem Jarrell invokes "that strange speech/In
which each sound sets out to seek each other." In poems like
"The Emancipators" the sounds set out to seek each other but,
not finding, settle for other sounds, more accessible, merely
because they are there. The sounds have a better chance when
they are less portentously directed, left to find their own companions. This is to say that Jarrell's poems are best when scored
for a voice, like Cordelia's, "soft, gentle, and low"; even when
the words are large in content:

                              nothing comes from nothing,
        The darkness from the darkness. Pain comes from the
            darkness
        And we call it wisdom: It is pain.

There is nothing remarkable in these lines except the tone of
their delivery. The crucial moment is in the gap between the
last two sentences: what is said, in the words, is only important because it frames the silence between one apprehension
and the next. Among the modern poets Eliot is the greatest
master of these silences. But Jarrell is more than Eliot's pupil
in this resource. He is particularly vivid in the relation between silence and speech, the flow of feeling between them.
So he does wonderful things with a full stop, a colon, a question mark. In "A Street off Sunset" the voice speaks of Mama,
her face "half a girl's," wringing a chicken's neck; and the
child thinking:

                    . . . Could such a thing
        Happen to anything? It could to a rabbit, I'm afraid;
        It could to—
                "Mama, you won't kill Reddy ever,
        You won't ever, will you?"

This experience, which recurs in several poems, is beautifully registered. Its horror is domestic: this is not to say that the horror is small. Jarrell's special area of feeling is the private loss, held but not resolved in the structure of daily things; where the domestic order conceals—but not really, and not for long—the private anarchy; where speech is bewildered in silence. His sad hearts are most warmly felt at the supermarket, his wounded souls at the Washington Zoo. This is why the conversational idiom is so close to the shape of the poems, the shape of their feeling; why, too, this poet got so much, in this way, from Hardy, Yeats, and Frost. Saying "Oh, it's not right" is momentous when things seem to be right: right, meaning normal, ordinary, daily. There is no point in saying "Oh, it's not right" if you are in Hiroshima. In "Three Bills" we are to imagine a man, the poet perhaps, in the restaurant at the Plaza, breakfast time, overhearing a conversation between a man, his wife, and another woman, all rich. The man goes off to the lavatory and his wife complains to her friend:

"We can't stay anywhere. We haven't stayed a month
In one place for the last three years.
He flirts with the yardboys and we have to leave."

The friend is sorry; and the poet in turn, is sorry; sorry that the wife, the blonde, "the suffused face about to cry/Or not to cry—"

was a face that under different
Circumstances would not have been beautiful, a woman's.

I.e.: "Oh, it's not right."

Act III: "An English Garden in Austria"; a voice asking, "And how shall we bear it?" The first answer is: by recalling everything else. Jarrell is a little Proust to whom, as someone has said, the only real paradises are lost paradises, spectrally recovered in memory and vision. Memory is compulsive in this poet, as if he feared that by losing anything he would lose everything. This is why so much of Jarrell's experience is seen under glass, and the death of the ball turret gunner, in a famous poem, is a sinister version of the boyhood image, the magic gone wrong. In "Children's Arms":

> The glass encloses
> As glass does, a womanish and childish
> And doggish universe. We press our noses
> To the glass and wish

In "The One Who Was Different" the poet thinks of a dead woman and, rearranging the conditions, thinks of her, instead, lying

> Encased in crystal, continually mortal,
> While the years rolled over you . . . .

Hence the mirror's magic, sometimes black, sometimes the whitest white; as in "Woman," where the morning sun, "grayer for its mirroring," is "perfected" in the wife's shining eyes. Hence also the dream poems, sometimes nightmare, sometimes what we see when we press our noses to the glass and wish. In "A Sick Child" the child longs so hard for things to be different that they must be different, mustn't they?

Jarrell has a wonderful feeling for dreams and for the children who attend them, for those countries to which a child creeps "out of his own life." He wrote many poems to chart those countries, planting them with their proper vines. In the nightmare poems the proof of desolation is the thought that the dream things are just the same as daily things. In "The Truth," when the bombs on London drive a child away from father and mother and the father is lost in one way and the mother in another, the child knows that the mother is no longer the same:

> Sometimes she was the same, but that was when I
> dreamed it.
> I could tell I was dreaming, she was just the same.

The wounded soldier in "A Field Hospital" comes out of his dream: "the old mistake." Dream is a way of bearing it. So is fiction, anything to make it new. Jarrell wrote several poems about children seen in a lending library. He speaks of "one cure for Everychild's diseases/Beginning: *Once upon a time there was.*" We live, the same poem has it, by "trading another's sorrow for our own"; trading "another's/Impossibilities, still unbelieved in, for our own . . . ." Stevens said of the

Supreme Fiction: "It Must Change." To Jarrell, that kind of change is the fiction itself, "dear to all things not to themselves endeared." So in "Children's Arms" the island sings to the child: *"Believe! Believe!"* We bear it, if we can, by make-believe, dreams, figments, fictions. The verbal equivalent, in the detail, is wit; where the poet, almost a child, creeps out of his own life, fighting the good poetic fight, slaying the prosaic dragon. Mostly the dragon comes as authority, the way of the world, Army Regulations, public cliché. The poet bears these things by gulling them, tripping them on their own banana skins. In "A War":

> There set out, slowly, for a Different World,
> At four, on winter mornings, different legs . . .
> *You can't break eggs without making an omelette*
> —That's what they tell the eggs.

When the poet asks, "And how shall we bear it?" his answer is "Lightly, lightly." This is his way into Act IV, the place where, traditionally, the dramatist releases "the pity of it all." Jarrell is lavish in pity. Indeed, he is never afraid of his feelings, or ashamed of them, or even proud of them. He is always pleased to appreciate the natural thing, liking the way a baby bat holds on tight to its mother's tail and the different ways an owl tests the corners of the night. The poet's special feeling in Act IV is care; its particular cadence, "And yet, and yet." He does not parade his care. Simply, he cares. It is typical of his sensibility that in an art gallery he notices the guard before he looks at the pictures; that when a girl talks of "the dailiness of life," he saves the day with an image of water:

> Water, cold, so cold! you cup your hands
> And gulp from them the dailiness of life.

After the cruelty of the gods we have to care for what remains, such as it is. If the rules of the game are unjust, so much the worthier those men of chance who play it well. Character is a game splendidly played: therefore good like the other good things, "to go on being," life itself with all its cruelty, ordinary things like sunshine, rain, childhood, the life of Nollekens. Or literature, one of the best ordinary things.

In criticism, in teaching, praise was the highest form of Jarrell's care. Robert Lowell has written that eulogy was Jarrell's glory as a critic, praise that moved mountains of inertia and condescension. Who has ever spoken so well for Whitman's lists merely by saying of them: yes, but what lists! Jarrell's own lists make an impeccable anthology, the classic unexpected poems from Hardy, Ransom, Rilke, Frost, Williams, Shakespeare, Marianne Moore. When he was wrong, as I think he was wrong in that early essay on Stevens, he found an occasion to try again and this time got it right. Indeed, his reading of favorite poets was so devoted that he seemed to think his response a paltry effort until he had almost made himself over in their image. So I think of "A Soul" as a Ransom poem, "To the New World" an Auden poem, "The Märchen" a Tate poem. And if someone loved Hardy so much that he wanted to write a Hardy poem, could he do better than Jarrell in "The Blind Sheep"? I am often surprised that Jarrell did not write a Yeats poem, but there are Frost poems, like "Money" and "Field and Forest." These poems are thank-you notes mailed to the poets who showed Jarrell what might still be done.

I am not sure about Act V. We are accustomed to muted endings, as in *King Lear* when Edgar says simply, "The weight of this sad time we must obey." In Jarrell's Act V the crucial poem is "Thinking of the Lost World." A man goes back, in reverie, to California, finding smog in Los Angeles where a child knew sunshine. "The orange groves are all cut down. . . ." So he tries to bear it, lightly:

> I say to my old self: "I believe, Help thou
> Mine unbelief."

The images of boyhood, the strangled chicken and the woman with the lion, are now parts of science fiction: this is not to say that they have been replaced, in belief, by anything else. There is a moment in *Timon of Athens* when Timon, who has been composing his epitaph, says to Flavius:

>                            My long sickness
> Of health and living now begins to mend,
> And nothing brings me all things.

It is a moment entirely in keeping with that all-or-nothing play. "Thinking of the Lost World" is also written, imaginatively, at the end of the line. So it goes back to the old images and gestures: one thing copying its opposite, a shadow miming a shadow, trading one emptiness for another. The poem ends, the last poem in Jarrell's last book:

> Where's my own hand? My smooth
> White bitten-fingernailed one? I seem to see
> A shape in tennis shoes and khaki riding-pants
> Standing there empty-handed; I reach out to it
> Empty-handed, my hand comes back empty,
> And yet my emptiness is traded for its emptiness,
> I have found that Lost World in the Lost and Found
> Columns whose gray illegible advertisements
> My soul has memorized world after world:
> LOST—NOTHING. STRAYED FROM NOWHERE.
>     NO REWARD.
> I hold in my own hands,in happiness,
> Nothing: the nothing for which there's no reward.

Gloucester speaks to Edmund of "the quality of nothing." Stevens speaks, in "The Snow Man," a poem dear to Jarrell, of the "mind of winter," the superbly qualified mind of one who willingly sees wintry things:

> the listener, who listens in the snow,
> And, nothing himself, beholds
> Nothing that is not there and the nothing that is.

This second nothing is the one that brings all things, Timon's nothing in Act V. In "Prologues to What Is Possible" Stevens writes of

> The way the earliest single light in the evening sky, in
>     spring,
> Creates a fresh universe out of nothingness by adding
>     itself.

This is what the mind of winter comes to, after the long sickness. Where there is nothing, Stevens implies, there is man, there is his imagination. Stevens thinks of it as a wonderful resilience of perception. It is what Jarrell comes to, at the end:

winter, and then, "in happiness," the mind of winter. In his
case I think of it as a resilience, equally wonderful, of love.
Call it gallantry. As Yeats sang:

> Man is in love and loves what vanishes,
> What more is there to say?

# Robert Lowell:
# A Poetry Of Rebellion

*by* HUGH B. STAPLES

Contemporary American poetry is marked by a return to formalism on the one hand and by a violent rebellion against traditional forms on the other. As Robert Lowell said recently:

"Our modern American poetry has a snarl on its hands. Something earth-shaking was started about fifty years ago by the generation of Eliot, Frost and William Carlos Williams. We have had a run of poetry as inspired, and perhaps as important and sadly brief as that of Baudelaire and his successors, or that of the dying Roman Republic and early Empire. Two poetries are now competing, a cooked and a raw. The cooked, marvellously expert, often seems laboriously concocted to be tasted and digested by a graduate seminar. The raw, huge blood-dripping gobbets of unseasoned experience are dished up for midnight listeners. There is a poetry that can only be studied, and a poetry that can only be declaimed, a poetry of pedantry, and a poetry of scandal."[1] Lowell's own work fits

"A Poetry of Rebellion" by Hugh B. Staples. From *Robert Lowell: The First Twenty Years*, pp. 13-21. Copyright © 1962 by Hugh B. Staples. Reprinted by permission of the author and Farrar, Straus and Cudahy.

[1] Programme of the Boston Arts Festival (June 1960), 13. The quotation is from Lowell's acceptance speech on the occasion of receiving the National Book Award in 1960.

into neither of these categories; neither "academic" nor "Beat,"
it is both learned and savage. His four volumes of verse, the
result of more than twenty years of poetic activity, represent
a canon of sufficient stature and complexity to warrant a sys-
tematic survey. My aim in this introductory study is to place
the individual poems and volumes in the context of the work
as a whole, and through such perspective to illumine his intention and achievement more fully than has yet been done
in the scattered criticism. In tracing the outlines, at least, of his
poetic career so far — of his development from the conflicts
and agonies of *Land of Unlikeness* to their partial resolution in
*Lord Weary's Castle;* from the preoccupations with the meaning of human experience as they are dramatized in *The Mills
of the Kavanaughs* to their mature handling in *Life Studies,*
my hope is to assist the reader to a clear understanding of the
individual poems and to a recognition that, as Elizabeth Bishop
put it: " . . . in the middle of our worst century so far, we
have produced a magnificent poet."

Many of Lowell's best poems require a knowledge of his
background, his local allusion and his special religious atti-
tudes. Another difficulty is style: the harsh, grating diction of
his early work is occasionally so disruptive as to prevent the
reader from seeing the mosaic pattern of his jagged bits of
language. His subjects are varied; the problem at the outset is
to discover a general characteristic common to all these pray-
ers, meditations, visions, jeremiads, tributes, monologues and
elegies, and then to posit a principle of development in the
successive poetic techniques by which they are rendered.

The most immediate and general impression is that these
poems, from the pessimistic meditations of "The Park Street
Cemetery" to the carefully understated horror of "Skunk Hour"
reflect a profound and constant dissatisfaction with humanity
and with the universe. His lyrical preachments against an idea,
a society or a symbolic human figure are stern and sombre,
ranging in mood from violent antipathy to muted scorn. No
stranger to graveyards, Lowell is fascinated by the ultimate
negation. As he states in "Colloquy in Black Rock":

> All discussions
> End in the mud-flat detritus of death.

His landscapes are filled with rubble, sewage and filth — the end products of erosion, corruption and decay. Human success, normal love, conventional beauty have no place in his vision of the modern world. At the outset, Lowell's rebellion is total. His war is not with a time, a place, the fabric of a specific society or a particular political system, but against the pressures of reality itself. To understand his development as a poet, we have to see how Lowell's sense of antagonism to the order of things in general becomes increasingly focused on more clearly defined targets; the history of his career is the history of his gradual delimitation of his subject, which ultimately becomes himself.

Perhaps this is too bleak a picture. Nothing can come of nothing, and it would be wrong to suppose that Lowell's programme is one of mere anarchy and iconoclasm. His poetry as a whole can be seen as a constructive search for positive values — in Catholic mysticism, in the perspectives of history, in human relationships. In his latest volume, Lowell begins to find in the operation of the memory a means of investing the events of his personal life with a measure of permanence and satisfaction. In this sense, his gradual accommodation to reality reaches its climax in two of the *Life Studies* poems: "Home After Three Months Away" — a tender and affectionate lyric to his infant daughter, and "Man and Wife" — his only published love poem.

But such affirmations are few and late; typically the conflicts in his poems remain unresolved, and the theme of rebellion remains dominant. His long quarrel with actuality focuses upon two main targets: society (past and present) and authority, through whose agency history becomes a chronicle of human suffering. In his first volume, Lowell appears so horrified by the spectacle of contemporary chaos that he can scarcely bring himself to comment on it in realistic terms. Cut off from the sight of God, modern man wanders about in his Land of Unlikeness, driven by greed and cruelty. Boston is as arid and as unreal as the Waste Land itself — a place where "the ground has settled in *saecula saeculorum*," where "the ancient blood of Cain is burning, burning the unburied grain." "Cistercians in Germany" captures the mindless brutality of the Third Reich, but Lowell's indictment of the American war effort in "Christmas Eve in the Time of War" is equally bitter.

Though the latter poem is subtitled "A Capitalist Meditates by a Civil War Monument," in most of the poems there is little social satire as such, for humanity seems to have become corrupted beyond the reach of satire. The note of lamentation is only balanced by a not very confident plea for personal salvation. Two lines from "The Drunken Fisherman" could serve as the book's epigraph:

> Is there no way to cast my hook
> Out of this dynamited brook?

The title of the first poem in *Lord Weary's Castle* — "The Exile's Return" — takes on an added significance if we see in the volume as a whole Lowell's attempt to relocate his conflicts on solider ground, to grapple with reality in a more intimate way. To be sure, his hostility towards the actual still provokes him into such flights of fantasy as "Where the Rainbow Ends" (a vision of the Last Judgment descending on Boston) and to such *cauchemar* as this from "As a Plane Tree by the Water":

> Darkness has called to darkness, and disgrace
> Elbows about our windows in this planned
> Babel of Boston where our money talks
> And multiplies the darkness of a land
> Of preparation where the Virgin walks
> And roses spiral her enamelled face
> Or fall to splinters on unwatered streets.
> Our Lady of Babylon, go by, go by,
> I was once the apple of your eye;
> Flies, flies are on the plane tree, on the streets.

But even here the locale is more particularized than in such earlier lamentations as "Scenes from the Historic Comedy," or "The Wood of Life." Similarly, Lowell places his diatribes against the secular nature of society, its materialism and inhumanity in actual settings: Black Rock, Concord, Dunbarton, Nantucket.

This tendency towards increasing specificity becomes most pronounced in *Life Studies,* where every poem has its own address, thus:

This is the way day breaks in Bowditch Hall at McLean's;
                              ("Waking in the Blue")

Nautilus Island's hermit
heiress still lives through winter in her Spartan cottage . . .
                              ("Skunk Hour")

Given a year,
I walked on the roof of the West Street Jail . . .
                    ("Memories of West Street and Lepke")

As the geographical limits of his poetry contract, Lowell's vision turns inward, so that in his latest work, he is concerned less with cosmic conflicts or social satire than with his own emotional reactions to people and situations important to his personal life. The note of rebellion is still present, though diminished; instead, there is a note of compromise, of at least a partial acceptance of the order of things.

For Lowell, as for Blake, the human dilemma is symbolized in the conflict between experience and innocence, between the representatives of authority: generals, kings, tyrants, bigots and exploiters — and their victims: children, primitives, animals. Even in *Land of Unlikeness,* where the centre of the stage is usually reserved for Divine antagonists, several poems have for their theme the futility of secular power and the evil that results from it. "What are Sam Adams and Cotton Mather?" he asks, and it is a dusty answer that comes from the tombstones of Park Street Cemetery. Because "the Puritan Dracos" used religion to justify their greed and hatred, their "stocks and Paradises" have become a heritage of evil. [2] Similarly, the suffering of the innocents at the hands of the powerful is symbolized by the death of a child in both "The Boston Nativity" and "Christmas Eve in the Time of War." Here too are the first of a series of poems denigrating the man on horseback: "Napoleon Crosses the Beresina" and "Dea Roma." In *Lord Weary's Castle,* Lowell's sense of outrage at the

---

[2] The point is made clearer in the *Lord Weary's Castle* version of the same poem, which is expanded and re-titled "At the Indian Killer's Grave". Also, Lowell has added this epigraph — from Hawthorne's "The Gray Champion":
"Here also, are the veterans of King Philip's War, who burned villages and slaughtered young and old, with pious fierceness, while the godly souls throughout the land were helping them with prayer."

abuse of power by historical figures continues to assert itself
in the satirical portraits of Charles V and Louis XVI, and his
rebellion against the falsity of the New England Calvinist tradition reaches a new pitch of intensity in the two masterful
indictments of Jonathan Edwards. But his dissatisfaction with
the present is equally strong: as he protests in "The Holy Innocents":

> Still
> The world out-Herods Herod; and the year,
> The nineteen-hundred forty-fifth year of grace,
> Lumbers with losses up the clinkered hill
> Of our purgation . . . .

In this volume too, the conflicts of *Land of Unlikeness* are
treated in more personal terms in the poem entitled simply
"Rebellion." This enigmatic nightmare-vision of patricide is
more than an expression of psychological hostility towards the
father-figure as a symbol of authority; the identification of the
father with the heirlooms makes it clear that the murder is a
rejection of tradition as well:

> There was rebellion, father, when the mock
> French windows slammed and you have backward,
>     rammed
> Into your heirlooms, screens, a glass-cased clock,
> The highboy quaking to its toes. You damned
> My arm that cast your house upon your head
> And broke the chimney flintlock on your skull.

The same antagonism to parents as symbols of a paralysing
tradition supplies the motive power for the long poem "Between the Porch and the Altar" and is further adumbrated in
"The Death of the Sheriff." However, the expiation of inherited guilt receives its most extended treatment in *The Mills
of the Kavanaughs*. Here the sins of the fathers, symbolized
by the patriarchal Red Kavanaugh

> . . . who burned and buried child
> And squaw and elder in their river bed
> A pine-tree shilling a scalp . . . .

are visited upon the children, whose fate it is to enact the last
scene in the fall of the House of Kavanaugh.

Lowell's rebellion is the expression of a very complex mind and imagination. Most of his poems are networks of interlocking ironies; they are composed of elaborate patterns of synthesis and disintegration, doubt and faith, affirmation and rejection. A good part of their difficulty arises out of his characteristic ambivalence towards his subject and this ambivalence is seen most strongly in his attitude towards tradition. For example, as we have noted, Lowell's satirical analysis of the deficiencies of the rulers of early New England is a dominant feature of the early poetry. Yet even in *Land of Unlikeness* there is a kind of wistful admiration for their achievements and an acknowledgement that they, too, were involved in the rebellion. Thus, in "In Memory of Arthur Winslow" Lowell explains his grandfather's pursuit of wealth this way:

You must have hankered for our family's craft:
The block-house Edward made, the Governor,
At Marshfield, and the slight coin-silver spoons
Some Winslow hammered thinner than Revere,
And General Stark's coarse bas-relief of bronze
Set on your granite shaft
In rough Dunbarton; for what else could bring
You, Arthur, to the veined and alien West,
But devil's notions that your gold, at least,
Would give back life to men who whipped the British
      King?

Similarly, in the later poem, "Mother Marie Therese," the epicureanism of the rebellious, aristocratic nun is favorably compared to the pious asceticism of her associates. Finally, in *Life Studies,* Lowell begins to find positive values in the leisurely world of his Victorian grandparents and in the tradition for which they stand.

In his personal as well as his poetic career, Lowell has not been content with mere iconoclasm; his rejection of one tradition has often been accomplished by his adherence to another. Dissatisfied with the Protestantism of his ancestors, he was not content to take up a merely agnostic position—instead he sought for spiritual values in the dogma of the Catholic Church. Finding Harvard, to which his family heritage had consigned him, something less than a nest of singing birds, he removed to Kenyon, where a new creative tradition was being developed by John Crowe Ransom. Unable to become, like his father, a naval officer, Lowell chose the role of conscientious objector, which he seems to have embraced with the zeal of a Christian martyr. In all these actions, as in all his poetry, he reveals a deep absorption in the historical sense without which, as T. S. Eliot pointed out in his famous essay, the individual talent cannot grow.                    ·

It is, at any rate, only in terms of some such notion of modifying tradition *within its own framework* that we can account for the central paradox of his poetry: that this poetry of rebellion is cast into highly traditional forms, that these outcries against order are themselves ordered by rigidly formal rhyme schemes and conventional stanzaic patterns adapted from the poetic achievements of the past.

As Allen Tate notes in his introduction, every poem in *Land of Unlikeness* has a strict formal pattern either of Lowell's devising or borrowed from other poets. Thus "In Memory of Arthur Winslow" is cast in the exact rhyme scheme of Matthew Arnold's "The Scholar Gipsy," "Satan's Confession" has a stanzaic structure adapted from Drayton's "To the Virginian Voyage"; "Concord" and "Salem" are examples of the Italian and Shakespearean sonnet respectively. Lowell's adherence to traditional forms in his first volume may perhaps be explained in part as an apprentice's acceptance of the disciplines of his craft, but these poems are more than mere "school figures" turned out for an instructor's approval. In each of them he attempts to get at the meaning of the universe and human experience, and an expression of rebellion against the order of things. In deliberately accepting the artistic demands imposed by traditional forms, Lowell has found a means of controlling the volcanic flow of his imagination.

This pouring of new wine into old bottles is not always successful in the earliest work. Sometimes Lowell seems unable to abide by the arbitrary metrical laws he has imposed on himself, with the result that individual lines are choked and cramped in an angry stutter:

Gall, or spiked bone-vat, siphons His bilged blood . . . .
("Christ for Sale")

Here the stamped tabloid, ballot, draft or actress....
                              ("Cistercians in Germany")

Sometimes too, the bondage of rhyming leads him into inappropriate, even faulty, decisions as in this stanza from "Satan's Confession":

The Hypocrite will plaster
Brimstone of the Abyss
    On Adam's every whim
    And life and limb
Abjure their Master
Man is a syphilis!

But on the whole, by casting his effusions into traditional moulds, Lowell has gained a measure of control over his material without any loss of force.

By *Lord Weary's Castle,* he has obviously acquired more experience and skill. Here there is less sense of strain; style, form and matter merge harmoniously. In the best poems, such as "Colloquy in Black Rock" and "The Quaker Graveyard in Nantucket," form becomes functional — no longer the mere container or limiting device it sometimes is in *Land of Unlikeness.* Here, too, Lowell depends much less on rigidly traditional forms; instead, he begins to introduce marked variations of his own in such poems as "Rebellion" and "At a Bible House." This process of experimentation continues in *The Mills of the Kavanaughs,* where the sixteen-line stanzas of the title poem consist of apparently conventional heroic couplets. On a second reading, however, it becomes obvious that the intricately varied rhyme scheme exceeds what is needed simply to avoid monotony. What seems to be happening in *The Mills of the Kavanaughs* is that Lowell, having mastered the traditional forms, is engaging in a search for a more individualized style. That is to say, reacting against the conventional, he is preoccupied with setting for himself increasingly difficult formal problems to solve. The direction that his ingenuity takes at this point is towards more and more complicated rhyme schemes combined, as in "Thanksgiving's Over," with a fantastically elaborate metrical pattern. This poem is almost unintelligible, partly becouse of the very odd religious symbolism involved, but more importantly because in this poem, Lowell has reached the point where decadence begins—where considerations of style and form become so obsessive as to obscure meaning and intention.

"Thanksgiving's Over" is the last poem in *The Mills of the Kavanaughs,* and it marks the climax of Lowell's preoccupation with form for its own sake. In *Life Studies,* published after an interval of eight years, the structure of his poetry is much looser than anything written earlier. Just as the sense of strain, conflict and rebellion is markedly reduced as Lowell tends towards an acceptance of reality, so the rigidity of his early period gives way to a more informal, even casual, blend of free verse and occasional rhyme. To be sure, there are a few reminders of his old contention with the order of things in such poems as "Beyond the Alps" and "Skunk Hour"; significantly, it is these poems that bear the closest resemblance on a formal level to his earlier work.

In its broadest outlines, then, the curve of Lowell's development as a poet in his first two decades is from a posture of rebellion towards a position of acceptance. And the parallel tendency away from his initial formalism towards relative flexibility is not the paradox it seems, but a function of his poetic needs.

# The Poetry of
# Richard Wilbur

*by* FREDERIC E. FAVERTY

Everything in the world is strange and marvellous to
well-open eyes. This faculty of wonder is the delight . . .
which leads the intellectual man through life in the per-
petual ecstasy of the visionary. His special attribute is the
wonder of the eyes. Hence it was that the ancients gave
Minerva her owl, the bird with ever-dazzled eyes. (Jose
Ortega y Gasset, *Revolt of the Masses.*)[1]

For a comparatively young poet, Richard Wilbur (b. 1921)
has received considerable recognition from official quarters:
the Harriet Monroe Prize in poetry, 1948; the Oscar Blumenthal
Prize, 1950; the Edna St. Vincent Millay Memorial Award,
1957; the National Book Award, 1957; and the Pulitzer Prize,
1957. In recognition of his promise as well as his achievement
he has been granted fellowships by the Guggenheim Foundation

"The Poetry of Richard Wilbur" by Frederic E. Faverty. From *Poets
in Progress*, ed. by Edward Hungerford, pp. 59-72. Copyright © 1962 by
Northwestern University Press. Reprinted by permission of the author
and Northwestern University Press.
[1]Quoted under "The Owl" in *A Bestiary*, compiled by Richard Wilbur, illustrated by Alexander Calder (Pantheon Books, 1955).

(1952) and by the American Academy of Arts and Letters (1945). Currently he is a professor of English at Wesleyan University.

One of his central interests has been animals, an interest that culminated in *A Bestiary,* compiled by Wilbur and illustrated by Alexander Calder (Pantheon Books, Inc., 1955). In this work there are thirty-three separate treatments: the frog, the dog, the fly, the spider, the hawk, the whale, etc. Fabulous animals like the centaur, the mermaid, and the unicorn are also included. For each creature there are four or five brief descriptions in prose or verse drawn from the voluminous literature on animals, from ancient books like Aesop's *Fables* and Pliny's *Natural History* to the works of contemporaries like Richard Eberhart and Marianne Moore. A few of the poems are Wilbur's own; some, like the one on the pelican, are his translations from other languages.

For more than a thousand years the *Bestiary* was one of the chief reference books on animals. In the earliest form of the work. *The Physiologus* of the second century, the legendary attributes ascribed to animals were given symbolical interpretations. By ingenious parallels the lion and the whale, for example, were shown to represent Christ. In many a medieval tapestry the unicorn dominates the scene. According to legend, it was an exceedingly dangerous beast; yet at sight of a virgin it would approach gently and place its head in her lap. So, Christ, mightiest of celestial beings, took on human form in the womb of the Virgin Mary. Animal allegories of this sort were favored by the Greek and Latin Church Fathers: Origen, Ambrose, Jerome, and Augustine. Through their influence the *Physiologus* came to be translated as the *Bestiary* into most of the west European vernaculars. Wilbur draws particularly upon the Middle English *Bestiary.* For translation from the twelfth century Anglo-Norman Philippe de Thaun's *Bestiaire* he selects "The Pelican," in which sophistication and naïveté are skillfully blended. The father pelican angered by the attacks his infant offspring make upon him, slays them. Moved by compassion he returns after three days, draws blood from his side and sprinkles it upon the lifeless forms. The little birds revive. In similar fashion, mankind condemned to death has been restored to life through the shedding of Christ's blood.

In definition and range, however, Wilbur's *Bestiary* goes

far beyond its medieval original. It includes classical and modern accounts that have no trace of allegory. Thorstein Veblen's diatribe on "the filthiest of the domestic animals," the dog, is an example. Of Wilbur's translations, one of the best is "A Prayer to Go to Paradise with the Donkeys," by the late nineteenth century French poet, Francis Jammes. In its humble subject, its simple diction, and its unquestioning faith, it recaptures something of the charm of the middle ages. Wilbur's faithful translation deserves to be quoted in full:

When I must come to you, O my God, I pray
It be some dust-roaded holiday,
And even as in my travels here below,
I beg to choose by what road I shall go
To Paradise, where the clear stars shine by day.
I'll take my walking-stick and go my way,
And to my friends the donkeys I shall say,
'I am Francis Jammes, and I'm going to Paradise,
For there is no hell in the land of the loving God.'
And I'll say to them: 'Come, sweet friends of the blue
    skies,
Poor creatures who with a flap of the ears or a nod
Of the head shake off the buffets, the bees, the flies . . .'
Let me come with these donkeys, Lord, into your land,
These beasts who bow their heads so gently, and stand
With their small feet joined together in a fashion
Utterly gentle, asking your compassion.
I shall arrive, followed by their thousands of ears,
Followed by those with baskets at their flanks,
By those who lug the carts of mountebanks
Or loads of feather-dusters and kitchen-wares,
By those with humps of battered water-cans,
By bottle-shaped she-asses who halt and stumble,
By those tricked out in little pantaloons
To cover their wet, blue galls where flies assemble
In whirling swarms, making a drunken hum.
Dear God, let it be with these donkeys that I come,
And let it be that angels lead us in peace
To leafy streams where cherries tremble in air,
Sleek as the laughing flesh of girls; and there
In that haven of souls let it be that, leaning above

Your divine waters, I shall resemble these donkeys,
Whose humble and sweet poverty will appear
Clear in the clearness of your eternal love.[2]

In his own animal poems, only a few of which are included in the *Bestiary*, Wilbur strikes an original note. He takes for his themes such things as the locust's song in "windless summer evenings," the southern flight of blackbirds in autumn, the death of a toad. Unlike Aesop, he provides no narrative, no moral; unlike Pliny, he is not concerned mainly with the animal's attributes, real or fabulous. In each instance, his animal is a medium through which he moves to larger, deeper issues. The poem about the locust, or cicada, rests upon a paradox. The cicada's song has always puzzled and delighted men; "chanters of miracles" have even taken it for a sign. Yet, as the scientist Fabre proved, the cicada cannot hear. In trying to catch in words the impression that the flight of blackbirds makes upon him, he discovers the shifting nature of reality, learns,

By what cross-purposes the world is dreamt.

In imagination he follows the dying toad as it sinks back toward its origins in primal oceans, toward "cooling shores," and "lost Amphibia's emperies." But the particular and profounder quality of these animal poems is illustrated best, perhaps, in "A Grasshopper," which appeared in *The New Yorker*, August 22, 1959. The familiar and invidious contrast with the ant has no place in this poem. There is no sermon on industry *vs.* idleness. Instead, the poem is an attempt, and a successful one, to catch the stillness of a summer day, the peace that for "a brief moment" descends on a field of grass, when a grasshopper pauses on a chicory leaf. The leaf rocks briefly under the weight and then is still. The quiet spreads to the surrounding flowers. The wind shrinks away. All cries fade out. Peace seems to extend "to the world's verge." But suddenly, and with no apparent purpose, the grasshopper leaps away, "giving the leaf a kick." By a kind of chain reaction, the grasses begin to sway again, the cricket's cry is heard, the entire field awakes. So, the macrocosm is shown in the microcosm. In little, the

[2]From *Things of This World*, copyright, 1956, by Richard Wilbur. Reprinted by permission of Harcourt, Brace and Company, Inc.

incident illustrates the larger ebb and flow of things, the universal alternation of opposites which is the dance of life, the cosmic harmony.

The *Bestiary* can be used to indicate another aspect of Wilbur's work, the equal attraction that comic and serious themes have for him. Under "The Fly" he has an entry drawn from Laurence Sterne and another drawn from William Blake. Uncle Toby in Sterne's *Tristam Shandy* is of so gentle a disposition that he has "scarce a heart to retaliate upon a fly." Having caught a particularly large and persistent one that has buzzed around his nose through dinner, he ceremoniously conveys it to the window, and after a long, grandiloquent, semi-Biblical speech of forgiveness and benediction, sets it free. The passage is remarkable for its lightness of touch and its comic overtones. A striking contrast is provided by Blake's serious thoughts on the same subject:

> Little Fly,
> Thy summer's play
> My thoughtless hand
> Has brush'd away.
>
> Am I not
> A fly like thee?
> Or art not thou
> A man like me?
>
> For I dance,
> And drink, & sing,
> Till some blind hand
> Shall brush my wing.

That Wilbur includes selections from authors so different in type as Sterne and Blake indicates a range of interests that is to be found also in his own work — his translations and his original poems.

It is significant that among French authors the two with whom Wilbur is most concerned are Molière and Voltaire. For sophisticated repartee, the satiric give-and-take of drawing-room conversation, few plays in the world's repertory can match Moliere's *Misanthrope*. And Wilbur's translation of the play [Harcourt, Brace, and Company, Inc., 1955] is as lively as any thus far in English. Furthermore, it is done in verse, preserving, as Wilbur says, "the frequently intricate arrangements of balancing half-lines, lines, couplets, quatrains, and sestets." All this, too, without sacrifice of accuracy and faithfulness to the original. How difficult such a feat is the Italians recognize in their adage, "*traduttore, traditore.*" Too frequently the translator is a traitor. In Wilbur's English dress, however, Molière's epigrams retain their polish and their poison. The double-edged nature of the satire — the simultaneous ridicule of society on the one hand, and its chief critic, Alceste, on the other — is admirably maintained. For conversational ease and naturalness combined with deadly verbal thrusts, as in a duel, no scene surpasses the one in which two drawing-room belles, Arsinoé and Célimène, tear each other's reputations to shreds. It is the scene that Wilbur selects for inclusion in his collection, *Poems 1943-1956* (Faber and Faber, 1957). The play as a whole shows his genuine talent as a translator.

After his success with Molière, he was a natural choice when Leonard Bernstein and Lillian Hellman wanted someone to write the lyrics for *Candide,* their comic operetta[3] on Voltaire's famous philosophical romance. Of all the spirited and amusing lyrics, the best is "Pangloss's Song," Wilbur's contribution, on which the opera closes. Through the ravages of syphilis, Pangloss the philosopher of optimism, has lost an eye, and his nose is half eaten away. Yet he remains faithful to his philosophy, still sings a song of praise to the Goddess of Love in this best of all possible worlds:

> Dear boy, you will not hear me speak
>     With sorrow or with rancour
> Of what has paled my rosy cheek
>     And blasted it with canker;
> 'Twas Love, great Love, that did the deed
>     Through Nature's gentle laws,
> And how should ill effects proceed
> From so divine a cause.
>
> Sweet honey comes from bees that sting,
>     As you are well aware;

[3]*Candide: A Comic Operetta Based on Voltaire's Satire.* Book by Lillian Hellman. Lyrics by Richard Wilbur (and others). Random House, 1957.

To one adept in reasoning,
    Whatever pains disease may bring
Are but the tangy seasoning
    To Love's delicious fare.

Columbus and his men, they say,
    Conveyed the virus hither
Whereby my features rot away
    And vital powers wither;
Yet had they not traversed the seas
    And come infected back,
Why, think of all the luxuries
    That modern life would lack!

All bitter things conduce to sweet,
    As this example shows;
Without the little spirochete
    We'd have no chocolate to eat,
Nor would tobacco's fragrance greet
    The European nose.

Each nation guards its native land
    With cannon and with sentry,
Inspectors look for contraband
    At every port of entry,
Yet nothing can prevent the spread
    Of Love's divine disease;
It rounds the world from bed to bed
    As pretty as you please.

Men worship Venus everywhere
    As plainly may be seen;
The decorations which I bear
    Are nobler than the Croix de Guerre,
And gained in service of our fair
    And universal Queen.[4]

There is a sprinkling of poems of the light and humorous sort
in each of Wilbur's books thus far published. Two clever
couplets, for example, are devoted to Dr. Samuel Johnson's
kicking a stone in refutation of Berkeley's idealistic philosophy

[4]Reprinted by permission of the author and of Random House, Inc.

("Epistemology"). Don Quixote riding abroad in search of glory
and adventure comes to a crossing and allows his horse to
choose the way. The horse, wiser than the master, heads back
for the barn ("Parable"). A graceful dancer pirouettes on a
museum wall ("Museum Piece"). It is a painting by Edgar Degas
who once bought an excellent El Greco

> To hang his pants on while he slept.

Degas, to whom Wilbur devotes two poems ("Museum Piece"
and "L'Etoile"), is not the only painter, however, to interest
him. "My Father Paints the Summer" is another poem on the
kindred art. Eugene Delacroix receives a tribute in "The Giaour
and the Pacha." A painting by Bazille is the subject of "Ceremony." And Pieter de Hooch's art inspires "Objects" and "A
Dutch Courtyard." In the work of these painters it is evident
that Wilbur finds principles operative that are of value, also,
to him as a poet. There is, for example, the peculiar power the
painter Pieter de Hooch has of making "objects speak." This
power Wilbur also possesses. From many possible illustrations,
"Driftwood" can be selected as representative. Cast up by the
sea, at rest finally on the sand, a few gnarled relics have a
tremendous significance. They tell of years of growing in the
forest; of service as mast, or oar, or plank; of eventual ship-
wreck; of floating in deep waters by which they were "never
dissolved"; of being "shaped" and "fitted" by ocean tides until
now they have

> the beauty of
> Excellence earned.

To the present generation faced by so many difficult problems,
these relics should have a special meaning, for through all
their ordeals — the wrecks and the wash of the seas — they
have preserved their "ingenerate grain."

In his *Weltanschaaung* Wilbur does not belong to the school
currently in fashion. Today the reigning favorites are the
authors who possess the tragic vision. There is a revival of
interest in Hawthorne and Melville with their sombre musings.
Dostoevsky's schizophrenics and psychopaths, characters who
have lost their spiritual bearings, are taken to be the fore-
runners of twentieth century man. The dominant philosophy

in Europe is existentialism, which has its origin partly in Nietzsche's dictum, "God is dead." Existentialism's leading exponent is the French philosopher Sartre, whose first novel, Nausea (1938), expresses in its very title his attitude toward existence. And the titles of the French novelist, Camus, who in 1957 won the Nobel Prize for literature, are similarly revealing: The Outsider (1942), The Plague (1947), The Fall (1956). Among German writers of the twentieth century, few have received more attention than Kafka, whose story "The Metamorphosis" is representative. In it the chief character, Gregor Samsa, is filled with such contempt for himself, and so strongly desires to evade his responsibilities, that he longs to become, and in fact does turn into a cockroach.

For these dark readings of the human enigma there is, of course, considerable basis in twentieth century experience. Camus never allows us to forget "that over a period of twenty-five years, between 1922 and 1947, 70 million Europeans — men, women, and children — have been uprooted, deported, and killed." It is no reflection on these powerful writers, however, to say that their philosophy is not the only one possible. At other times, or in other places, or by a different light existence may be viewed more favorably. For Wilbur, at any rate, black is not the only color, nor anguish the only theme. A writer's view of life depends largely on his temperament. And in temperament Wilbur differs from Sartre, Camus, and Kafka. Not that he is deaf or blind so far as social, political and economic questions are concerned. He, too, has witnessed the world conflict of the forties. In "Mined Country" he describes the aftermath. "War," he says, "hits at childhood more than churches." In "First Snow in Alsace," the gutted buildings and the ammunition dumps are gradually covered and changed by the snowfall. And a mile or two outside the town, the snow also

> fills the eyes
> Of soldiers dead a little while.

He refers in passing to such things as the Negro problem, and "the single-tax state" ("Water Walker"). Five of his quatrains berate the Philistines in the suburbs ("To an American Poet Just Dead"). But he is not at his best on these subjects. They lie on the periphery of his thought.

Essentially, Wilbur's note is one of affirmation. He is attracted, for example, by an Italian fountain ("A Baroque Wall-Fountain in the Villa Sciarra"), by the carved fauns at their innocent games. They never grow weary of the sun. They are happy in the loose waterfall and spray,

> Reproving our disgust and our ennui
> With humble insatiety.

It is possible, Wilbur implies ["A Problem from Milton"], that men reflect too much on the nature of things, do not enough enjoy the natural phenomena of which they are a part, the life force evidencing itself in the coiled vine, the lush tree, the comber dashing itself on the rocks. Adam in Eden was the first offender. Not content simply with being, he lost Paradise in his attempt to understand it. For splendid vitality there is no better example than the sea

> Whose horses never know their lunar reins.

As Ortega y Gasset says in the passage quoted at the beginning of this article, "Everything in the world is strange and marvellous to well-open eyes." Unquestionably, Wilbur would meet with the Spanish philosopher's approval. For he discovers the strange and the marvellous in the commonest objects. Like the painter, Pieter de Hooch, whom he admires ("Objects" and "A Dutch Courtyard"), he is entranced by the way in which a courtyard seems to burn in the sun, finds pleasure in "true textures," true integuments," magic in "the weave of a sleeve." Even the lowly potato inspires a lyric ("Potato") ten stanzas long.

Yet he is aware, as Wordsworth earlier was aware, that when he invests the commonplace with magic, he half perceives and half creates the objects of his vision. In "My Father Paints the Summer," the setting is a beach hotel on a chilly, rainy July day. While the other guests shiver by the "lobby fire," the father in his room puts on canvas his conception of the perfect season. It is "a summer never seen," having its origin in the heart, for

> Caught summer is always an imagined time.

On occasion, as in "La Rose des Vents," the poet may be too

prone to journey to the lands of his imagining, to cultivate the "roses of the mind." His lady calls him back to reality so that he may

> tend the true
> The mortal flower.

Deep within the heart of reality, however, dwells the miraculous, requiring for its perception no perversion or distortion of things, only "well-open eyes." This is the theme of "Praise in Summer":

> Obscurely yet most surely called to praise,
> As sometimes summer calls us all, I said
> The hills are heavens full of branching ways
> Where star-nosed moles fly overhead the dead;
> I said the trees are mines in air, I said
> See how the sparrow burrows in the sky!
> Perverts our praise to uncreation, why
> And then I wonder why this mad *instead*
> Such savour's in this wrenching thing awry.
> Does sense so stale that it must needs derange
> The world to know it? To a praiseful eye
> Should it not be enough of fresh and strange
> That trees grow green, and moles can course in clay,
> And sparrows sweep the ceiling of our day?"[5]

Many of Wilbur's works are songs of praise. His love poems, delicate and restrained, trace the forms the beautiful takes in its many changes ("A Simile for Her Smile" and "The Beautiful Changes"). Reading in the *Notebooks* of G. M. Hopkins he comes upon a quotation from another poet: "The young lambs bound/As to the tabor's sound." And at once he thinks of Nijinsky's "marvellous mid-air pause" in his dancing; the amazing sure-footedness of the dining-car waiter "in the shaken train"; Hamlet's thought and Flaubert's speech — all instances of grace that he remembers with pleasure ("Grace"). And along with "Grace" his tributes to "Clearness," "Lightness," and "Ceremony" should be mentioned. In effect, they are what he calls one of his poems, a "Conjuration."

[5]From *The Beautiful Changes and Other Poems*, copyright, 1947, by Richard Wilbur. Reprinted by permission of Harcourt, Brace and Company, Inc.

From all these examples cited, it is evident that Wilbur is a versatile poet. Nothing has been said of his verse forms and metres, but they are as varied as his themes, and as skillfully handled. He is deeply and widely read in at least two literatures, English and French. In his techniques as in his subjects he sometimes draws upon earlier authors: Nash, Traherne, Milton, La Fontaine, Baudelaire, Valéry. But always he supplies his own distinctive touch, beats his own music out. In the difficult and insufficiently appreciated art of translation he is a master. Most of all, in his own, original work he imparts to the familiar an air of newness and strangeness. He is what Ortega y Gasset desires — an intellectual man who has not lost the sense of wonder. He is one of those poets of whom in a recent anthology Robert Frost says that they "need live to write no better, need only wait to be better known for what they have written."

# James Dickey:
# The Expansive Imagination

### by RICHARD CALHOUN

As the 1960's draw to a close, the major poets at the beginning of the decade — Eliot, Frost, and Williams — are dead;
and American literature seems to be without a poet of major
stature. John Berryman, Richard Eberhart, and Anthony Hecht
are among our most recent Pulitzer Prize winners; but the two
poets most often considered to be the prime candidates for the
role of "major poet" are Robert Lowell and James Dickey. That
Lowell is so highly regarded is not surprising because, as the
decade began, it was he and Theodore Roethke who seemed to
be the trail blazers of new directions for American poets in
both subject matter and technique. Lowell's *Life Studies,* published in 1959, apparently signaled the final severing of the
bonds which Eliot's theory of impersonality and the canon of
the objective correlative had forged for modern poets. It is
now regarded as Lowell's major work even by those critics
who had misgivings about his poetic metamorphosis, partly because of its influence and partly because he has not consistently been successful in transcending the limitations of a
style so personal that many reviewers have referred to his
poetry as "confessional."

Although only six years younger than Lowell, James Dickey was practically unknown as a poet at the beginning of the decade. To the few who were aware of his literary existence he was the rather opinionated poetry reviewer for the *Sewanee Review*, who had just recently deserted a successful business career to turn to poetry. For Dickey to rival Lowell would require a massive explosion of poetic energy. This explosion has taken place with the appearance of *Into the Stone* (1960), *Drowning With Others* (1962), *Helmets* (1964), and *Buckdancer's Choice* (1965) — four books within five years, integrated into the work of a decade in his *Poems 1957-1967*.

There is even an historical appropriateness that Lowell and Dickey should be poetic rivals at this particular moment, for they represent a good many of the polarities evident in modern American poetry. Lowell's poetry owes much to tensions inherent in his being a member of a patrician New England family. In his poetry the past often coexists with the present. From the very first he was of the establishment, sponsored by John Crowe Ransom and Allen Tate in the dominant literary magazine of the 1940's, the *Kenyon Review*, progressing by the 1960's to a position of prestige as one of the resident intellectuals of the *New York Review of Books*. With Kenyon, Boston, Harvard, and the Poetry Center in New York as his bases of operation, he had won a Pulitzer Prize by the time he was thirty. In contrast, James Dickey is a sturdy, middle-class son of the New South. His first literary appearances were in the *Sewanee Review* at a time when it was breaking with the tenets of the New Criticism; and, like Whitman, his coming to poetry was comparatively late, in his mid-thirties, after an apprenticeship in the Air Force and in the business world as an advertising copywriter. His essay, "Barnstorming for Poetry," is an amusing account of a middle-aged poet earning his reputation the hard way, with one-night readings on the poetry circuits in the Mid-West, South, and Far West.

It is important to note that the poet Dickey has felt most akin to was Lowell's "rival" at the beginning of the decade, Theodore Roethke. Roethke was not a personal poet in the apparently literal sense that Lowell was, and neither is Dickey. Both have sought the condition of joy that Roethke declared to be the aim of his poetry, and each has attempted to transcend the limitations of his literal personality through a ver-

sion of something pretty close to what 19th-century aesthe-
ticians called the empathetic imagination. Roethke's version
was regressive, moving "downward" towards communion with
the minimal forms of nature, but never quite escaping from
the isolation of the self. Dickey's has progressively become
the expansive imagination, moving "upward," seeking connections between the human world and all the dynamic forces of
nature, destructive and vital, that might transform and intensify
the merely human self.

Peter Davison, who regards Dickey as potentially a major
poet, has suggested that he knew his subject when he began
publishing at the age of thirty-four — "the thousand variations
of one song" he refers to in "Buckdancer's Choice."[1] What he
needed to do was to develop the techniques that would permit
him to realize his variations of that song. This view is supported by Dickey's own critical theories in his reviews for the
*Sewanee Review,* recently reprinted in *From Babel to Byzantium.* The significance of the title lies in Dickey's belief, evidenced in his reviews, that each poet has his special vision,
his Byzantium. What he must do is find the right language and
the right voice among the many tongues of Babel to express
it. Poetry is "suspect" when it displays a manipulation of language for its own sake and becomes a sort of intellectual game
for poets who have forgotten something more important than
their craftsmanship — how to communicate what they really
feel. To Dickey technique should be a means of discovery,
since he regards poetry not as the reworking of known or established forms but rather as a personal exploration in which
content is as important as form and inseparable from it. A
poet's technique should provide him with the means of communicating to the reader a subject matter that for Dickey could
best be expressed in "Lawrence's magnificent little jotting:
'We don't exist unless we are deeply and centrally in touch
with that which can be touched but not known.' "[2] This is the
"song" that is developed with variations in a good many of
his poems.

Much of Dickey's work has been directed towards finding
the necessary poetic forms to make connections with what

[1] "The Difficulties of Being Major: The Poetry of Robert Lowell and
James Dickey," *Atlantic Monthly,* CCXX (Oct., 1967), 116-121.
[2]*Babel to Byzantium* (New York, 1968), p. 149.

cannot be ordinarily known, the archetypal "other," both as it has manifested itself in his experiences and as it has appeared to his imagination. He is a personal poet to the extent that he believes that a poet's best poems are related to "intense episodes and events in his own life," describing his own poetic efforts as attempts to find "some way to incarnate my best moments — those which in memory are the most persistent and obsessive."[3] From the very beginning, his poems have reflected the events of his domestic life — the dead brother whom he never knew; his invalid mother, whistling "Buck-dancer's Choice"; his father, whose hunting sweater he dons; and himself in the role of a middle-aged father, responsible for the lives of his children. There are poems dealing with his favorite activities of both the past and the present — hunting, fishing, swimming, and flying.

But if Dickey's critical theory is related to his practice, the "song" that he had made "a thousand variations of" must be necessitated by experiences more deeply imbedded in his memory; and, in fact, Dickey, the poet, seems obsessed by two traumatic events, both involving death and engendering a guilt which his poems have attempted to come to terms with. The first obsession, recurrent in his early poems, arose from his parents' accounts of the brother who was "dead before I was born." The second obsession is the guilt of a "survivor" (his own favorite image of himself), haunted by memories of those who died in World War II. Beginning with "The Performance" in *Into the Stone*, Dickey wrote a series of poems in which he tries to establish connections with these dead.

The poet has mentioned "The Performance" as the first poem in which he realized the importance of empathetic identification, a technique that he later refined into what H. L. Weatherby has called "The Way of Exchange."[4] The last time Dickey saw Donald Armstrong, he was performing, standing not too steadily on his hands in the sun. Having learned of his beheading, the poet tries to create in his imagination a second, more nearly perfect performance which almost transcends the moment of his death and establishes a human bond between victim and executioner:

[3]*Ibid.*, p. 292.
[4]*Sewanee Review*, LXXIV (Summer, 1966), 669-81.

Yet I put my flat hand to my eyebrows
Months later, to see him again
In the sun, when I learned how he died,
And imagined him, there,
Come, judged, before his small captors,

Doing all his lean tricks to amaze them —

Even in his early poems Dickey seems to have had an obsession to understand through an act of faith in his imagination
events which reason alone could not comprehend. What was
lacking then was the mastery of techniques which could make
the necessary connections and assuage the guilt of one alive in
the presence of the dead. In "The String," for instance, he has
difficulty imagining his dead brother:

Except when he enters my son,
The same age as he at his death,
I cannot bring my brother to myself.
I do not have his memory in my life,
Yet he is in my mind and on my hands.
I weave the trivial string upon a light
*Dead before I was born.*

In his late poetry, however, he has been able to move more
deeply into the experiences that he desires to explore by employing three important techniques — his split line, his symbols
(what he calls "big basic forms"), and, until very recently, his
"way of exchange."

Dickey has indicated that his first departure from traditional forms was his discovery during the composition of an
early poem, "Sleeping Out At Easter," that the simple declarative sentence "had exactly the qualities I wanted my poems to
have."[5] Thus the sentence became an important unit in his
early poetry as he felt it capable of communicating his experiences to the reader with the directness he desired. The poem
just mentioned begins like this:

All dark is now no more.
This forest is drawing a light.
All Presences change into trees.

---

[5]*Babel to Byzantium*, p. 287.

But in actual practice Dickey soon saw that he must use the short sentence sparingly, saving it for his climaxes, as in the conclusion of "The Hospital Window":

> I have just come down from my father, . . .

or resorting to short, one-sentence stanzas, as in another fine poem, "The Dusk of Horses":

> Right under their noses, the green
> Of the field is paling away
> Because of something fallen from the sky.

Later, he tended to break his sentences up into lines formed from the separate phrasal units of his sentences, slightly run-on, as in "Cherrylog Road":

> Restored, a bicycle fleshed
> With power, and tore off
> Up Highway 106, continually
> Drunk on the wind in my mouth,
> Wringing the handlebar for speed,
> Wild to be wreckage forever.

But apparently neither the traditional lines of prosody, nor the sentence, nor the phrase, was entirely satisfactory in conveying the sense of immediacy he was after.

It was in *Buckdancer's Choice* (1965) that Dickey arrived at the basic unit of his recent poetry, what his reviewers have called space punctuation, or the split line. When questioned about the reason for adopting this much longer line, broken up into phrasal units, Dickey has suggested that he was trying to get closer to the way people actually associate their thoughts, also hinting at an analogy between this line and the rhythms of guitar playing. It would suggest two somewhat different analogies. First, in his search for a poetic line which would be more expressive of the rhythms inherent in the experiences he seeks to communicate, Dickey has produced something closer to vocal music, with the pauses similar to breath pauses. He has always admired "the windless, elemental quality" of the sound of the voice in Roethke's poetry;[6] and his purpose here may be clarified by noting the im-

---

[6] *Ibid.,* p. 150.

portance he places in his criticism on the sound of a "voice"
in good poems as a means of taking the reader into the experience of the poem.

In commenting on Dickey's practice in his recent poetry
of using verse-paragraph breaks instead of stanzas, Laurence
Lieberman has used the analogy of the film strip.[7] This analogy
might even be extended to compare the split line unit with a
single film frame. Many of Dickey's space punctuation units
seem to seek the status of separate observations, separate
sense perception, or distinctive images, while contributing to
the rhythmic flow of the poem as a whole much as each frame
contributes to the flow of the film. A selection from "Falling"
will illustrate my point:

Arms out      she slow-rolls over      steadies out      waits for
          something great
To take control of her  trembles near feathers      planes head-
          down
The quick movements of bird-necks turning her head      gold
          eyes the insight —
eyesight of owls blazing into the hencoops      a taste for chick-
          en overwhelming
Her      the long-range vision of hawks enlarging all human
          lights of cars
Freight trains      looped bridges      enlarging the moon racing
          slowly
Through all the curves of a river      all the darks of the mid-
          west blazing
          from above. A rabbit in a bush turns white      the
          smothering chickens
Huddle . . . .

Dickey has identified another staple of his poetry as
" 'the big basic forms' — rivers, mountains, woods, clouds,
oceans . . . ."[8] Forms of nature do recur in Dickey's poetry,
and the most important seem to be those rather basic ones of
water and air. The former predominates in his early poetry;
the latter, in the later poems. In *Into the Stone* (1960), *Drowning With Others* (1962), and *Helmets* (1964), the ocean, under-

----

[7]In "Notes on James Dickey's Style," to be published in *The Canadian
Journal of Modern Literature.*
[8]*Babel to Byzantium*, p. 291.

ground streams, rivers, salt marshes, the movement of fish and man in water, the activities of fishing, swimming, and drowning recur. Beginning with *Buckdancer's Choice* (1965), memories of flying return with "The Firebombing," and images of climbing, leaping, falling become central in his poetry. In short, in the early poems movement through water is a central action, while in the later poems Dickey's increasingly obsessive themes of rebirth, resurrection and reincarnation tend to be expressed through images of air rather than the more traditional symbol of water. Laurence Lieberman has stressed the increasing importance of symbols to Dickey through the developing stages of his art, commenting in particular on the personal importance of the symbol of air.[9] In his desire to get in touch with what cannot be ordinarily known, Dickey has moved (in his imagery) more and more towards archetypal images and, in his subjects, towards identification with the archetypal "other."

Perhaps the most important device Dickey has employed in achieving his goal of conjunction with the "other" is his own version of empathetic identification — "The Way of Exchange" — which first appears in *Drowning With Others* [1962]. In this book and in the next, *Buckdancer's Choice,* the "exchange" occurs between man and his opposites, particularly between men and animals ("A Dog Sleeping on My Feet" and "Springer Mountain"), but also between men and machinery ("Drinking From a Helmet"). Weatherby has made it clear that Dickey's process of "exchange" is more than just a one-way empathetic projection. It is a reciprocal process. In "A Dog Sleeping on My Feet" Dickey gains immediacy of perception through the creation of a composite *persona*, part animal and part human. The poet gains new sensuous impressions, and the irrational animal is given the power to reflect on what he experiences:

> Before me the fox floats lightly,
> On fire with his holy scent.
> All, all are running.
> Marvelous is the pursuit,
> Like a dazzle of nails through the ankles, . . .

Even though entering the animal realm is desirable, this state

---

[9]"Notes on James Dickey's Style."

cannot be indefinitely maintained; and the poem concludes with a return "From the dream of an animal" for the poet, as

> . . . all rushes on into dark
> And ends on the brightness of paper.
> When my hand, which speaks in a daze
> The hypnotized language of beasts,
> Shall falter, and fail
>
> Back into the human tongue, . . .

In "Approaching Prayer" Dickey is able to put on the boar's head and through the eyes of his victim see himself shooting his arrow. In "Springer Mountain" he is able through the "exchange" not only to gain immediacy but to feel for the first time, as he strips himself naked and runs with the animals, something that has increased significance in his later poetry — the power and vitality of nature that can be gained from such a process. In "Drinking From a Helmet" he is able to effect an "exchange" between the living and the dead as he puts on the helmet of the dead soldier, and the dead man's past seems to enter his own:

> I threw my old helmet down
> And put the wet one on.
> Warmed water ran over my face.
> My last thought changed, and I knew
> I inherited one of the dead.

Dickey's "exchange" is not *always* possible. In "The Driver," while seeking the understanding of death through an exchange with one who has drowned, he becomes aware of the danger of staying under:

> . . . I was becoming no more
> Than haunted, for to be so
> Is to sink out of sight, and to lose
> The power of speech in the presence
> Of the dead, with the eyes turning green,
>
> And to leap at last for the sky
> Very nearly too late, . . .

In one of the finest poems in *Buckdancer's Choice,* "The Fire-

bombing," Dickey tries to transpose himself from his plane
down to the destruction he is creating below. But his imagination is incapable of penetrating the aesthetic distance created
by the space barrier to overcome sufficiently his memories of
the beauty and skill of his flight, or of transcending the barriers posed by the present comforts of suburban American life.
He is

> . . . still unable
> To get down there or see
> What really happened.
>                         But it may be that I could not,
> If I tried, say to any
> Who lived there, deep in my flames: . . .
>
> Come in, my house is yours, come in
> If you can, if you
> Can pass this unfired door. It is that I can imagine
> At the threshold nothing . . . .

Having said so much about Dickey's "way of exchange,"
I must now speak of its limitations, which, happily for his poetry, Dickey seems to have realized before his critics did. A
primary danger was that it might become too one-directional,
emphasizing the beatitude of the animal state without using
it to dramatize what man in his very un-natural human state
stood in need of. If Dickey was to continue in this direction,
the only paths left were that of mysticism, descriptions of salvation through conjunction with the "other," or the writing of
merely pastoral poetry. In fact, there are poems that seem experiments in these directions. The most successful is entitled
"The Heaven of Animals," in which the animals are beautiful
and incapable of evil because they have no human guilt and
can accept nature's cycle of kill and be killed, the roles of
hunter and hunted. Both predator and victim are permitted to
walk

> Under such trees in full knowledge
> Of what is in glory above them,
> And to feel no fear,
> But acceptance, compliance.
> Fulfilling themselves without pain

At the cycle's center, . . .

In "Fog Envelops the Animals" Dickey himself is able to enter this animal heaven momentarily and "stand with all beasts in a cloud" because the fog "is eating / My visible self alive."

And I drift forward
Through the hearts of the curdling oak trees,
Borne by the river of Heaven.

Though the animals may be unaware of a human presence, the human hunter is "deadly aware" of them and thus ultimately separated from their natural world:

My arrows, keener than snowflakes,
Are with me whenever I touch them.
Above my head, the trees exchange their arms
In the purest fear upon earth . . . .

In "Reincarnation II" the poet is allowed the experience of being reborn as a bird. But this long poem is, in my opinion, not effective, even as a description of the human consciousness becoming aware of its new freedom. Despite the fact that Dickey has revealed a social conscience in poems like "The Firebombing" and "Slave Quarters" and despite evidence that guilt has been an obstacle to any liberating effect his "exchange" might have had, certainly if he had continued writing in this vein the charge of militants of the New Left that his poetry is socially irresponsible[10] might have been justified.

The poems that bring the animal-nature cycle of his poetry to a close are "The Sheep Child" and "Encounter in a Cage Country." Both poems stress *change*, but each in its way suggests a new concern (of the poet). In "The Sheep Child" Dickey presents the "exchange" in terms of legend and inner psychological fears — an account of the act of bestiality and its offspring, half human and half animal. The sheep child may actually be a fiction for farm boys to "keep themselves off / Animals . . . ." But since, like all legends, it holds forth the possibility of truth, Dickey gives the embalmed monstrosity a voice to recount its brief existence:

[10]See Robert Bly, "The Collapse of James Dickey," *The Sixties* (Spring, 1967), 72-80.

In the summer sun of the hillside, with my eyes
Far more than human, I saw for a blazing moment
The great grass world from both sides,
Man and beast in the round of their need,
And the hill wind stirred in my wool,
My hoof and my hand clasped each other,
I ate my one meal
Of milk, and died
Staring . . . .

In "Encounter in a Cage Country" the black leopard, like the sheep child, gives the stare of the "other." Behind his green glasses, the poet returns the stare, acts out before the caged animal the charade of hunter, and receives without any exchange of being a message regarding his own human resources:

. . . and something was given a life-
mission to say to me hungrily over

And over and over          *your moves are exactly right*
*For a few things in this world: we know you*
*When you come, Green Eyes, Green Eyes.*

It seems to me that in the "Falling" section of *Poems 1957-1967* the thrust of Dickey's imagination has reversed its direction from the self to the "other," back towards the self. His mystical tendencies have become, as some critics have described Whitman's, inverted. His imagination is still expansive in that he seeks some means of not being strapped in the everyday self; but he is, in Laurence Lieberman's phrase, "a worldly mystic" who must reconnect with the world."

Dickey's current interest seems to be less in "exchange" than in creating *personae* whose situations are symbolic of how people trapped in the confines of time and flesh may find at moments of existential encounter the hidden resources for transcending the mundane self. Perhaps this new emphasis coincides with his awareness that his own youth is gone, that his life space, like that of the hostess in "Falling," has contracted. In such a situation one must learn how to employ all the hidden resources of both the body and the soul, what is accessible from both the inner and the outer world.

---

11"The Wordly Mystic," *Hudson Review*, XX (Autumn, 1967), 513-20.

In "Falling" Dickey is able to enter into the last moments of an airline hostess as she plummets to her death. On the way down she realizes that she must give up her fantasies of flying, of rescue *deus ex machina* (by "those sky-divers on TV"), and of salvation by immersion in water with its associations of institutional religious symbolism. Instead she realizes, under the extreme pressures of her contracted life-span, that the only possibility of transcendence lies in making her death a mystery for the farm boys below. Consequently, she affirms her life at the very moment of her death, stripping herself naked and preparing her body for its last fatal sacrifical re-union with the fertile earth. Her performance at the moment of encounter with death "works" (transcends), as Donald Armstrong's does not, because Dickey is able to associate her death with one of the oldest and most obsessive of man's symbols, the rites of fertility. She discovers within herself a resource which permits transcendence.

"Power and Light" is perhaps a less successful poem but one of Dickey's most metaphysical. There is certainly a suggestion that the pole climber represents a new concept of the poet in that he is able to find the sources of his power — his ability to make connections for "the ghostly mouths" carried over the lines — *underground*, in the silent dark of his basement. There he feels "the wires running / Like the life-force along the limed rafters," and he discovers that

> . . . in the deep sway of underground      among the roots
> That bend like branches      all things connect      and
>      stream
> Toward light and speech . . . .

Here it seems that the "secret" of existence that Dickey has been pursuing comes from a confrontation not with the natural world but with the "dark" of one's own death. One passage from this poem seems both to look back towards his earliest personal poems and ahead to new directions:

> . . . Years in the family dark have made me good
> At this   nothing else is so good   pure fires of the Self
> Rise crooning in lively blackness . . . .

The conclusion of his recent poem "The Eye-Beaters"

(*Harper's*, Nov. 1968), would seem to give credence to Dickey's public statements that he would like to write "poems about cave men," a further indication of his interest in describing encounters with the most basic possible life experiences. His reviewers have commented on the new sexual realism — a combination of eroticism and fertility ritual — in poems like "The Fiend," "Falling," "The Sheep Child," and "May Day Sermon to the Women of Gilmer County, Georgia, by a Woman Preacher Leaving the Baptist Church." In an introduction to a collection of poetry by young American poets, Dickey has cited the ultimate promise of poetry as being "to bring the reader to the place where the flame breaks forth from the pit and the gods speak from the burning bush."[12]

When confronted with statements like this, critics like myself, who regard Dickey as an important poet, can take comfort from the fact that he has also shown a tendency to adopt comic poses, to assume on occasion tones of self-mockery. With the risks that he takes in his poetry he may need to control his excesses with some kind of built-in whimsy, irony, or humor, what Robert Penn Warren has called "coming to terms with Mercutio." Justification for the terrible risks he is now taking will ultimately lie, however, in his accomplishments — a terrible but nevertheless an exhilarating poetry. In his comparison of Robert Lowell and James Dickey as potentially our next major poets, Peter Davison states:

> Such writing as Dickey's requires a vast fire to keep the cauldron boiling. If he were to encounter a slight recession of energy, such as that which seems lately to have overtaken Robert Lowell, Dickey's value as poet might easily enter into a decline just at the moment when his reputation, like Lowell's today, has reached its apogee.[13]

I doubt the danger of such a decline. Dickey's expansive imagination seems capable of finding forces either outside in the world or deep inside the poetic self to justify his claiming as a poet to be what his pole-climber is:

> And I am a man
> Who turns on. I am a man.

[12]In *The Young American Poets*, ed. by Paul Carroll (Chicago, 1969).
[13]"The Difficulty of Being Major," p. 121.

# Postscript:
# American Poetry in The 60's

## by Guy Owen

What is American poetry like in the 60's? For one thing, the subject is far too complicated to lend itself to a brief essay. In 1945 Karl Shapiro tried to sum up the condition of American poetry in his *Essay on Rime*. The poem grew into a long one, and what he seemed to discover everywhere was confusion — confusion in prosody, language and belief. Much of what he wrote then still obtains, though there would be no need to comment on Marxist poetry today.

In the 1960's the landscape of our poetry is still a confused one — no doubt a good thing. Certainly no one or two figures dominate our verse in the way T. S. Eliot and Ezra Pound did in the late 20's. Today there are Activists, Beats, neo-Beats, Academics, Projectivists, Concretists, etc. How does one suggest the flavor of a body of poetry that includes the classic precision of J. V. Cunningham, the cool elegance of Richard Wilbur, the urbane wit and archaic mannerisms of John C. Ransom — as well as the dithyrambic howls of Allen Ginsberg and the anti-intellectual automatic droolings of Gregory Corso or Peter Orlovsky? I hope merely to point out a few directions here, and at the risk of producing a dry catalogue, to touch on what seems to me to be the significant new talents.

To begin with, anyone approaching our poetry today must feel a deep sense of loss. During the last decade most of the giants have died, those hardy pioneers who in the 20's forced American verse to surrender its provinciality and made important breakthroughs in imagery and free verse. The old masters are gone: T. S. Eliot, Wallace Stevens, Robert Frost, E. E. Cummings, Robinson Jeffers and Dr. William Carlos Williams, as well as the younger Theodore Roethke, whose restless talent might have provided the leadership in opening up new fields had he lived. Other poets who helped shape the new poetry of the 20's have felt their powers wane: Marianne Moore's late work offers nothing new, and Ezra Pound has subsided into political snarls and the murky later Cantos. Thus far the giants have not been replaced.

It has been a commonplace in recent years to say that all our "young" poets were either old men or dead. Like most commonplaces, this one contains a great deal of truth, for during the 40's and 50's it was the poets I have just mentioned who wrote most of the fresh and dynamic verse. What is "new" in the younger poets — both Beat and Academic — was mostly borrowed and adapted from the pioneers of the 20's. Although they are now dead or silent, their influence still pervades much of the poetry of the 60's.

Which of the giants remain as vital influences? It is difficult to single out a major influence — though if one counted the number of young disciples, the honor would probably go to Dr. Williams. However, there is no problem in pointing out "the Big Four": Stevens, Eliot, Pound and Williams — with Ransom as a lesser force among the Academics. (I omit here the major "foreign" influence of Auden and Yeats and the minor impact of Dylan Thomas.) At the time of his death, Wallace Stevens had a large following of young sophisticates, most of them at the universities, who were enamored of his Frenchified diction and dandified stance. His grace and wit and elegance can be seen in the work of Richard Wilbur, among others. T. S. Eliot's influence on poetry has diminished ever since he joined the Anglican Church, though he still carries considerable weight. His brilliant diction, his juxtaposition of the literary and the colloquial, his use of literary and mythical allusions, his use of irony — indeed much of his poetic technique is still very much a part of the poetic scene, though there has been an unmistakable revolt against his brand of classicism since World War II. For example, the recent "confessional poets" have repudiated his emphasis on objectivity. Such poets as Allen Tate, R. P. Warren and Randall Jarrell have gone to school to Eliot — though they have, obviously, not been overwhelmed by him. Pound and Williams have made the most impact upon the young rebels of the late 50's and the 60's, especially among Beatnik poets. Pound has proved useful for his early experiments with images and metrics — his insistence upon "the musical phrase" rather than the metronome; Williams for his emphasis upon colloquial native speech and rhythms, notably for his spontaneous effects and his rebellion against iambics and rhyme. One can also detect the voice of Robert Frost here and there among post-war poets who employ conservative patterns and pastoral themes, but of course he has never been a major influence, in spite of his brilliant achievement.

Second, there is active today a group of poets who began producing during World War II: many of them have consolidated their reputations during the 60's — but they must be passed over rapidly here. After the dreary Marxist verse that flooded the 30's, American poetry went to war in the 40's. Out of the turbulent war years came little lasting verse. Among the best war poets were Randall Jarrell, John Ciardi, Karl Shapiro and Richard Eberhart. All of them moved on from war poetry to establish solid reputations as poets and, in the case of the first three, as critics. Ciardi and Shapiro possess the most restless talents of their generations. Shapiro in the 60's has attacked the use of iambics and rhymed forms; his *The Bourgeois Poet* (1964) is a volume of prose poems. I think Shapiro, and the late Theodore Roethke, are the most interesting and most talented poets of their generation — they are certainly the most daring. (No doubt other commentators would suggest John Berryman or Stanley Kunitz.)

Finally, we come to the poetry of our post-war generation and the talent which is just now asserting itself. American poetry in the late 50's divided itself into two camps at war with each other; in fact, it has been suggested that the 60's might be remembered for its own "battle of the books." This state of declared war has been the situation for the last decade, though the lines of battle at present are not so clear and the noise of battle has diminished — perhaps because the Beats have exhausted themselves. On the one side, there are the young Turks, the Beats; on the other are the traditionalists, the poets labeled Academics by the Beats — though they represent no school or movement in the sense that their vociferous enemies do. Although they tend to be conservative — they are said to write "English" verse, not American — the Academics are a diverse group rather difficult to define. Certainly they don't all teach or live in university circles.

Their work has been anthologized in *The New Poets of England and America* (1957) edited by Donald Hall, Robert Pack and Louis Simpson and *New Poets: Second Selection* (1962), edited by Hall and Pack. The poets represented in these two collections were at the time under forty years old; included is the best work of Robert Lowell and James Dickey, unquestionably the most gifted of their age group, as well as selections from such promising poets as W. D. Snodgrass, William Meredith, Vassar Miller, James Wright, X. J. Kennedy and a dozen or so others. Interestingly enough, not one of the poets in the first anthology is included in Donald Allen's *New American Poetry: 1945-1960,* which represents the enemy camp. However, Donald Hall had relented enough by 1962 to include three poets who are generally associated with the Beat movement in his *Contemporary American Poetry:* Denise Levertov, Robert Creeley and Gary Snyder.

Robert Lowell has referred to the preceding decade as "the tranquilized 50's," and Glauco Cambon in *Recent American Poetry* alluded to "the academic quiescence in the mid-fifties" — soon to be shocked by Ginsburg's explosive *Howl.* In 1950 John Ciardi wrote that "barbaric yawps a la Whitman, as well as daredevil experimentation, were through." The wild "redskin" poets had to make way for the "pale face." No doubt all of these statements over-state the case, yet they do point to the central shift in serious poetry in our time. After the war, American poets found a home, or a refuge, in the universities, as students on the GI Bill and as teachers, and today dozens of them are poets-in-residence scattered throughout America. This does not mean that poetry became "ivory tower" overnight; however, this mass movement to the groves of academe has had enormous impact. Universities are notoriously conservative, departments of English especially so. As one might ex-

pect, the post-war poets, many of them shaken to the depths
by war, sought a sense of balance and order in their art. Inevitably, they tended to distrust wild emotions and risky experiments. What they did, in fact, was to consolidate the gains
made by older poets, often producing carefully polished and
beautifully controlled poetry: witness the work of John Hol-
lander, X. J. Kennedy, and Edgar Bowers. There is no question
about the accomplishments of most of the young poets presented in *New Poets of England* and *America*; it represents a
high level of achievement and gives promise of better things
to come as the poets mature.

Yet for all the abundant skill and artistry of the poets collected in these two anthologies, I must confess to misgivings as
I read them, for the world they create is severely limited.
There seems to be a lack of intensity and a haunting sameness
here. I am reminded of the unity of tone and diction in Eigh-
teenth Century verse and can easily see why our age has been
often called the Silver Age of poetry. Aside from being almost
always solemn, Academic poems are too obviously in the
"minor mode"; they are too carefully casual, occasional and
personal, too often understated and ironic. The speaking voice
seems to be cultivated at the expense of the singing voice, for
the lyrical drive is noticeably suppressed, the emotions held in
check. The typical Academic poem is patently the work of the
intellect: it is a carefully "made" work of art — and no acci-
dents allowed. No doubt the will and the intellect are often
forced to do the work of the imagination. Since writing poetry
has become fashionable in America (it was not in the 20's), one
feels that too many poets create poems as an exercise, not
because they are compelled to express themselves. In the end,
there is too much control, too much tightness of form and
clever juggling of ambiguities, too many signs of erudition. At
the worst, the poems are brilliantly dull. One wishes for more
intensity and less polish, for more daring even at the expense
of an uneven texture or the risk of failure.

Moreover, one notes the same subjects being endlessly
treated, or avoided. There are inevitably poems about places
where one has traveled (foreign scenes are much in vogue),
poems about memories of the war or childhood, and, always,
poems about works of art and the books one has read. And, of
course, the ubiquitous poems about being a poet, about the

process of creating the poem, the favorite theme of Wallace Stevens' disciples. In a given year *Poetry* magazine, which is the chief organ of the Academics — and an enemy of the Beats — will publish a dozen poems centered on the creative process — and scarcely one on fallout, racism, the atom bomb, or the poor in America. Finally, there are everywhere poems about family relationships. Our young talents are rather tame domestic poets. It is as though the young poet had lost all faith in society and its institutions, plus his sense of the past; he feels thrown back upon himself and his family and a small circle of friends — who are, likely as not, other poets.

(A further development of this situation has been the recent wave of "confessional poetry." W. D. Snodgrass won the Pulitzer Prize for *Heart's Needle,* a collection that grew out of his divorce and separation from his young daughter; and Robert Lowell followed with *Life Studies,* personal poems that deal with his mental illness, his jail sentence and family relationships. This paved the way for the tormented later poems of Sylvia Plath and the poems of personal crises by Anne Sexton, who writes of her stay in a mental institution, her cancer operation, and other personal problems. The end is not yet in sight, but already one is weary of poems that center on the poet's poor eyesight or his mistress's latest miscarriage. As John Ciardi has commented, some confessional poets have very little to confess — or they fail to confess in an artistically engaging manner.)

However, if one can trust the evidence of Donald Hall's latest anthology, *Contemporary American Poetry* (1962), a new direction can be discerned: the lines of the young Academics are loosening up and they are becoming less cerebral, trusting the heart and the unconscious more. As Glauco Cambon puts it, the younger poets are growing less timid; "they are releasing their pressing [poetic] genie from the 'bottle' of rhymed iambics" — though certainly not to the extent of the Beats. No doubt Robert Lowell is a major influence here; for example in his *Life Studies* he has moved away from the tight forms of *Lord Weary's Castle.* In any case, in the 60's one can see a development away from formalized patterns in such "traditional" poets as Donald Hall, James Wright and Richard Wilbur. In fact, the little magazines are now being flooded with neo-surrealistic poems by such young poets as Peter Wild and

William Matthews. On the other hand, W. D. Snodgrass and
X. J. Kennedy continue to employ the old forms in fresh and
brilliant ways.

And now a word on the young Turks. The Beat movement
began in the middle 50's and it obviously began dying in the
mid 60's. There are some critics, like John Ciardi, who argue
that this rebellious group is not really a literary movement at
all (it has produced very little literature), but merely a fad,
created in part by journalists. However, they cannot be ignored in any essay on American Poetry of the last decade.

It is difficult to trace the origins of the movement; the term
itself seems to have been invented by the novelist Jack
Kerouac. John C. Holmes has said that *beat* means "more than
mere weariness, it implies the feeling of having been used, of
being raw. It involves a sort of nakedness of mind, and, ultimately, of soul; a feeling of being reduced to the bedrock of
consciousness." Many of the first Beatniks studied under
Charles Olson at Black Mountain College and were associated
in one way or another with *The Black Mountain Review,* which
included Kenneth Rexroth on its editorial board. This nucleus
included Robert Duncan, Jonathan Williams and Robert Creeley.
The movement later spread to San Francisco, where Duncan
helped stimulate the so-called San Francisco renaissance —
recorded in Lawrence Lipton's sympathetic *The Holy Barbar-
ians* — and on to New York, where it quickly gathered adher-
ents in Greenwich Village. Allen Ginsburg and Lawrence Ferlinghetti are important West Coast figures. Le Roi Jones and the
late Kenneth Koch are perhaps representative of the New York
group. In addition to Charles Olson, these "angry young men"
of the U. S. were championed by Kenneth Rexroth (who later
repudiated them), Henry Miller and Dr. W. C. Williams.

The Beat movement is, of course, not merely a literary
movement. It is made up of a small minority of the generation
that grew up during World War II and its uneasy aftermath.
These young bohemians, somewhat like the lost Generation of
the 20's — though thus far they have not been nearly as significant — are in revolt against a world they never made. They are
non-conformists, gleefully satirizing every facet of "square"
American society, including Christianity, for which some of
them have substituted an ill-digested Zen Buddhism. They are,

above all, anti-tradition, anti-academic and, in the end, anti-intellectual.

The reader interested in the quality of Beatnik verse need go no further than the well known (notorious?) anthology edited by Donald Allen, *The New American Poetry: 1945-1960,* a collection that pointedly ignores the most accomplished — though traditional — poets of the postwar generation, such as Robert Lowell and James Dickey. In his preface Mr. Allen asserts that his collection represents "a total rejection of all those qualities typical of academic verse. Following the practice and precepts of Ezra Pound and William Carlos Williams [in some cases Walt Whitman], it has built on their achievements and gone on to evolve new conceptions of the poem ... They are our avantgarde, the true continuers of the modern movement in American Poetry." In many ways their poetry is allied to jazz and abstract expressionist painting. For a time it was fashionable for the Beats to read their wildly free verse with a jazz combo improvising in the background, and through readings and recordings such poets as Lawrence Ferlinghetti have created a popular oral poetry.

What is the typical Beat poem like? Obviously it represents a revolt against current literary conventions, against stiff prosody, fixed patterns, "poetic" diction, etc. Too often it seems, at least to me, a spewing up of images yoked together arbitrarily and with little or no control. Such poems lack a sense of direction and design; raw energy is substituted for the discipline of art. It is the ultimate in the Romantic approach to poetry. As Gene Baro has written,

It [Beat poetry] is spontaneous, ungoverned, often to the point of incoherence. Frequently, it is centered in a mood or a moment and is so wedded to the components of its occasion that much of its meaning must elude the uninitiated reader. It is colloquial, even slang-ridden, and despises conventional organizations, traditional syntax and spelling, fixed subject matter . . . It is involved in the uninhibited exposure of personal feeling and is therefore often embarrassingly sentimental or pathetic by common standards of **taste.**

This is a succinct description of most Beat verse. I would add only that the greatest failure of this large body of poetry is that it is simply dull — it does not successfully engage the mind. The reader soon grows weary of four letter words that no longer shock, of repetitious allusions to Zen and drugs, of the inevitable sexual references which seem to obsess the young rebels. At its worst, one feels that behind many of these poems is only an energetic mindlessness that is impelled to express itself.

Mr. Allen has claimed that the Beat movement has produced a new poetry. This is hardly accurate. The typical Beat poem is one of content, not of style. The Beats have made no genuine contribution to prosody; they simply stress natural speech rhythms. However, Charles Olson has emphasized "the pressures of the breath" in determining the length of the line: "And the line comes (I swear it) from the breath, from the breathing of the man who writes, at the moment that he writes . . . . " In Olson's poems the reader often wonders just how his breathing dictates the line breaks.

Perhaps a brief quotation from Olson will suggest the flavor of his influential "projective verse." The following is from *The Maximus Poems:*

>                    Colored pictures
>     of all things to eat: dirty
>     postcards
>         And words, words, words
>     all over everything . . . .

On the other hand, Allen Ginsburg, in the most famous poem to come out of the movement, *Howl* (1956), employs a longer line:

>     I saw the best minds of my generation destroyed by
>         madness starving hysterical naked,
>     dragging themselves through the negro streets at dawn
>         looking for an angry fix . . . .

Unfortunately, this technique offers little that is new; it is merely Walt Whitman updated with hip slang.

In spite of my conviction that is has produced more newspaper copy than literature, no doubt some good has come out of its sensational explosion on the poetic scene and in the popular press. For one thing, it took poetry out of the classrooms and into the streets; it gave poetic treatment to subjects the traditionalists shy away from. Everywhere it placed a premium upon energy rather than politeness and control, and certainly Beat poets were willing to take risks the Academics would not — in subject matter and in experiments. They have, for example, helped make surrealism once more a viable option for the poet. As Gene Baro wrote, "On the whole, the 'new' poetry has had a desirable liberating effect; it has restored the colloquial, the occasional, the journalistic, the argumentative, the perverse, the disorderly, the vulgar, and the wildly imaginative. Time will redress the balance and shape yet another taste." Moreover, there have been poets associated with the Beat movement who are more then merely promising talents, among them Denise Levertov, Robert Duncan and Gary Snyder.

Finally, Reed Whittemore has said that American poetry is moribund today. I do not agree, though in these remarks I have been largely critical and negative. The truth is that there is more interest in poetry in America than ever before, there is a larger and more perceptive audience and there are unquestionably more poets who are intelligent and knowledgeable concerning their craft. Every month new magazines, both avant-garde and traditional, are founded; and publishing houses are issuing paperback series that help poets find a large audience. In addition, universities and colleges are hiring poets-in-residence, who are communicating their skill and enthusiasm to thousands of students.

No, poetry in the 60's is neither moribund nor tranquilized — though it does lack the rowdy excitement of the 20's. American poetry is merely waiting for the next breakthrough.

# About the Contributors

A. ALVAREZ (Hart Crane) was born and educated in England.
He has taught at Oxford, where he received his B. A.
and M. A. degrees. In 1958 he gave the Gauss Seminars
at Princeton and later was Visiting Professor in English
at Brandeis. His books include *The School of Donne*
and *Stewards of Excellence*, studies in modern English
and American poetry.

CLEANTH BROOKS (T. S. Eliot) is one of the most famous of
the New Critics who emerged from Vanderbilt University
in the 1920's, where he was an undergraduate. He received his M. A. from Tulane and studied at Oxford as a
Rhodes Scholar. He was co-editor of *The Southern Review* from 1935-1942. Among his most influential books
are *The Well Wrought Urn* and *Poetry and the Tradition*.
In 1963 he published *William Faulkner: the Yoknapa-
tawpha Country*. He is Gray Professor of Rhetoric at
Yale University.

RICHARD J. CALHOUN (James Dickey) received his M. A. from Johns Hopkins and his Ph. D. from the University of North Carolina. He is now Alumni Professor at Clemson University, where he is an assistant editor of the recently founded *South Carolina Review*. He has written numerous articles on contemporary American poetry and criticism and is the author of a forthcoming study of Randall Jarrell. His book on James Dickey will be published by Everett/Edwards, inc. in 1972. He has edited a collection of taped lectures on important American poets for the same company.

DENIS DONOGHUE (Randall Jarrell) is Professor of Modern English and American Literature at University College, Dublin. He has been a visiting lecturer in America and has published frequently on modern American poets. He is the author of *Connoisseurs of Chaos,* a study of modern American poetry, and *The Third Voice: Modern British and American Verse Drama.*

JAMES DICKEY (Edwin Arlington Robinson), one of the most widely known poets to emerge in America since World War II, is the author of six collections of poetry, including *Buckdancer's Choice* and *Poems: 1957-1967*, as well as a best-selling novel, *Deliverance*. His honors include the National Book Award in Poetry and an appointment as Consultant in Poetry to the Library of Congress. His criticism was collected in 1968 in *Babel to Byzantium,* and he is the subject of a forthcoming volume edited by Richard J. Calhoun. At present Mr. Dickey is Poet-in-Residence at the University of South Carolina.

FREDERIC E. FAVERTY (Richard Wilbur), formerly chairman of the Department of English at Northwestern University, is at present Morrison Professor of English Literature. He received both of his graduate degrees at Harvard and has published numerous critical and scholarly articles in the field of Victorian literature. Among his books is *Matthew Arnold the Ethnologist.*

VIVIENNE KOCH (Marianne Moore) before her untimely death made a significant contribution to the study of modern American and British poetry. Her study of

John Crowe Ransom has been frequently reprinted and her pioneering book on William Carlos Williams is still widely used. She was the recipient of a Rockefeller Grant, and her study in England resulted in *W. B. Yeats: the Tragic Phase.*

RICHARD M. LUDWIG (Ezra Pound) received both of his graduate degrees from Harvard. He is now Professor of English at Princeton University, where he teaches courses in American poetry and the English and American novel. Among his numerous books are *Major American Writers* and *Guide to American Literature and its Backgrounds Since 1890.* Recently he has edited *Aspects of American Poetry* and *Letters of Ford Madox Ford.*

RALPH MILLS JR. (Theodore Roethke) received his M. A. and Ph. D. degrees from Northwestern University and is now Professor of English at the University of Illinois at Chicago Circle. He is the author of *Richard Eberhart* and *Theodore Roethke* and has edited *On the Poet and His Craft: Selected Prose of Theodore Roethke* and *Selected Letters of Theodore Roethke.* In addition, he has published essays on such modern British and American poets as Edith Sitwell, Kathleen Raine and Wallace Stevens.

LOUIS MARTZ (Wallace Stevens) received his Ph. D. from Yale, where since 1957 he has been Tracy Smith Professor of English and American Literature. His books include *The Later Career of Tobias Smollett, The Poetry of Meditation* and *The Poem of the Mind.* In 1968 he was elected a member of the American Academy of Arts and Sciences.

GUY OWEN (John Crowe Ransom and American Poetry in the Sixties) is Professor of English and teacher of Creative Writing at North Carolina State University. He is the author of three novels, *Season of Fear, The Ballad of the Flim-Flam Man* and *Journey for Joedel,* and a recent collection of poetry, *The White Stallion and other Poems.* He is the founder and editor of *Southern Poetry Review.*

ROY HARVEY PEARCE (Robert Frost) has taught at Johns Hopkins, the University of California at Berkeley and is at present Professor of Literature at the University of

California at La Jolla. Among his numerous publications are books on Whitman, Hawthorne, Wallace Stevens and *The Continuity of American Poetry,* published by the Princeton University Press. He was the winner of the 1961 Chap-Book Award of the Poetry Society of America.

KARL SHAPIRO (William Carlos Williams) is well known as editor, critic and poet. He received the Pulitzer Prize for *V-Letter and Other Poems* in 1944; since then his collections have included *Poems 1942-1953, Poems of a Jew* and *The Bourgeois Poet.* His critical essays have been published in *Beyond Criticism* and *In Defense of Ignorance.* He is a member of the National Institute of Arts and Letters, and since 1967 has been Professor of English at the University of California at Davis.

HASKELL S. SPRINGER (E. E. Cummings) received his M. A. and Ph. D. in English at Indiana University. He has taught at the University of Virginia and is at present a member of the English Department at the University of Kansas. He has written on William Dean Howells and is currently the textural editor of Washington Irving's *Sketch Book,* part of Irving's complete works being published by the University of Wisconsin Press.

RADCLIFFE SQUIRES (Robinson Jeffers) received his M. A. from the University of Chicago and his Ph. D. from Harvard; he is now Professor of English at the University of Michigan. He is the author of *The Major Themes of Robert Frost, The Loyalties of Robinson Jeffers,* and *Frederic Prokosch.* In addition to his critical work, he is a poet and the author of a collection published in 1967, *The Light Under the Islands.*

HUGH B. STAPLES (Robert Lowell) was educated at Harvard and Berkeley and has taught at Northwestern and The University of California at Davis. At present he is Director of Graduate Studies in English at the University of Cincinnati. His most recent book is *The Ireland of Sir Johan Barrington,* and he now considers that his primary interest lies in the area of Irish literature, especially the writings of James Joyce.